QUEERING

BLACK

ATLANTIC

RELIGIONS

RELIGIOUS CULTURES OF AFRICAN
AND AFRICAN DIASPORA PEOPLE

Series editors:

Jacob K. Olupona,
Harvard University

Dianne M. Stewart,
Emory University

& Terrence L. Johnson,
Georgetown University

The book series examines the religious, cultural, and political expressions of African, African American, and African Caribbean traditions. Through transnational, cross-cultural, and multidisciplinary approaches to the study of religion, the series investigates the epistemic boundaries of continental and diasporic religious practices and thought and explores the diverse and distinct ways African-derived religions inform culture and politics. The series aims to establish a forum for imagining the centrality of Black religions in the formation of the "New World."

QUEERING BLACK ATLANTIC RELIGIONS

ROBERTO STRONGMAN

Transcorporeality in Candomblé, Santería, and Vodou

Duke University Press   Durham and London   2019

© 2019 Duke University Press
All rights reserved
Printed in the United States of America on acid-free paper ∞
Designed by Courtney Leigh Baker
Typeset in Minion Pro and Knockout by Westchester Publishing Services

Library of Congress Cataloging-in-Publication Data
Names: Strongman, Roberto, [date] author.
Title: Queering Black Atlantic religions : transcorporeality
in Candomblé, Santería, and Vodou / Roberto Strongman.
Description: Durham : Duke University Press, 2019.
| Series: The religious cultures of African and African diaspora people |
Includes bibliographical references and index.
Identifiers: LCCN 2018035547 (print)
LCCN 2018042517 (ebook)
ISBN 9781478003458 (ebook)
ISBN 9781478001973 (hardcover : alk. paper)
ISBN 9781478003106 (pbk. : alk. paper)
Subjects: LCSH: African diaspora. | Christianity—African influences.
| Religions—African influences. | Sex—Religious aspects.
| Homosexuality—Religious aspects. | Vodou—Haiti. |
Santeria—Cuba. | Candomblâe (Religion)—Brazil.
Classification: LCC BL625.25 (ebook) | LCC BL625.25 .S77 2019 (print)
| DDC 299.6/7—dc23
LC record available at https://lccn.loc.gov/2018035547

Cover art: Entranced male initiate dressed in female garb, sacramentally
performing as an *iyáwó*, or bride of the Spirit. Changó soundidé ceremony,
Ouidah, Dahomey (Benin), circa 1948. Courtesy of Fundaçao Pierre Verger,
Salvador da Bahia, Brazil.

To my great-grandmothers,

ANITA MATHÉLLY ROSEMOND   *Je t'écoute . . . Mwen tande'w*

LAURA GRABILL STRONGMAN   *I hear you . . .*

JOSEFINA MONTOYA SALDAÑA

VIRGINIA JIMÉNEZ GUEVARA   *Las escucho . . .*

Ma-Liz, DeLois, Louise Briscoe, Aunt Anni, Linda, and Genevieve; Mawu-Lisa, thunder, sky, sun, the great mother of us all; and Afrekete, her youngest daughter, the mischievous linguist, trickster, best-beloved, whom we must all become. —AUDRE LORDE, *Zami: A New Spelling of My Name*

CONTENTS

ACKNOWLEDGMENTS

One of the most important lessons I have learned from working with the *orishas* and *lwas* is that the greatest form of reverence and the most pleasing offering of all is gratitude.

Any research is always the result of collective undertaking, and I would like to thank those colleagues and mentors who have contributed to making this project a reality. My deepest respect to all my informants for having shared their time, knowledge, and devotional practice with me all the while knowing that most ethical research practices dictate that they remain anonymous. Their selflessness encapsulates the sublime moment of egoic-transcendence that this book is about. To all of you, named and unnamed: *Ashé!*

A LIBATION TO THE ANCESTORS: Horacio Roque-Ramírez, José Muñoz, O. R. Dathorne, Karen McCarthy Brown, Cedric Robinson, Clyde Woods, and Otis Madison. Your light illuminates our path.

MÈSI! I WOULD LIKE to thank the dean of social sciences, Charles Hale, and all the very supportive colleagues at my home institution, the University of California, Santa Barbara (UCSB). My deepest appreciation to my dear friends at the Department of Black Studies: Jeffrey Stewart, Ingrid Banks, Jude Akudinobi, Stephanie Batiste, Jane Duran, Terrance Wooten, Jaime Alves, and Christopher McAuley.

Thanks also to all of my partners in matters sacred and profane at Religious Studies: Rudy Busto, José Cabezón, William Ellison, Barbara Holdrege,

Kathleen Moore, Elizabeth Pérez, Dwight Reynolds, Inés Talamántez, Vesna Wallace, and David White.

To my Comparative Literature family, my gratefulness, especially to Catherine Nesci, Elisabeth Weber, Dominique Julien, Bishnupriya Ghosh, Dorota Dutsch, Claudio Fogu, Eric Prieto, Chela Sandoval, and Paul Amar.

And where would I be if not for my *camaradas* from Spanish? Thanks to Silvia Bermúdez, Leo Cabranes-Grant, Jorge Luis Castillo, Juan Pablo Lupi, Francisco Lomelí, Sara Poot-Herrera, Viola Miglio, Micaela J. Díaz-Sánchez, and María Herrera-Sobek.

And of course, my thankfulness to my colleagues from Feminist Studies: Mireille Miller-Young, Edwina Barvosa, Eileen Boris, Grace Chang, Laury Oaks, Leila Rupp, and Jennifer Tyburczy.

A big applause to my colleagues in Theater and Dance for bringing the orishas alive to the UCSB community through conferences and plays: Ninotchka Bennauhum, Risa Brainin, Christina McMahon, Carlos Morton, Christopher Pilafian, and Brandon Whited.

MERCI! I WOULD ALSO like to acknowledge the organizers and representatives of several learned societies who gave me the opportunity to present my work at their meetings and provided useful feedback as I completed the manuscript.

From the Australian Association of Caribbean Studies, my deepest appreciation to Anne Hickling-Hudson, Sue Thomas, Anne Collett, and Barry Higman. From the Caribbean Studies Association, thanks to Carole Boyce-Davies, Holger Henke, Percy Hintzen, Elisabeth Paravisini-Gebert and Aisha Khan. Many thanks to Anja Bandau from the Society for Caribbean Research, to Karina Smith from the Society for Caribbean Studies, and to Lucy Wilson from the Modern Language Association.

I would also like to acknowledge the outstanding cooperation of all the members of the UC Black Atlantic Religions Faculty Working Group: Patrick Polk (UCLA), Andrew Apter (UCLA), Jeroen de Wulf (UC Berkeley), Jeffrey S. Khan (UC Davis), Elisabeth Pérez (UCSB), Rachel Sarah O'Toole (UCI), Robin Derby (UCLA), and Katherine Smith (UCLA).

¡GRACIAS! I WOULD ALSO like to recognize the sources of funding for the fieldwork carried out in association with this book. Thanks to the following organizations for their generous financial contributions: Hellman Founda-

tion, UCSB Academic Senate, the Institute for Social, Behavioral and Economic Research, the Center for Black Studies Research, and the Center for Chicano Studies.

OBRIGADO! AN APPLAUSE TO all my dedicated mentors over the years: Sylvia Wynter, Fredric Jameson, Diane Middlebrook, Marc Prou, Raphaël Confiant, Randy Matory, Rosaura Sánchez, Jaime Concha, Louis Montrose, Ann Pellegrini, Anna Wexler, Carlos Decena, Tom Schmid, Bob Esch, Mimi Gladstein, Marianne Phinney, Feroza Jussawalla, Grant Goodall, Scott Michaelsen, Jon Amastae, Teresa Meléndez Hayes, and Page Dubois.

Thanks to all those counselors who helped me to keep the book and an academic career in a proper perspective within the larger context of life: Michael Riley, Vinnie Carafano, Scott Claassen, Tymi Howard, Terra Gold, and Kathleen Baggarley.

A heartfelt tribute also to the editors of this book series for their faith, dedication, and endurance: Jacob K. Olupona, Dianne M. Stewart, and Terrence L. Johnson.

And, I could not finish these brief acknowledgments without thanking my dear friend Geoffrey Gartner and, of course, Jacky, both of whom are learning that love is eternal.

INTRODUCTION
Enter the *Igbodu*

The entrance of inductees into the initiation chamber of an Afro-Atlantic spiritual community uncannily resembles the practice of reading you are currently performing. Your opening of this book mirrors the neophytes' unlocking of the doors to the space in which their new consciousness will gestate. Whether within the *djevo* of Haitian Vodou, the *camarinha* of Brazilian Candomblé, or the *igbodú* of Cuban Lucumí/Santería, this sacred place is a space of intellectual, physical, and spiritual nourishment, the first step in a rite of passage that will mark the death of the old, illusory self and foster the rebirth of the new, spiritually aware subject.

Much like one's indecision before a shelfful of clamoring books at a bookstore or library, the process of committing to the temporal and monetary rigors of the *igbodu* is often marked by much vacillation and postponement. But eventually the seekers succumb to the mysteries within, pledging themselves to whatever temporary privations might be required for the sake of spiritual transformation. The initial disorientation and pervasive loneliness are compensated with the wholesome enrichment of learning the secrets of each lesson, ceremony, or chapter.

The igbodu is the place where the community's secrets are kept.[1] They are shared only with the select few who make their abode within for a predetermined period—a year historically, but increasingly, due to the demands of urban and industrialized societies, as little as a month or a few days. This is the paradigmatic space of cultural regeneration and demographic propagation in these religious societies in which orality has superseded textuality as the main conduit of information and ritual transmission.

As in the acts of reading and writing, the novices in the igbodu spend most of their time in seclusion. This is a space of meditation where, through the cultivation of silence, one may hear the West African divinities called *orishas* speak.[2] But the isolation is punctuated by the periodic incursions of priests and elders who tend to the initiates' physical needs. As infants in the practice, the initiates are fed, bathed, and dressed by the community of saints. Even their bodily excretions are removed from the space by their new brothers and sisters. The igbodu is a place of humility, where one learns to trust others through the sacred simulacrum of renascence.

Welcome to the scholarly igbodu that this book represents. In it, you will learn about *transcorporeality*, the distinctly Afro-diasporic cultural representation of the human psyche as multiple, removable, and external to the body that functions as its receptacle. This transcorporeal view of the self obtains clear visual representation in a tropical fruit that is largely unknown in Europe and North America because the fragility of its skin impedes exportation. Nevertheless, this emblematic and queer fruit, emerging from the flora of the geographical and climatic region covered in this book, is widely cultivated and consumed on both sides of the black Atlantic by humans and gods, as it is one of the favorite offerings of the orishas Changó and Oshún. The cashew pear (Fr. *pomme de cajou*, Sp. *marañón*, Pg. *caju*, Kreyòl *pom kajou*, also known by the taxonomical name *Anacardium occidentale*) allows us to readily see how the transcorporeal conceptualization of the body holds the kernel of the self, not within the meat of the fruit, but on the outside. Unlike the lesser-known fruit, the seed is a prized and popular nut worldwide. The easy removability of this seed and its wide commercial dissemination as an export crop to distant, often high-latitude and temperate lands where it releases the photosynthesized power of the tropical sun speaks to the externality, flight, and Ashé-power of the transcorporeal Spirit. This unique view of the body in which the ego, soul, or anima exists in an outward orientation vis-à-vis the physical body—preserved in its most evident form in African-

FIG. I.1. Cashew pear, displaying external seed. Photograph by Jacob Abhishek.

diasporic religious traditions—allows the regendering of the bodies of initiates, who are mounted and ridden by deities of a gender different from their own during the ritual ecstasy of trance possession. By discussing novels, paintings, films, interviews, and ethnographies, my book assembles and interprets a representative collection of such transcendental moments in which the commingling of the human and the divine produces subjectivities whose gender is not dictated by biological sex. In so doing, it demonstrates that, while transcorporeality is rooted in the religious practice of trance possession, its effects spill over into the everyday life of participants and observers of these religions and it becomes a leading feature of nearly every aspect of Afro-diasporic cultural production.

The purpose of this book-cum-igbodu is to impart knowledge of this black transatlantic conceptualization of corporeality among a readership inside and outside the academy ready for such new information. It means to achieve this goal by utilizing cultural studies' critical methodologies to expose and explain the occurrence of transcorporeality in literary, aesthetic, and performative contexts. It also employs ethnographic interviews to produce self-reflective personal narratives that give voice to queer priests and practitioners of the Afro-diasporic religions that have preserved and transformed transcorporeality, adapting it to the exigencies of various historical and geographical contexts across the Atlantic world. The counterpoint between theoretical discourse and interpretive first-person accounts offers multiple points of entry to readers at various stages of familiarity with academic discourse.

The term "transcorporeality" was introduced by Graham Ward in his seminal book *Cities of God*. My use represents neither a derivation nor an adaptation but a fuller elucidation of the term. Using the Christian imagery of the broken body of Christ, the sacrament of the Eucharist, and incarnation theology, Ward employs "transcorporeality" to illustrate the proliferation of Christianity: "Continually called to move beyond itself, the transcorporeal body itself becomes Eucharistic, because endlessly fractured and fed to others. It becomes the body of Christ, broken, given, resurrected and ascended. . . . The transcorporeal body expands in its fracturing, it pluralises as it opens itself towards external growth" (2000, 95). Because he focuses exclusively on Christianity, the full potential of transcorporeality is beyond the bounds of Ward's important contribution. Where is the "trance" of "transcorporeality"? More than fanciful word play, this question forces us to look beyond a view of the incarnation as a singular historical event or as the logical domain of Christianity. My work furthers Ward's exploration of the transcorporeal by studying how incarnation theologies are universalized through the phenomenon of trance possession, the quotidian rite through which humans understand themselves as embodiments of the divine in Afro-diasporic religions.

This reworking of the idea of transcorporeality through Afro-Atlantic religion has profound philosophical implications for the understanding of the black body. The imposition of a European discourse of identitarian interiority onto colonized and enslaved populations renders the black body's representation an empty shell. While many theorists have endeavored to fill this personal vacuum with a unitarian form of consciousness, I fear this produces neither an epistemologically accurate account of Afro-Atlantic consciousness nor a politics of enablement. The philosophies of African peoples conceive of the body as an open vessel that can be occupied temporarily by a variety of hosts. During the height of the slave trade, the real act of imperialism was not so much to label Africans soulless as to close off their philosophical corporeal openness while at the same time legislatively prohibiting precisely those religious rituals of trance possession that render black bodies inhabited or soulful. While endowing Europeans with individuality, the discourse of interiority trapped the black body into a physical image projection that obstructed the full, plural communion with the spiritual hosts that had animated it prior to its capture by the West and its philosophy. It is the capture of the black body, not its evolution, that rendered it empty. The African bodily house received many visitors until the guests were rudely expelled and the door shut and sealed by monopolizing newcomers. However, the multiple forms of consciousness knocking at the door are loosening the bolts of this subversive manipulation of the corporeal construction and restructuring their ancient abode according to familiar forms, as a physical craft, opening it to welcome them once again.[3]

Chapter 1, "Of Dreams and Night Mares: Vodou Women Queering the Body," examines the initiatory-critical works of five female anthropologists to study how women's perspectives on Haitian Vodou corporeality problematize the Cartesian mind/body problem. Deploying the theory of transcorporeality, I argue that Zora Neale Hurston's *Tell My Horse* (1938), Maya Deren's *Divine Horsemen* (1953), Katherine Dunham's *Island Possessed* (1969), Karen McCarthy Brown's *Mama Lola* (1991), and Mimerose Beaubrun's *Nan Dòmi* (2010) document the development of a feminist and queer canon that is concerned with the potential of Vodou to develop more enabling models of embodiment.

Chapter 2, "Hector Hyppolite èl Même: Between Queer Fetishization and Vodou Self-Portraiture," utilizes the concept of twinning prevalent in Afro-diasporic religions, and Vodou in particular, to frame a queer counterpoint between the works of Haitian painter Hector Hyppolite and those of white ethnographers such as Hubert Fichte and Pierre Verger. I suggest that Hyppolite's paintings avail themselves fully of the cross-gender identificatory possibilities of Vodou in order to respond to the fetishistic queer gaze of these ethnographers.

In chapter 3, "A Chronology of Queer Lucumí Scholarship: Degeneracy, Ambivalence, Transcorporeality," my objective is to elucidate the existence of a queer Lucumí tradition of scholarship by anthropologists from Cuba, the United States, and France and to trace the evolution of this research through the release of the movie *Fresa y Chocolate*, which I see as representing a pivotal moment in the chronology and lineage of this scholarship. The chapter proposes that *Fresa y Chocolate* is as much about Lucumí as it is about queerness.

Chapter 4, "Lucumí Diasporic Ethnography: Fran, Cabrera, Lam," continues the exploration of Lucumí as a cultural arsenal of non-heteronormative identifications and representations through a reading of Lydia Cabrera's lifework and Wifredo Lam's tableaux. This exposé is framed around a conversation with an initiate and informant, Fran, in order to foreground the dialogic quality of field research, the need to give voice to the practitioners of Afro-diasporic religions, and to afford the ethnographer a moment of public self-reflection.

Chapter 5, "Queer Candomblé Scholarship and Dona Flor's S/Exua/lity," provides a historization of queer Candomblé scholarship as the contextual framework of a discussion of Jorge Amado's novel *Dona Flor e seus deus maridos* and the Bruno Barreto film adaption bearing the same title. Here I argue that the trickster quality in Brazilian Candomblé's orisha Exu makes possible a prominent non-heteronormative thematic element in Amado's novel, whose main protagonist, Dona Flor, allegorizes the orisha Exu in its feminine version: Exua. Further, I propose that Dona Flor is the fulcrum of a homoerotic triangle, as her two husbands allegorize orishas with plural gender identifications. The novel is therefore a prime example of the rich queer cultural potential of Candomblé and Afro-diasporic religions in general.

Chapter 6, "Transatlantic Waters of Oxalá: Pierre Verger, Mário de Andrade, and Candomblé in Europe," utilizes ethnographic interviews and literary analysis to investigate the role of Europe as the next frontier for Candomblé. The chapter examines visits to Candomblé communities in Brazil and Portugal and provides a reading of Mário de Andrade's novel *Macunaíma* to ascertain how a religion with African origins and substantial creolizations in the New World is now adapting in its third passage to the former European colonial center.

Queering Black Atlantic Religions seeks to make significant interventions and contributions to a wide range of academic fields by fomenting hemispheric understanding of black cultures while moving beyond US and Latin American models of analysis. In so doing, it attempts to intervene in current discussions regarding the scope of the ethnic studies disciplines within black studies and Latino studies. In a related sense, this work contributes to Latin American and Caribbean studies as it foregrounds the black experience as an important component of the ethnic makeup of Latin America and makes visible important linkages between the Hispanophone, Lusophone, and Francophone Caribbean that are often overlooked in the language-specific disciplines prevalent in the academy. Furthermore, the field of diaspora studies has been dominated by works attempting to understand South Asian migration to England and the United States. This study seeks to add to a growing body of work that expands on the understanding of diaspora from the perspective of other migrant trajectories. This project makes an important contribution to the field of gender and sexuality studies as it contributes to an understanding of how First World categories of sexual difference often fail to correspond to non-heterosexual categories elsewhere. This observation builds on queer ethnic works such as *Global Divas* (2003) by Martin F. Manalansan and *Aberrations in Black* (2003) by Roderick Ferguson. Certainly there is a need for a greater understanding of Lucumí, Candomblé, and Vodou within religious studies.[4] When the topic of syncretism emerges within religious studies, it is not viewed as a multilayered formation that can acquire new strata through current migrations. Similarly, it addresses gaps in other fields such as the discussions of migrancy in American studies that are almost entirely devoid of the topic of religion. The confluence of theoretical and ethnographical writing on religious ritual ensures that this book should be of interest to scholars and students of anthropology, cultural studies, and performance studies.

Toward an Afro-diasporic Philosophy
of Corporeal Receptacularity

The Western philosophical tradition presents the concept of a unitary soul within the hermetic enclosure of a body. In *Sources of the Self*, historian of philosophy Charles Taylor presents a genealogy of the Western self in which Descartes marks the most important milestone:

> The internalization wrought by the modern age, of which Descartes's formulation was one of the most important and influential, is very different from Augustine's. It does, in a very real sense, place the moral sources within us. Relative to Plato, and relative to Augustine, it brings about in each case a transposition by which we no longer see ourselves as related to moral sources outside us, or at least not at all in the same way. An important power has been internalized. (1989, 143)

It becomes important for us to place Taylor's claims concerning Descartes in the historical context of the Enlightenment. The theocentric philosophical tradition delineated by Plato and Augustine is characterized by the human search for an identity beyond the individual, in the divine without. The intense secularization of the Enlightenment disrupts this theocentrism by foregrounding the individual, a move that brings about the internalization of identity. This sense of inwardness, however, is dependent upon a clear demarcation between the new boundaries of the self and the body. In the following passage, Descartes reasons how even if the mind or soul might be within the body, the two remain distinct parts of the individual:

> Pour commencer donc cet examen, je remarque ici premièrement qu'il y a une grande différence entre l'esprit et le corps, en ce que le corps de sa nature est toujours divisible, et que l'esprit est entièrement indivisible; car en effet, quand je le considère, c'est-à-dire quand je me considère moi-même en tant que je suis seulement une chose qui pense, je ne puis distinguer en moi aucunes parties, mais je connais et conçois fort clairement que je suis une chose absolument une et entière; et quoique tout esprit semble être uni à tout le corps, toutefois lorsqu'un pied ou un bras ou quelque autre partie vient à en être séparée, je connais fort bien que rien pour cela n'a été retranché de mon esprit; et les facultés de vouloir, de sentir, de concevoir, etc., ne peuvent pas non plus être dites proprement ses parties, car c'est le même esprit qui s'emploie tout entier à vouloir, et tout entier à sentir et à concevoir, etc.; mais c'est tout le contraire dans les choses corporelles ou étendues, car je n'en puis imaginer aucune, pour petite qu'elle soit, que je ne mette aisément en pièces par ma pensées, ou que mon esprit ne divise fort facilement en plusieurs parties, et par conséquent que je ne connaisse être divisible: ce qui suffrait por m'enseigner que l'esprit ou l'âme de l'homme est entièrement différente du corps, si je ne l'avais déjà d'ailleurs assez appris. (1948, 130–31)

In order to begin this examination, then, I here say, in the first place, that there is a great difference between mind and body, inasmuch as the body is by nature always divisible, and the mind is entirely indivisible. For, as a matter of fact, when I consider the mind, that is to say, myself inasmuch as I am only a thinking thing, I cannot distinguish in myself any parts, but apprehend myself to be clearly one and entire; and although the whole mind seems to be united to the whole body, yet if a foot, or an arm, or some other part, is separated from my body, I am aware that nothing has been taken away from my mind. And the faculties of willing, feeling, conceiving, etc. cannot be properly speaking said to be its parts, for it is one and the same mind which employs itself in willing and in feeling and understanding. But it is quite otherwise with corporeal or extended objects, for there is not one of these imaginable by me which my mind cannot easily divide into parts and which consequently I do not recognize as being divisible; this would be sufficient to teach me that the mind or soul of man is entirely different from the body, if I had not already learned it from other sources. (1996, 105–6)

Clearly, Descartes's concern here is to negate the full absorption of the soul by the body through the process of subjective internalization. The two remain distinct entities, even if one resides within the other. Apart from remarking on Descartes's famous cogito in his description of the "I" as the "thinking thing," we should note his concern for divisibility and indivisibility as tests for integrity. For Descartes, the possibility that the body can be separated into parts implies that it is of a different nature than the indivisible mind/soul. In fact, Western philosophy does not prove capable of developing a discourse for the parts of the mind until the twentieth century, with Freud's 1923 *Das Ich und das Es* (*The Ego and the Id*) and with Sartre, who in his 1943 *L'être et le néant* (*Being and Nothingness*) claims that "l'altérité est, en effet, une négation interne et seule une conscience peut se constituer comme négation interne" (1943, 666; Alterity is, really, an internal negation and only a conscience can constitute itself as an internal negation).[5] Nevertheless, through his reasoning, Descartes crystallizes the notion of a self within a body, establishing this self as internal, unitary, and inseparable from the body.

In the twentieth century, a strong Western philosophical current attempts to amend Descartes's internal subject. Bataille, for example, posits the divine as a self inside the body: "J'entends par *expérience intérieure* ce que d'habitude on nomme *expérience mystique*: les états d'extase, de ravissement, au moins d'émotion méditée" (1943, 15; By *internal experience* I mean that which is normally called *mystical experience*: ecstasies, rapture, as a form of meditative emotion). Bataille suggests here that even though inwardness initially requires secularization, once established, it can become sacramental again without forcing the self to exit the body. Similarly, Michel Serres in *Variations sur le corps* uses an aesthetic discourse to claim that the body's internalization of the self does not imply a rejection of the profound and transcendental mystery of artistic appreciation:

> Voilà les cycles admirables de support réciproque entre le labyrinthe de l'oreille interne, chargé du port, et les volutes spiralées de l'externe, qui entend et produit la musique, convergeant dans un centre noir et secret, commun à ses deux réseaux, où je découvre soudain la solution aux mystères sombres de l'union de l'âme qui ouït la langue et du corps porteur. (1999, 23)

> Let us consider the admirable cycles of reciprocal support between the labyrinth of the internal ear and the spiraling corrugations of the external ear, which hears and produces music, converging into one dark and secret center, common to both networks, where I suddenly

discover the solution to the shadowy mysteries of the union between the soul that hears language and the body that carries it.

While Bataille and Serres are interested in recuperating the divine for the internal self, for Sartre, "tout autre conception de l'altérité reviendrait à la poser comme en-soi, c'est-à-dire à établir entre elle et l'être une relation externe, ce qui nécessiterait la présence d'un témoin pour constater que l'autre est autre que l'en-soi" (1943, 666; All other conceptualizations of alterity will end up presenting it as in-itself, in other words, to establish between it and Being an external relationship, which would require the presence of a witness to verify that the other is different from that which is in-itself). This French philosophical internalization of the self acquires its most recent expression in Foucault's "repressive hypothesis," presented in his *L'histoire de la sexualité* (*History of Sexuality*, [1979] 1976) as the popular belief that since the seventeenth century discourses of sexuality have been driven underground and made secretive while in fact narratives and "confessions" about sex have nothing but proliferated since then. If we believe we are repressed, it is because of the Cartesian model of a bodily entrapped soul—a culturally conditioned image that is not shared by all phenomenological traditions across the world and historical periods.

In *Caliban's Reason: Introducing Afro-Caribbean Philosophy*, Paget Henry explains that Afro-diasporic philosophy does not exist as a tradition isolated from other manifestations of culture:

> Because traditional African philosophy emerged implicitly in the ontological, ethical, existential, and other positions taken in religious, mythic, genealogical, and folkloric discourses, its presence and visibility depended upon the continued vitality and growth of these systems of thought. Their contraction or decay would mean decline and eclipse for traditional African philosophy. . . . In the Caribbean . . . traditional African philosophy experienced an even greater eclipse as a result of the rise of colonial discourses and a literate, hybridized local intelligentsia. (2000, 43, 45)

Henry's statement implies the need to investigate Afro-diasporic religion as a repository of philosophical information that can overcome the imposition of Western philosophical discourses on colonized peoples. In fact, a thorough study of Afro-diasporic religions reveals how—unlike the Western idea of the fixed internal unitary soul—the Afro-diasporic self is removable, external, and multiple. This idea has antecedents in J. Lorand Matory's

"Vessels of Power," his 1986 anthropology master's thesis, and in his *Sex and the Empire That Is No More* (2005b), where he discusses how African pots, calabashes, baskets, and other concave ritual, representational, and utilitarian objects provide Oyo-Yorùbá metaphors of personhood. My work is inspired by his statement that "the Cartesian notion of the body is the detachable and disposable vessel of an invisible mind or soul" (2005b, 169) and extends it to interrogate just how the notion of the body as vessel allows for queer resubjectifications that are rare or impossible under the containment model provided by Descartes.

In *An Essay on African Philosophical Thought: The Akan Conceptual Scheme*, Kuame Gyekye presents a tripartite plan of the self, consisting of the *honam*, the material body; the *okra*, the immaterial soul; and the *sunsum*, the quasi-material spirit (Gyekye 1995, 89). In *Cultural Universals and Particulars: An African Perspective*, Kwasi Wiredu explains Gyekye's systematization of Akan personhood by comparing it with Descartes's mind/body binarism:

> One thing, in any case, should be absolutely clear: Neither the okra nor the sunsum can be identified with the immaterial soul familiar in some influential Western philosophical and religious thinking (with all its attendant paradoxes). This concept of the soul is routinely used interchangeably with the concept of mind while the concept of okra and sunsum are categorically different from the Akan concept of mind (adwene), as our previous explanation should have rendered apparent. Thus Descartes (in English translation) can speak indifferently of the soul or the mind and appear to make sense. In Akan to identify either the okra or the sunsum with adwene would be the sheerest gibberish. (Wiredu 1996, 129)

The multiplicity of the self displayed in the Akan scheme is prevalent in Western African societies and has been noted by Haitian Vodou scholar Guérin Montilus in his study of Adja philosophy:

> The Vodu religion of the Adja taught these same Africans that their psychic reality and source of human life was metaphorically symbolized by the shadow of the body. This principle, represented by the shadow, is called the *ye*. There are two of these. The first is the inner, the internal part of the shadow, which is called the *ye gli*; that is, a short *ye*. The second, the external and light part of the same shadow, is called the *ye gaga*; that is, the long *ye*. The first *ye gli*, is the principle

of physical life, which vanishes at death. The second, *ye gaga*, is the principle of consciousness and psychic life. The *ye gaga* survives death and illustrates the principle of immortality. It has metaphysical mobility that allows human beings to travel far away at night (through dreams) or remain eternally alive after the banishment of the *ye gli*. After death, the *ye gaga* goes to meet the community of Ancestors, which constitutes the extended family and the clan in their spiritual dimensions. (2006, 2)

This multiplicity of the self found in African philosophy survives in the Caribbean diaspora. The African duality of the immaterial self—the okra and sunsum of the Akan and the ye gli and ye gaga of the Adja—become the *tibonanj* and the *gwobonanj* in Haitian Vodou. In *Creole Religions of the Caribbean: An Introduction from Vodou and Santería to Obeah and Espiritismo*, Margarite Fernández Olmos and Lizabeth Paravisini-Gebert define these two elusive terms:

The head, which contains the two elements that comprise the soul—the ti bònanj or ti bon ange (the conscience that allows for self-reflection and self-criticism) and the gwo bònanj or gros bon ange (the psyche, source of memory, intelligence, and personhood)—must be prepared so that the gros bon ange can be separated from the initiate to allow the spirit to enter in its place. (2003, 118)

Here we begin to see that there is a cooperative relationship between the tibonanj and the gwobonanj. Alfred Métraux further expounds on this cooperation:

It is the general opinion that dreams are produced by the wanderings of the Gros-bon-ange when it abandons the body during sleep. The sleeper becomes aware of the adventures of the Gros-bon-ange through the Ti-z'ange who remains by him as a protector and yet never loses sight of the Gros-bon-ange. He wakes the sleeper in case of danger and even flies to the rescue of the Gros-bon-ange if this faces real danger. (1946, 85)

For the self to achieve altered states of consciousness—in trance possessions, dreams, or death—the tibonanj allows the gwobonanj to become detached from the body. In the case of trance possession, the gwobonanj surrenders its place and its authority to the *mètet*, "the main spirit served by that person and the one s/he most often goes into trance for" (McCarthy Brown 2006, 10).

In her landmark book *Mama Lola: A Vodou Priestess in Brooklyn*, Karen McCarthy Brown further explains the multiple concept of the self in Vodou by presenting the notion of the mètet, roughly translated as "the master of the head": "The personality of the *mèt tet* and that of the devotee tend to coincide, an intimate tie hinted at in the occasional identification of the 'big guardian angel' (*gwo bònanj*), one dimension of what might be called a person's soul, with the Vodou spirit who is his or her *mèt tet*" (1991, 112–13). Here we see how the gwobonanj is the central element of the self in Vodou. Not only is it the seat of individuality but it also maintains links between mètet and the tibonanj, two aspects of the self that are not directly connected to each other. These links are broken after the death of the individual, in the Vodou ceremony of *dessounin*:

> In a certain sense, the maît-tête is the divine parent of the gros-bon-ange, the psychic inheritance from the parents. The ceremony of *dessounin* thus accomplishes two separate but related actions: it severs the loa cord of the gros-bon-ange; and it separates the gros-bon-ange from its physical parent—the now defunct matter of the body—launching it as an independent spiritual entity into the spiritual universe, where it, in turn, becomes either part of the general spiritual heritage of the descendants of that person, or even, perhaps, the divine parent, the loa maît-tête of some subsequent gros-bon-ange. (Deren 1970, 45)

We can summarize the roles of the two most important aspects of the self by saying that the gwobonanj is consciousness, while the tibonanj is objectivity. The gwobonanj is the principal soul, experience, personality (Agosto 1976, 52), the personal soul, or self (Deren 1970, 44). The tibonanj is described as the anonymous, protective, objective conscience that is truthful and objective, the impersonal spiritual component of the individual (Deren 1970, 44), whose domain also encompasses moral considerations and arbitration (Agosto 1976, 52). The tibonanj is a "spiritual reserve tank. It is an energy or presence within the person that is dimmer or deeper than consciousness, but it is nevertheless there to be called upon in situations of stress and depletion" (McCarthy Brown 2006, 9).

The complex relationship between the gwobonanj and the tibonanj has at times not been correctly understood by Western scholars, who have disseminated erroneous information, further mudding our collective understanding of the self in Vodou.[6] For example, Desmangles ascribes to the tibonanj characteristics that most scholars attribute to the gwobonanj: "The ti-bonanj is the ego-soul. It represents the unique qualities that characterize an

FIG. I.2. Representation of the gwobonanj as the Blue Angel. Hector Hyppolite (1894–1948), *L'ange blue* (*Blue Angel*), ca. 1947. Oil on cardboard, 0.65 × 0.65 m. Musée d'Art Haïtien. Photograph: Mireille Vautier / Art Resource, NY.

individual's personality" (1992, 67). Comparisons to Western philosophy underscore his confusion:

> The Vodou concept of the ti-bon-anj in heaven seems to correspond to the Roman Catholic doctrine of the soul, for Vodouisants believe that it "appears" before Bondye to stand before the heavenly tribunal where it is arraigned for its misdeeds, and must suffer the appropriate penalties. (Desmangles 1992, 69)

Wade Davis also ascribes to the tibonanj attributes that most scholars use to define the gwobonanj: "the Ti bon ange [is] the individual, aura, the source of all personality and willpower" (1986, 185). Furthermore, Davis (1986, 182) says that the tibonanj travels during sleep, while most scholars agree that it is the gwobonanj who does so (McCarthy Brown 2006, 9; Montilus 2006, 4).

In addition to the gwobonanj, the tibonanj, and the mètet, there remain three components of the Vodou concept of personhood. The *nam* is the "spirit of the flesh that allows each cell to function" (Davis 1986, 185) or "the animating force of the body" (McCarthy Brown, 2006, 8). The *zetwal* is the "celestial parallel self, fate" (McCarthy Brown 2006, 9) and the "spiritual component that resides in the sky," "the individual's star of destiny" (Davis 1986, 185). The *kòkadav* is "the body itself, the flesh and blood" (Davis 1986, 185), "the dead body of a person," and "a material substance separable from these various animating spiritual entities" (McCarthy Brown 2006, 9).

The phenomenon of trance possession needs to be explained through the multiplicity of the self in Vodou. The projection of Western philosophical concepts by certain schools of anthropology onto Vodou has been responsible for inaccurate understandings of trance possession: "Dans sa phase initiale, la transe se manifeste par des symptômes d'un caractère nettement psychopathologique. Elle reproduit dans ses grands traits le tableau clinique de l'attaque hystérique" (Métraux 1958, 120). "The symptoms of the opening phase of the trance are clearly pathological. They conform exactly in their main features, to the stock clinical conception of hysteria" (Métraux 1959, 107).

Nevertheless, it is important to note how other scholars from the Haitian national elite have questioned the uses of Western philosophy to understand Afro-diasporic trance possession:

> Si le phénomène de la possession—la transe ou l'extase—chez les criseurs du Vaudou est une psycho-névrose, peut-on la classer dans la catégorie de l'hystérie selon l'une ou l'autre doctrine ci-dessus exposée? Nous ne le croyons pas. Les possédés de la loi ne sont pas de criseurs dont on peut provoquer l'attaque par suggestion et qu'on peut guérir par persuasion. (Mars 1928, 128)

> Even if the phenomenon of possession—trance or ecstasy—among Vodou practitioners implies a psychological breakdown, can one classify it within the category of hysteria according to one or another doctrine here presented? We do not believe this to be a correct approach. Those possessed by lwa are not psychotics who can be induced into such a state by the power of suggestion or healed through persuasion.

However, even as Métraux inaccurately equates trance possession with the already questionable notion of hysteria, he does provide one of the clearest definitions of this phenomenon during the 1950s, the early period of serious scholarly investigation of Vodou:

> L'explication donnée par les sectateurs du vaudou à la transe mystique est des plus simples; un *loa* se loge dans la tête d'un individu après en avoir chassé le "gros bon ange," l'une des deux âmes que chacun porte en soi. C'est le brusque départ de l'âme qui cause les tressaillements et les soubresauts caractéristiques du début de la transe. Une fois le "bon ange" parti, le possédé éprouve le sentiment d'un vide total, comme s'il perdait connaissance. Sa tête tourne, ses jarrets tremblent. Il devient alors non seulement le réceptacle du dieu, mais son instrument. C'est la personnalité du dieu et non plus la sienne qui s'exprime dans son comportement et ses paroles. Ses jeux de physionomie, ses gestes et jusqu'au ton de sa voix reflètent le caractère et le tempérament de la divinité qui est descendue sur lui. (Métraux 1958, 106)

> The explanation of mystic trance given by disciples of Voodoo is simple: a *loa* moves into the head of an individual having first driven out "the good big angel" (*gros bon ange*)—one of the two souls everyone carries in himself. This eviction of the soul is responsible for the tremblings and convulsions that characterize the opening stages of trance. Once the good angel has gone, the person possessed experiences a feeling of total emptiness as though he were fainting. His head whirls, the calves of his legs tremble; he now becomes not only the vessel but also the instrument of the god. From now on it is the god's personality and not his own which is expressed in his bearing and words. The play of these features, his gestures and even the tone of his voice all reflect the temperament and character of the god who has descended upon him. (Métraux 1959, 120)

Métraux's quote is helpful for us in that it allows us to locate the seat of selfhood in the corporeal head of the individual. In Haitian Kreyòl, *tèt* has an interesting double meaning. It is a noun referring to the anatomical head and, in its function as a reflexive prefix attached to personal pronouns, it also means "self." This synecdoche becomes important, as it establishes the head as a referent for selfhood, in a part-for-whole metaphor. It also presents the head as the physical location for the multiple parts of the self. Writing in the interstices between African and European philosophies, Métraux describes trance possession using an ambiguous language implying penetration and hovering. This vacillation between metaphors for possession continues in the following quote:

> Le rapport qui existe entre le *loa* et l'homme dont il s'est emparé est comparé à celui qui unit un cavalier à sa monture. C'est pourquoi on dit du premier qu'il "monte" ou "selle" son *choual* (cheval). . . . Elle est aussi un envahissement du corps par un être surnaturel qui s'en approprie; d'où l'expression courante: "le *loa* saisit son cheval." (Métraux 1958, 106)

> The relationship between the *loa* and the man it has seized is compared to that which joins a rider to his horse. That is why a *loa* is spoken of as mounting or saddling his *chual* (horse). . . . It is also an invasion of the body by a supernatural spirit; hence the often-used expression: "the *loa* is seizing his horse." (Métraux 1959, 120)

Métraux's use of in/out metaphors for the phenomenon of possession is a Western importation. The rider metaphor popularized by early scholars of Vodou like Zora Neale Hurston, Maya Deren, and Katherine Dunham—whose works are discussed in chapter 1—articulates the symbolic language used by the initiates themselves.

Afro-diasporic religions operate under a transcorporeal conceptualization of the self that is radically different from the Western philosophical tradition. Unlike the unitary soul of Descartes, the immaterial aspect of the Afro-diasporic self is multiple, external, and removable. These various subjectivities rest upon a concave corporeal surface reminiscent of a saddle or an open calabash.

Unlike the Western idea of the body as the enclosure of the soul, the kòkadav is an open vessel that finds metaphoric and aesthetic expression in the *kwi*, *govi*, and *kanari* containers of Haitian Vodou. As Thompson explains, one of the most arresting sights for a newcomer into an Afro-diasporic religious setting is the collection and assortment of ritual containers:

> The close gathering of numerous bottles and containers, on various tiers, is a strong organizing principle in the world of vodun altars. That unifying concept, binding Haitian Rada altars to Dahomean altars in West Africa, precisely entails a constant elevation of a profusion of pottery upon a dais, an emphasis on simultaneous assuagement (the liquid in vessels) and exaltation (the ascending structure of the tiers). (1983, 182)

In fact, some of the most striking art objects of the African diaspora are anthropomorphic receptacles, as noted by Falgayrettes-Leveau, in her exhibition catalogue *Réceptacles*: "Les Kuba et les peuples apparentés du Zaïre ont priv-ilégié de façon presque systématique, mais avec raffinement, la représenta-tion de la tête dans la conception des plus beaux de leurs réceptacles: les coupes à boire le vin de palme" (1997, 32; The Kuba and their kin in Zaire have privileged in an almost codified, yet refined, manner the representation of the head in crafting the most beautiful of their receptacles: the cups for drinking palm wine). These cephalomorphic receptacles emblematize the function of the head—and through synecdoche, the body—as an open con-tainer. This association of the head with such ritual containers is evident in the use of a specific receptacle called *pòtet*, literally "container heads":

> This part of the initiation also involves the preparation of the pò tets, as containers for the new selves, repositories for ingredients symbolic of the new union of spirit and human being: hair, sacrificial food, herbs, and oils. When the initiates join the community for their presenta-tion as ounsis, they walk with these pots balanced on their heads and place them in the altar, as symbol of their entering the community as initiated ounsi. (Fernández Olmos and Paravisini-Gebert 2003, 118–19)

Wade Davis explains how the separation of the corporeal and immate-rial aspects of the self involving such containers effects the phenomenon of zombification:

> The spirit zombi, or the zombi of the ti bon ange alone, is carefully stored in a jar and may later be magically transmuted into insects, animals, or humans in order to accomplish the particular work of the bokòr. The remaining spiritual components of man, the n'âme, the gros bon ange, and the z'étoile, together form the zombi cadaver, the zombi of the flesh. (1986, 186)

This very detached description of the process of zombification is consis-tent with Davis's (1988, 7) clinical view of zombification as purely the result of neurotoxin poisoning. Davis views the tibonanj as the principal soul and the seat of individuality. However, this view is incongruent with the work of other scholars, who believe that "the famous zombies are people whose Gros-bon-ange has been captured by some evil hungan, thus becoming living-dead" (Métraux 1946, 87). Moreover, apart from zombification, there are various forms of spiritual embottlement, all of which involve the cap-turing of the gwobonanj, not the tibonanj. For instance, when the individual willingly decides to bottle up part of himself, it is the gwobonanj:

A certain amount of immunity against witchcraft may be obtained by requesting an hungan to extract the Gros-bon-ange from the body and to enclose it in a bottle. The soul, removed from its bodily envelope, may either be hidden or buried in a garden or entrusted to the hungan for safekeeping. (Métraux 1946, 86)

While this procedure protects the gwobonanj, it does not prevent bodily damage to the material body from which it proceeds. This creates a potentially dangerous scenario in which people who have sustained severe bodily injury— through either spells or accidents—will beg to have their gwobonanj liberated from the bottle, in order to end their corporeal suffering through death.

The gwobonanj must be ritually removed from the person's head shortly after death through the ceremony of *desounnen*, in which

the Oungan calls the spirit, or in some cases the name of the dead, then removes the lwa and puts it in a pitcher or bottle, called a *govi*. In death, the link between the spirit and its human vessel must be broken, so that the individual's spirit can move beyond death, and beyond revenge, joining the ancestors under the waters in the mythical place called *Ginen* (Guinea). (Dayan 1995, 261)

Then, a year and a day after death, the gwobonanj is called up from the water in a ceremony referred to as *relemònandlo* (calling the dead from the water) and installed in a govi clay pot (McCarthy Brown 2006, 8).

Davis is correct in his assessment of zombification as constituting the embottlement of one part of the self. However, he is mistaken in saying that this part is the tibonanj, since this and other types of spiritual embottlements involve the containment of the gwobonanj. Beyond noticing these important discrepancies, what is important for us here is to consider how regardless of what aspect of the self is bottled, according to all of these authors, any type of hermetic enclosing of the self is seen as potentially dangerous or associated with death. The fact that one of the most dreaded Afro-diasporic states of being should be so similar to the Cartesian view of the hermetically sealed soul points to the contestatory and critical relationship between these two philosophical traditions. Curiously, the zombified body of Haitian Vodou bears striking similarities to the body without organs that Gilles Deleuze and Félix Guattari elaborate in *L'anti-Oedipe*:

Instinct de mort, tel est son nom. Car le désir désire *aussi* cela, la mort, parce que le corps plein de la mort est son moteur immobile, parce que les organes de la vie sont la *working machine* . . .

FIG. I.3. The container substitutes for the body of the deceased in the process of zombification. Hector Hyppolite, *Vol de zombis*, 1946–48. 66 × 81 cm. Musée d'Art Haïtien.

Le corps sans organes n'est pas le témoin d'un néant originel, pas plus que le reste d'une totalité perdue. Il n'est surtout pas une projection; rien à voir avec le corps propre, ou avec un image du corps. C'est le corps sans image. Lui, l'improductif . . . le corps sans organes est de l'anti-production. (1972, 15)

Death instinct, that is its name. Because desire *also* desires that, death, because the body full of death is its immobile motor, because the organs of life are the *working machine* . . .

The body without organs is not the witness of an original nothingness, no more than the remains of a lost totality. It is not a projection; it has nothing to do with the body itself or with an image of the body. It is the body without an image. The unproductive itself . . . the body without organs is antiproduction.

In this sense, both the Western and African view of personhood can be seen as coinciding. By presenting the most abject state of being as that of the individual that is deprived of its constitutive elements—organs, gwobonanj—

both traditions present an image of the exploited, enslaved, unremunerated, and incomplete worker. Descartes's body as clockwork and Vodou's kòkadav are more similar than previously thought.

Unlike the Western idea of a unitary self that is fixed within the body, the African diasporic philosophical-religious tradition conceives of the body as a concavity upholding a self that is removable, external, and multiple. Allowing for a wider range of subjectivities than the more rigid Western model, the modular African diasporic discourse of personhood becomes a vehicle for the articulation of noncompliant identities that are usually constrained by normative heteropatriarchy.

Science and the Location of Consciousness

Recent scientific experiments in the area of perception and cognition present further evidence that the relationship between the self and the body is not a universal given, but imagined and constructed. Out-of-body experiments conducted by two research groups using slightly different methods expanded upon the so-called rubber hand illusion. In that illusion, people hide one hand in their lap and look at a rubber hand set on a table in front of them. As a researcher strokes the real hand and the rubber hand at the same time with a stick, people have the sensation that the rubber hand is their own. When a hammer hits the rubber hand, the subjects recoil or cringe. Various versions of this experiment have been repeated through the use of whole-body illusions created through virtual reality technology (Ehrsson 2007, 1048). The subjects wore goggles connected to two video cameras placed six feet behind them and, as a result, saw their own backs from the perspective of a virtual person located behind them. When the researcher stroked the subject's chest and moved the second stick under the camera lenses simultaneously, the subjects reported the sense of being outside of their own bodies, looking at themselves from a distance where the cameras were located. The scientists infer from these experiments that they now understand how the brain combines visual and tactile information to compute and determine where the self is located in space. These experiments are relevant to us in that they help us to understand that the location of the self vis-à-vis the body is culturally constructed through the senses. The body and its self need not be coterminous. The self need not reside inside the body, but may be imagined or placed externally. In different ways, current scientific discourse coincides with Afrodiasporic philosophy in its exposure of subjective inwardness as an illusion.

The Oyěwùmí/Matory Debate

A notable genealogical trajectory for my project can trace its roots to the debate between Oyèrónké Oyěwùmí and J. Lorand Matory, which took place at the 1999 Globalization of Yorùbá Religious Culture Conference at Florida International University in Miami. This debate—outlined in Matory's (2005a, 2005b) *Black Atlantic Religion* and *Sex and the Empire That Is No More*, Oyěwùmí's (1997) *The Invention of Women*, and Olupona and Rey's (2008) *Òrìṣà Devotion as World Religion*—concerns the cross-cultural applicability of the concept of gender and the politics of positionality in cultural criticism.

The debate has inspired multiple public lectures, a large number of scholarly articles, the founding of an online journal, one edited volume, hundreds of citations, and to date at least one book devoted exclusively to the topic (Matory 2008, 516). While it would be beyond the scope of this present study to delve at length into all the complexities of this interaction and into the abundant scholarship it has generated, it might be in order for us to revisit some of the main points of contention in order to provide inroads for readers wishing to become more fully acquainted with its details on their own.

Nostalgically alluding to a mythical African past and defying established feminist criticism, Oyěwùmí introduces the controversial idea that the category of woman did not exist in pre-colonial Africa. Oyěwùmí's argument is built on the premise that semantic analysis of kinship terms in Yorùbá reveals that seniority, not gender, was the definitive societal form of subjective categorization. Matory contradicts her hypothesis by providing alternative interpretations of Yorùbá lexical items and by exposing a current practice of transvestism in Yorùbá religions, going back to pre-colonial times in Africa. The ability to don the garments of another gender, as the femininely clad male priests of Ṣàngó have done in Nigeria for centuries, points to the social reality of gender. One cannot transgress a nonexistent boundary. While Oyěwùmí sees gender in contemporary Yorùbá society as a European colonial importation, Matory, on the other hand, understands gender as a long-standing reality of Yorùbá social life. Sacramental cross-dressing, far from evidencing the nonexistence of gender, for Matory implies clear categories that can under certain limited situations be transposed. Firmly staking her ground, Oyěwùmí takes issue with Matory's presentation of transvestism in Yorùbá religious life. Her genderless model would simply explain the female-clad and -coiffed male priests of Ṣàngó not as men who dress as women, but as wives of the orisha.[7]

The importance of the debate cannot be understood without some attention to the matter of authorial reflexivity. Oyěwùmí deploys her status as Yorùbá royalty for authenticity purposes (1997, xvi), and Matory, an African American, exposes the blind spots that class privilege can bestow upon such a "princess" (2008, 515). As much of the debate pivots around the correct English translations of key Yorùbá language terms, who has the ultimate right to linguistic—and cultural—interpretation among Afro-diasporic scholars over African languages' terminology is at stake. This became clearly visible in Oyěwùmí's choleric remarks when Matory corrected a missed Yorùbá plural marker in her spontaneous translation of another scholar's address (2008, 544). Undergirding the entire debate is the tacit fact that an African woman's definition of the category of "woman" is being challenged by a black man, confounding the gist of the debate with the specter of patriarchy and intra-ethnic gendered antagonisms. Matory notes that Oyěwùmí avoids all direct quotation of his work (2008, 526), and that instead of citing his book, she chooses to cite his relatively unavailable 1991 dissertation (515). There is no essay of Oyěwùmí's in the Olupona and Rey (2008) volume, and that her argument is recapitulated by another female scholar, Rita Laura Segato, only adds to the controversy over who has the right to speak for whom and in what manner. The fact that Oyěwùmí's book was the winner of the American Sociological Association Sex and Gender Section's 1998 Distinguished Book Award would have lent her argument something of a protective shield until the politics of representation again reared its head when it became known that not a single Africanist was among the panel of judges. Redressing this omission, the 2008 African Studies Association conference hosted a panel of Africanist scholars to discuss the work through the lenses of this regional specialist expertise.

Both scholars agree on the notion that the Yorùbá conception of gender defies the binary constraints of Western Cartesian representations of the body. This common platform may very well serve as the point of departure for a continued investigation into what has been one of the most polemic issues in Yorùbá religious studies for the past two decades: that is, the question of how Yorùbá culture constructs the body and how this construction might produce gender categories that surpass the constraints of Western modes of being. Neither Matory's nor Oyěwùmí's project asks where the body is in relation to the spirit/essence/anima, nor do they engage with the theories and testimonies surrounding spiritual embodiment, especially as they configure queer subjects. I surmise that the elucidation of the body/self relationship I present here can reorient the deliberation on gender they inaugurated in this new direction for the current and upcoming generation of scholars of black Atlantic religions.

Calling on the intellectual virtues of the orisha and lwa of wisdom, Oxalá-Dambala-Obatalá, it pleases me to present *Queering Black Atlantic Religions* as an offering to advance the terrestrial conversation about the divine in the black Atlantic on the twentieth anniversary of the 1999 conference in which the Matory-Oyěwùmí debate first emerged. Upon learning these introductory family secrets, you have firmly and irreversibly traversed the threshold. You may now confidently enter the igbodu, the Yorùbá "womb of the forest," a place where your psyche and body will be prepared for your new sacramental function as the "ìyáwó," the bride of the Spirit. As you turn the leaf onto this new chapter of your existence and settle into the silence of your cloister, await there the revelation of the hallowed technology allowing you to bear this matrimonial title, irrespective of your sexual anatomy and gender expression.

PART I

VODOU

OF DREAMS AND NIGHT MARES
Vodou Women Queering the Body

The matrix of Haitian Vodou scholarship contains an as-yet-uncharted an-thropological narrative thread that is distinctly female authored. Making up a veritable genre of Vodou *écriture féminine*, the corpus of this work coheres around the themes of embodiment, desire, and homosociality. All of these texts share the common narrative of a female anthropologist integrating herself into a Vodou community, originally for the sole purpose of writing a scholarly memoir and gradually becoming a practitioner and initiate. The narratives share a preference for dreaming as leitmotif and metaphor for me-diumship. They nearly always begin with an explanation of the horse and rider metaphor and end climactically with a trance possession experience, ideally the author's own but also those experienced by close acquaintances. In so doing, the narratives can be understood as constituting oneiric, abstracted, condensed, and abruptly ended Vodou ceremonies. In this first chapter, the ethnography as ceremony refracts the initiatory chamber metaphor developed in the introduction and foreshadows the notion of transcripturality revealed in the conclusion.

In order to understand the construction, evolution, and impact of this genre, this chapter examines the initiatory-critical works of five female anthropologists to study how women's perspectives on Haitian Vodou corporeality problematize the Cartesian mind/body problem. These five texts were published at an average interval of eighteen years from the early twentieth century to the early twenty-first century. These are, in chronological order, Zora Neale Hurston's *Tell My Horse* (1938), Maya Deren's *Divine Horsemen* (1953), Katherine Dunham's *Island Possessed* (1969), Karen McCarthy Brown's *Mama Lola* (1991), and Mimerose Beaubrun's *Nan Dòmi* (2010). Through the notion of transcorporeality, I propose that there is a feminist and queer convergence in the common deployment of Vodou potentialities to develop more enabling models of embodiment.[1]

The very title of the most recent book of this collection, *Nan Dòmi*, highlights the important role that dreams play in the process of becoming a Vodouisant. This latest book in the tradition outlined here stands as the culmination of an intertextual conversation that deploys dreaming as a metaphor for entering the metaphysical dimension of trance possession, initiation, communion with the divine, and mystical knowledge. Throughout the text, Beaubrun provides the reader with extended descriptions of dreams that function as commentaries, warnings, and exhortations about the waking world. Dreams become such an important part of the narrative that we begin to question whether dreams are in fact derivative from the so-called real. Perhaps dreaming is primary and the source of our waking actions, Beaubrun makes us ponder: "Le rêve, pour moi, c'était un monde imaginaire de souvenirs cachés. . . . Mais, pour tante Tansia, le rêve était un état du monde inconnu qui n'avait aucun rapport avec l'imagination. 'Il est réel,' m'apprit-elle" (2010, 41). "Dreaming, in my view, consisted of an imaginary world of hidden memories. . . . But for Aunt Tansia, dreaming was a state of the unknown world that had no connection to the imagination. 'It is real,' she taught me" (2013, 41). Paradoxically, the sleeper's eyes are open: "Rêver c'est voir. . . . Un rêveur est un *médium voyant*, un témoin de l'Inconnu" (2010, 73). "To dream is to see. . . . A dreamer is a medium, a witness to the unknown" (2013, 71).

Under the tutelage of her mentor, Aunt Tansia, Beaubrun begins to understand the importance of dreaming: "Rêver . . . c'est non seulement avoir la capacité de regarder le monde connu mais aussi d'être témoin de l'Inconnu" (2010, 68). "The purpose of dreaming was to develop the ability to see the known world, but also to be a witness to the Unknown" (2013, 67). This unknown world is populated by ancestral and divine spirits from Africa, a continent that is known mystically in Vodou as Ginen: Nan Dòmi is a state to master, "les manifestations de l'Esprit et le sèvis Ginen" (Beaubrun 2010, 45); "the manifestations of the spirit and the service of Ginen" (2013, 45). Regarding the referent for Ginen, Bien-Aimé, another spiritual mentor, deflects Beaubrun away from clear physical geographies: "'Qu'est-ce que le Ginen?' Il me répondit: 'Se sa w pa wè a'" (C'est l'Invisible)" (2010, 34). "'What is Ginen?' He answered, 'Se sa w pa we'a' (It is the Invisible)" (2013, 34). Dreaming is more than traveling or returning to an ancestral land; it is accessing an existing parallel dimension of knowledge and being. And for that it becomes necessary to expand one's sight. Much of Beabrun's apprenticeship with Aunt Tansia involves learning how to access and manage spiritual technologies of dreaming: "Pour entrer en état de rêve, me disait encore tante Tansia, il faut savoir faire silence en soi; il faut faire taire toutes les pensées" (2010, 68). "'To enter into the dream state,' Aunt Tansia repeated to me, 'it is necessary to silence oneself. One must silence all thoughts'" (2013, 67). The stilling of the mind renders the Vodouisant clairvoyant: "Le moun Ginen le peut, parce qu'il a le Je (pouvoir surnaturel de voyance, don de clairvoyance . . .)" (2010, 34). "Moun ginen can do it because he has Je (literally 'eye,' or 'opening,' can refer to supernatural power of seeing, clairvoyance . . .)" (Beaubrun 2013, 34). Katherine Dunham also records mystical eyes as referents for clairvoyance: "Prix des yeux: 'Prize of eyes,' or 'price of the eyes'; clairvoyance. Highest degree of vaudun initiates" (1969, 279).

Through the aperture provided by Nan Dòmi, we are able to appreciate the importance of dreaming in the worldview of Vodou and just how female ethnographers have been able to comment on the development of this mystical vision. Maya Deren, whose birth name is Eleanora Derenkowskaia, deploys the Sanskrit name for dreams and illusion—Maya—to craft a mystical authorial identity for herself. Her seminal book and film, both called Divine Horsemen, utilize stream-of-consciousness techniques to achieve a surrealistic, dreamlike quality of great psychological depth. She describes her trance possession at the end of her book as a dream (Deren 1970, 259). In contrast to this tail-end figuration of dreaming, Zora Neale Hurston, in Tell My Horse, presents how the spiritual journey starts with dreams: "How does a man know that he has been called? It usually begins in troubled dreams" (1990, 122). Dreams bookend the initiation narration of these female anthropologists, and this narrative frame encapsulates various other dreams, forcing us to consider how, if the book is a microcosm and mirror of life, perhaps we are dreaming that/what we are reading. In Mama Lola, Karen McCarthy Brown (1991, 206, 207, 213, 255) records how her informant's mother, Philo, communicates with the lwas in dreams. When

Philo wants to end her pregnancy, a white woman comes into her dreams to warn her against aborting (209). This old white woman tells her not to come to her house, the hospital, to have the baby (211). The hospital bears the name Our Lady of Lourdes, syncretized with Ezili Dantò. As a result of this warning, the baby is born into the chamber pot, at home, escapes an epidemic at the hospital, and receives a name that is a creolized form of the Catholic saint, Aloud or Alourdes (212). Years later, Dantò appears to Aloud in a dream—as she did to her own mother—to counsel her to keep her child (240). Here, McCarthy Brown reiterates Hurston's idea that the calling begins with a dream by narrating how these dreams do in fact launch the spiritual journeys of female mambos.

Constituents of the Self

Just as dreaming functions as a descriptor for the phenomenon of trance possession, we can see how the self itself is dreamed—that is, imagined, projected, symbolically represented—as constructed of many material and immaterial constitutive parts in the worldview of Vodou.

The constituents of the self in Vodou are multiple. There are three components that are understood as bodies. First is the *kòkadav*, or the physical body. Second is the *nannan*, an astral body that serves as a double, normally enveloped by the kòkadav. However, in the dream state, the physical body that represents the gwobonanj is contained by the nannan "pour pouvoir protéger le rêveur en lui donnant un sentiment de solidité" (Beaubrun 2010, 89); "to protect the dreamer by giving him a sense of solidity" (2013, 86). Third, there is the *nannan-rèv*, which is the dream body (Beaubrun 2010, 89; 2013, 86).

Among the immaterial aspects of the self, three are of central importance in the construction of the body in Vodou. There is some debate in the literature as to which one is the repository of the personality or character of the individual and which is more akin to the Western notion of the soul, but the important point to apprehend is that like the various bodies, the psyche in Vodou is multiple.

The first one is *esprit*, which can be translated as "intelligence," "energy and action of the mind," "source and the act of judgement, decision, desire and all of the motivation and the will projected in a man's visible action" (Deren 1970, 25). The esprit is a "person's 'life principle,' his nature or character rather than in an exclusive or mystical sense. In this sense it approximates English 'spirit' as in the 'spirit of the times'" (18).

The remaining parts of the psyche are given considerably more attention in the literature, as these are more active and engaged in the processes of living, dying, and trance. These two parts are the tibonanj or little guardian angel, and the gwobonanj or big guardian angel.

The tibonanj, also called *lanvè* or *selidò*, is the spiritual body, a portion of God, which controls the dream state: "The universal commitment towards good, the notion of truth as desirable, all that conscience which, in our culture is understood as a function of the soul is, for the Haitian, the function of a third element, the *ti-bon-ange*" (Deren 1970, 26), which is automatically liberated at the moment of death, is objective conscience, and, consequently, cannot lie (44).

On the other hand, the gwobonanj, known also as *ladwat* or *sèmèdò*, functions as the mental world or intellect (Beaubrun 2013, 42), personality, or consciousness (McCarthy Brown 1991, 384), the invisible nonmaterial character of an individual, as distinguished from the physical body—which is more like psyche than soul (Deren 1970, 18). The gwobonanj is the "metaphysical double of the physical being . . . the immortal twin of mortal man . . . similar to what we understand by a man's soul, if we think of the soul as duplicating the man and not as a moral force of a 'higher' nature . . . the repository of a man's history" (Deren 1970, 26–27).

It is the elucidation and the functioning of the gwobonanj to which most of the literature of body corporeality is devoted because this is precisely the part of the psyche that is movable during trance: "Those who serve the Vodou spirits believe that, in possession, the *gwobonanj* leaves the body and floats loose in the world" (McCarthy Brown 1991, 352). Deren explains that the lwa is itself a gwobonanj and it is this very nature that allows it to replace temporarily the gwobonanj of the devotee during trance:

> Man has a material body, animated by an *esprit* or *gros-bon-ange*—the soul, spirit, psyche or self—which, being non-material, does not share the death of the body. This soul may achieve . . . the status of a loa, a divinity and become the archetypal representative of some natural or moral principle. As such, it has the power to displace temporarily the gros-bon-ange of a living person and become the animating force of his physical body. This psychic phenomenon is known as "possession." (1970, 16)

As the most recent book among this collection of female-authored initiatory ethnographies, Beaubrun's *Nan Dòmi* is the most profoundly personal and the narrative that most clearly states the need to transcend the egoic self-hood that is the gwobonanj. Her book begins as an anthropology thesis and then becomes a personal journey (Beaubrun 2013, 32). Her movement from detached, idealized objectivity to a participatory subjectivity forces her to confront her strong sense of individuality. Aunt Tansia keeps telling her that she is limited in her growth by clinging to her personality, her "Moi/I" (Beaubrun 2010, 67; 2013, 66): "Tu n'es en sécurité que lorsque tu trouves des explications" (2010, 81); "You only feel safe when you have explanations" (2013, 78). "[Il faut] te défaire de ta raison" (2010, 74); "Free yourself of your reason" (2013, 72), Aunt Tansia tells her. "Danse, ma fille, danse. . . . Tout danse, l'univers et tout ce qu'il contient, les énergies dansent" (2010, 75). "Dance my child, dance. . . . Everything dances. The entire universe and everything it contains, the energies dance" (2013, 72–73). Throughout the narrative, Aunt Tansia urges Beaubrun to lose her personality. Her teaching insists that one's personality is not one's being: "Ta personalité a été fabriquée par ce monde-ci et pour le fonctionnement de ce monde. On t'a donné un nom, une classe et une éducation" (Beaubrun 2010, 105). "Your personality has been constructed by this world for the functioning of this world. You have been given a name, a class, and an education" (2013, 101). According to Aunt Tansia, societal norms and prohibitions play a large role in the construction of the personality. She urges Beaubrun (2013, 101) to look deep inside for that being who is a mystery. Many of Beaubrun's challenges in the transcending of her egoic self lie in her attachment to language. Aunt Tansia kindly chides her: "Tu aimes trop les mots. Tu deviens dépendante. C'est ce qui cause le blocage des poètes. Prisonniers des mots, ils restent d'éternels nostalgiques d'un monde qu'ils ont perçu sans pouvoir vraiment le décrire" (2010, 96). "You love words too much. You become dependent on them. That is what causes blockages in poets. Prisoners of words, they remain eternally nostalgic for a world that they have perceived, but never truly been able to describe" (2013, 93). Finally, in the epilogue, Beaubrun succeeds in her attempt to shed the egoic self. When her husband, Lòlò, tells her, "Tu vas laisser ta trace à travers ce livre" (You are going to leave your mark through this book), she firmly replies, "Non, au contraire, je vais plutôt l'effacer" (No, on the contrary, instead I am going to erase it) (Beaubrun 2010, 279; 2013, 267).

The modular nature of these different parts of the self becomes evident in various Vodou life-cycle rituals. *Kanzo* is a fire ritual of initiation that creates a composite life made up of the lwa, the initiate, and the sacrificed animal in the pòtèt (Deren 1970, 220–22). The ritual of *desounnen* separates all three parts of the initiate upon death: the body, the gwobonanj (the personal soul or self), and the *lwamètèt* (the spirit who is the master of the head; Deren 1970, 44). The gwobonanj, now liberated from the bond with the lwa and the material body of the deceased, is now free to become a lwa or a tutelary family spirit (45). The ritual of *retirer d'en bas de l'eau* is a ceremony that takes place one year and a day after the death of the initiate. It is the feast in which the spirit is freed and then reclaimed from the waters of the abyss to embody a *govi* (27, 220–22, 336). This govi becomes a replacement for the deceased body: "The clay jar, or *govi*, in which it is placed at this ceremony is a substitute for the vessel of flesh which once contained it. Out of the mouth of the jar issue the counsels and wisdoms by which the deceased continues to aid and advance his descendants" (28). The fact that the jar can substitute for the body underscores the image of the body as receptacular in nature.

Zombification is a process of desubjectification that further evidences the multiplicity of the immaterial self, the removal and substitution of these various parts, the role of the body as container, and the modularity of the dreamed, constructed self. Katherine Dunham provides a most apt definition of the zombie:

> The first definition of the creature is that of a truly dead person who by the intervention of black magic has been brought back to life, but by such a process that memory and will are gone and the resultant being is entirely subject to the will of the sorcerer who resuscitated him, in the service of good or evil. (1969, 184)

Perhaps the dread of zombification curtailed the need for specificity, for in the explanation of this matter Deren relapses into using the word "soul," which she finds so inadequate in the context of Vodou: "The dread zombie, the major figure of terror, is precisely this: the body without a soul, matter without morality" (1970, 42). Zora Neale Hurston also uses the terminology of "soul," this time evoking the image of it as "the breath of life," which can be sucked out, inhaled, and possibly smelled:

> After the proper ceremony, the Bocor in his most powerful and dreaded aspect mounts a horse with his face toward the horse's tail and rides after dark to the house of the victim. There he places his lips to the crack of the door and sucks out the soul of the victim and rides off in all speed. Soon the victim falls ill, usually beginning with a headache, and in a few hours is dead. (1990, 181–82)

After this, the houngan keeps the soul, either in a bottle or in his hand. He calls the dead body at midnight using the soul as bait. Then, "the dead man answers

FIG. 1.1. Zora Neale Hurston drumming in Haiti. Library of Congress, *New York World-Telegram and the Sun* Newspaper Photograph Collection, 1937, http://www.loc .gov/pictures/item/98511782/. *World-Telegram* staff photographer.

by lifting his head and the moment he does this, the Bocor passes the soul under the nose for a brief second and chains his wrist" (Hurston 1990, 182).

This feminine dreaming of the body becomes most visibly gendered in the mythical role that the womb plays in the construction of the Vodou body. In Haitian folklore, the phenomenon of *pèdysion* is the popular belief in the possibility of withheld pregnancies (McCarthy Brown 1991, 243). After conception, a pregnancy can be halted and resumed so that women may say that they have actually been pregnant for years. This allows women to claim that men with whom they had sexual relations in the distant past are the fathers of their newborns. This mythical imagining of the womb outlined by Karen McCarthy Brown illuminates Mimerose Beaubrun's statement, "La matrice, dit-elle, porte toutes nos frustrations, nos peurs, nos complexes, etc." (2010, 76); "The womb . . . contains all our frustrations, our fears, our complexes, and the like" (2013, 74). This is why Aunt Tansia urges her to *woule vant*, to roll her belly to exorcise her fears:

> Elle m'apprit le mouvement *woule vant* (danse du ventre), dans le deux sens, qui consiste à faire rouler la peau de mon ventre à partir de mon bassin en montant, puis dans le sens inverse. Elle me conseilla de faire ce mouvement jusqu'à ressentir une sensation pareille à celle de l'orgasme. Son dessein était de me porter à découvrir la perception de roule vant avec ma matrice. (Beaubrun 2010, 76)

> She taught me how to do the *woule vant* (belly dance) in two directions. The dance consisted of rolling my stomach from my pelvis up, then doing the same thing in the opposite direction. She advised me to perform this movement until I felt a sensation similar to an orgasm. Her plan was to lead me to become aware of the belly dance in the womb. (Beaubrun 2013, 73–74)

Herein we see the great allure of women's exploration of models of embodiment that could present an alternative to the soul-encased body schematization inherited from Descartes. If the gwobonaj, as the principal immaterial aspect of the self, can be external, removable, and temporarily replaced, how might a female subjectivity, particularly a queer female subjectivity, dream of using such a novel model for her own advantageous self-crafting?

Vodou Non-heteronormativities

The modularity of the self, preserved in these African-diasporic religions, allows for the temporary substitution of the gwobonanj by the lwa, allowing for cross-gender identifications to take place during trance:

> If a male loa possesses a female devotee, the name of the loa or the pronoun *he* will be used (as it always is in Voudoun) when referring

to the acting subject responsible for all events transpiring during that possession; and conversely, if a female loa possesses a male, the pronoun will be *she*. (Deren 1970, 17)

This regendering of the body has some very visible sartorial effects:

Baron Samedi delights in dressing his "horses" in shabby and fantastic clothes like Papa Guedé. Women dressed like men and men like women. Often the men, in addition to wearing female clothes, thrust a calabash up under their skirts to simulate pregnancy. Women put on men's coats and prance about with a stick between their legs to imitate the male sex organs. (Hurston 1990, 224)

The phenomenon of possession that enables this performative regendering of the body in the ritual context, far from being contained within the sacred space, spills over into the realm of the profane. For example, Carnival is one event in which such regenderings are visible:[2]

It is common for men and women to exchange clothes, perhaps with the desire to satisfy homosexual inclinations. With nightfall, all possible remaining restrictions are automatically cast aside, and the play element becomes decidedly orgiastic. . . . Homosexual activity is very common to these mass bands. It is not at all unusual to see two men in the embrace of the gouillé dance. A person who, in everyday life, shows no abnormal inclinations will, under the increasing momentum of the Mardi Gras, seek out persons of the same sex for the erotic dances. (Dunham 1983, 44–45)

Dreaming the body with the technologies of Vodou corporeality implies the possibility of constructing a gendered subjectivity with greater freedom and flexibility than that allowed by the interiorizing model of the European philosophical tradition. The cashew-nut-like external and removable anima allows for a modular bodily schema, accounts for trance possession, and enables the regendering of the female body in the sacred and profane realms of Haitian cultural life. In all of these accounts there is a diffused and buried self-awareness of an enabling malleability of the self that is alluring to the female and queer ethnographer. Yet it is the role of the critic to give voice to the impetus behind such research on Vodou embodiment, since for many of these female ethnographers, likely due to sociotemporal conventions, the desires animating their inquiry remain something of a taboo.

Transcorporeality, as the modular aspect of the self that allows the ritual and everyday flourishing of non-heteronormative performance and identifications, underpins the varied forms of female homosociality we encounter in this tradition of Vodou ethnographies written by women. Mimerose Beaubrun's husband is Theodore "Lòlò" Beaubrun (2013, 27), but he is largely absent from the body of the narrative. He is introduced at the beginning of the spiritual diary that the book is and only returns in a significant way at the end of the narrative, when one could almost say she is reconciled to him, as if there had been a marital estrangement. The fact that his nickname, Lòlò, means "penis" in Martinican Kréyòl seems to reduce him to a mere reproductive and practical sexual object. The renewed intimacy occurs as Beaubrun discovers her husband's spiritual sensitivity and intuition and learns that their "intimacy went beyond the marital bond" (Beaubrun 2013, 257; intimité allait au-delà des liens maritaux) (2010, 269). In the body of the narrative, the main relationship is that between initiate and mentor, Beaubrun and Aunt Tansia, who share a deep sensuous bond.

Nan Dòmi has an arc that begins and returns to the marriage between the author and her husband. This relationship seems to adopt Aunt Tansia and then evacuates her—she appears to be expiatorily sacrificed in her death—allowing the heterosexual couple the experience of a quasi-sexual trial that, in the end, serves to deepen their bond. Beaubrun (2013, 74) explicitly declares her love for Aunt Tansia, something she never does for her husband. Beaubrun composes a love poem, directed presumably to the earth, yet it seems obliquely addressed to Aunt Tansia. Using language that conveys a sense of erotic ecstasy and bliss, she writes,

Je veux te remercier Maman chérie!
Bénie sois-tu, Mère secourable
Oh! comme je t'aime!
J'aime ton odeur . . .
Apprends-moi à l'exhaler
Dans les grains
De poussières qui forment
Ton temple, ma chair
Fais-la-moi sentir dans l'air que je respire
À chaque seconde

Apprends-moi à vibrer suivant ton rythme
J'ai tellement besoin de toi! (2010, 243)

I want to thank you dear Mother!
Bless you helpful Mother
Oh! How I love you!
I love your scent . . .
Help me to exhale it
In the particles
Of dust that form
Your temple, my flesh
Make me sense it in the air I breathe
At every moment
Teach me to vibrate to your rhythm
I have such need of you! (2013, 233)

Beaubrun is sensuously captivated by Aunt Tansia's appearance: "Tansia était très belle. C'était la plus belle femme du pays. Elle avait la peau couleur de pêche, elle avait les cheveux épais et ondulés, des dents blanches, des yeux marron clair et mesurait un mètre soixante-quinze" (2010, 55). "Tansia was very beautiful. She was the most beautiful woman in the country. Her skin was the color of a peach, her hair thick and wavy, her teeth white, eyes a clear brown, and she was five feet seven inches tall" (2013, 55). The gaze of desire is perceptible enough that Aunt Tansia must question her about its nature:

> Pendant qu'elle parlait, son visage se transforma; ses traits devinrent ceux d'une jeune femme. Elle était très, très belle. Elle détacha son chignon, ses cheveux avaient une couleur de miel. Elle était agile, à l'aise, et se déplaçait avec coquetterie. Si ce changement d'apparence physique était surprenant, son changement d'humeur l'était encore plus. J'étais ébahie, je n'en croyais pas mes yeux. Elle vit ma surprise et me dit: "Pourquoi me regardes-tu comme ça." (2010, 54)

> While she was speaking her face was transformed; her features became those of a young woman. She was very, very beautiful. She unfastened her chignon. Her hair was the color of honey. She was agile, at ease, and moved coquettishly. If this change in her physical appearance was surprising, her changed mood was even more so. I was astounded. I could not believe my eyes. She saw my surprise and said, "Why are you looking at me like that?" (2013, 54)

Beaubrun describes her closeness to Tansia in a thinly veiled erotic language. The relationship is close enough for Aunt Tansia to tell Beaubrun to remember to wash her "*bouboun* (pubis)" (2010, 64; 2013, 64). Also, recalling the postlude of one of her possession/dreaming episodes, she writes, "Il faisait noir. J'ouvris grand les yeux, un moment je perçus du jaune safran puis du blanc, et je me réveillai blottie dans la jupe de tante Tansia. Mon corps tremblait, secoué de spasmes. Elle me fit boire l'eau, en passa sur mon visage. J'avais chaud" (2010, 58). "It was all black. I opened my eyes wide; at one moment I saw saffron yellow, then white, and I awoke nestled in Aunt Tansia's skirt. My body trembled, seized by spasms. She had me drink some water, pouring it over my face. I was hot" (2013, 58).

This coded lesbianism is also perceptible in Katherine Dunham's lifework. One of her biographers reads the caption describing the "gay good spirits" of Dunham's company as coded queerness. The male dancers' jutting hips only accentuate the queer implications. Many of the dancers were associated with Carl Van Vechten's gay social circle. George Chauncey's oral history confirms the reputation of the Dunham Company as one center for gay life in Harlem during the mid-twentieth century (Manning 2005, 262). Dunham's (1969, 60–61) *Island Possessed* is pervaded by sensuous descriptions of extremely close bodily contact with other female initiates in ceremonies. This culminates in a thinly veiled homoerotic situation:

> Guédé Nimbo should have waited before mounting the woman in my lap. . . . She had slept heavily since inserting herself again between us, angled backward into my lap, scarcely waking when we turned. . . . She breathed open-mouthed and I could smell Guédé's alcohol and pipe tobacco. (Dunham 1969, 78)

Her biographer identifies this woman as a lesbian (Aschenbrenner 2002, 76). Commenting on the non-heteronormativity that pervades popular and peasant culture in Haiti, Dunham writes, "There has been a fusion of the forms of polygamy which flourish in variety in Africa, to produce the Haitian system" (1969, 83). She appears to have lived and loved in accordance with this non-heteronormative polyamory, in which she had as lovers deities, men, and several unnamed, ungendered, anonymous people. Judging from the suggestions and intimations outlined above, would it be far-fetched to assume women were among them?

> At the time of my wedding to Damballa I was already married, though hardly mature enough of spirit to realize it, to someone who would

FIG. 1.2. Katherine Dunham as *Woman with a Cigar*, undated. Photograph by Alfredo Valenti. Used courtesy of Library of Congress. From Special Collections Research Center, Morris Library, Southern Illinois University, Carbondale.

perhaps rather remain anonymous; I felt myself in love with a dear friend who might also rather remain anonymous; I was smitten with one or more college professors, fascinated by Dumarsais Estimé, and engaged in more ways than one to Fred Alsop. (Dunham 1969, 111)

Lastly, this coded lesbianism is evident in her stage performance and commercial self-portraiture. In *Tropics—Shore Excursion*, Dunham performs "as the 'Woman with the Cigar.'" Personifying the phallic woman, Dunham uses the cigar to regender her body but also to "allude to the religious practices of Santería, a fusion of Yorùbá and Catholic practices that originated in Cuba. On the other hand, Dunham based the dance on Caribbean market women known as Madame Sara, market women who often supported 'wives'" (Manning 2005, 262). The fact that the body functions as the receptacle of an external anima allows for an imagination, a dreaming, of the relationship between sex and gender to be less fixed than in the Cartesian model of bodily soul entrapment. This allows for an exploration of female homosociality in the sacred and profane aspects of Haitian culture, even if these forms of same-sex bonding and queer desire require critical decoding to make them visible.

The Trope of the Tragic Lesbian

One of the distinguishing features of the corpus of female-authored Vodou initiatory ethnographies is their frank exposition of lesbianism, a bold move especially for those writing before the 1970s. Nevertheless, the presentation of same-sex-loving women largely ends in tragedy, evoking an early trope in the depiction of lesbianism in modernist European cultural works such as Radclyffe Hall's *The Well of Loneliness* (1928) and Leontine Sagan's *Mädchen in Uniform* (1931).

The first instance of lesbianism in these female-authored ethnographies is found in Zora Neale Hurston's *Tell My Horse*:

> A tragic case of a Guédé mount happened near Pont Beaudet. A woman known to be a Lesbian was "mounted" one afternoon. The spirit announced through her mouth, "Tell my horse I have told this woman repeatedly to stop making love to women. It is a vile thing and I object to it. Tell my horse that this woman promised me twice that she would never do such a thing again, but each time she has broken her word to me as soon as she could find a woman suitable for her purpose. But she has made love to women for the last time. Tell my horse to tell that woman I am going to kill her today. She will not lie again." The woman pranced and galloped like a horse to a great mango tree, climbed it far up among the top limbs and dived off and broke her neck. (1990, 222)

The fact that this scene immediately follows the revelation of the meaning of the title of the book highlights the importance accorded to same-sex desire by the author. Beyond illustrating the title of book, this passage is presented at a culminating point of the book, very near the end of the narrative. Given the thematic and narrative location of the scene, we could argue that the axis of the book is lesbian and that *Tell My Horse* is non-heteronormatively centered. Her discussion of lesbianism in 1938 is groundbreaking for the fields of black Atlantic religions and anthropology. The death of the lesbian is a literary cliché of the times, and it may have been the only way in which such a representation would have endured editorial censorship. Nevertheless, it remains important to note that it is spiritual infidelity, not necessarily homophobia, which prompts the lwa to kill her horse.

A similar rendition of the tragic lesbian occurs in Karen McCarthy Brown's *Mama Lola*, in the chapter "Dreams and Promises" when it is revealed that the spiritual grandmother of Alourdes is a lesbian:

"In Santo Domingo, there was a woman, a *manbo*. Madame Gilbert was her name, and she had a very strong spirit named Agèou. He worked, worked, worked. People came from all over the Dominicain to see Madame Gilbert and her Agèou. Any problem—any problem!—Agèou could treat it.

"But Agèou became angry with Madame Gilbert. She was . . . you know . . . a lesbian," Philo said, dropping her voice, "and she was always buying things for women. She bought them clothes . . . perfumes . . . jewelry. All her money she spent on those women. She did not give Agèou even one candle! She expected him to work, but she gave him nothing! There was one day Agèou came in Madame Gilbert's head, and he got so mad, he made her cut off her finger. He did that!" Philo sighed, and, for the first time since she began talking, she looked Rapelle in the eye. "That woman—so stupid!"

Philo's voice quickly fell back to its somber cadence, and her eyes locked on the cup of herbal tea she held in her hand. "Madame Gilbert changed nothing. She went right on buying, buying for all those women. She did not offer one little thing to Agèou. So he made her sick. She got tuberculosis . . . consumption. She started to vomit blood. They took her to the hospital. Finally she died—and do you know what happened?" Rapelle did not attempt to answer. "Not one of those women came to see her in the hospital. Not one came to the funeral. Not one." (1991, 206–7)

Also here, it becomes important to note how the mambo's death is not brought about by homophobia per se, but through sacramental infidelity, the neglect of spiritual duties and the jealousy that this produces in the lwa. In the passage, there is no hint of social condemnation for same-sex desire. Instead we find a frank discussion of sexual non-heteronormativity and the acceptance of women-loving women by the lwa, as long as they can maintain a balance between their sexual and spiritual lives. Nevertheless, the fact that narratives of same-sex-loving women are permitted so long as the love story ends in tragedy and death remains problematic and indicative of powerful hetero-patriarchal force in the discourse of Haitian cultural life.

Similarly, Alourdes loses a baby when her jealous husband kicks her as he misinterprets her sisterly affection for the maid as sexual (McCarthy Brown 1991, 240). Rather than a condemnation of lesbianism, what we have here is an exposure of the affront to patriarchy that such bonding between women represents. The tragic lesbian in this literary tradition is not a morality tale

in which reproductive heterosexuality asserts itself as victorious and virtuous. Rather, the power present in female homosociality and same-sex desire
between women is presented as a force that husbands and gods seek to channel for themselves at all costs. The fact that the tragedy in these lesbian narratives is incongruent with the overall story line points to tragedy's role as an
insincere disclaimer and forced retraction driven by discursive conventions.

The Two Erzulies: Freda and Dantor

Driven by a feminist impetus, the female ethnographers who composed the
canon of work studied here focus on the female lwa par excellence, Erzulie,
whose avatars, Erzulie Freda and Erzulie Dantor, respectively illustrate the
paths of sensuality and maternity. Like oil and vinegar, these two aspects of
femininity remain separate in the Vodou worldview, perhaps not to uphold
but instead to grapple with the patriarchal expectations of women in Haitian
popular culture. In order for Freda to remain sexually available, she must remain childless, but what to do with the offspring of such copious copulation?
Freda hands over her little girl, Anaïs, to her maternal sister, Dantor, who
cares for her as if the child were her own. While it would appear that these
split manifestations of Erzulie only serve to uphold reproductive heteropatriarchy by preventing the representation of women's coarticulated identities,
these writers prove that the overdeterminacy of her divine imagery enables
potent queer possibilities. Deren makes clear the heterosexual desire radiat-
ing from Erzulie: "Mistress Erzulie, in all her various aspects and aliases, is
the divinity who most frequently—more than any of the other loa—requires
such a marriage with the men who serve her" (1970, 263). Hurston clarifies
how, this heterosexual inclination notwithstanding, Erzulie Freda also sabo-
tages and forestalls opposite-sex coupling. Hurston points out how she sets
"aside for herself young and handsome men and thus bar[s] them marriage,"
and when they are already married she "throws herself between the woman
and her happiness" (1990, 122). Dunham reminds us that anyone can marry
Erzulie, including women: "Once married to Erzulie there is no mystery of
life or love left unknown and man, woman or child may be chosen by the
goddess of love" (1969, 61). Certainly, these women would be in same-sex
divine marriage, transgressing heterosexuality, at least symbolically. Furthermore, Hurston tells us that the few female devotees of Erzulie Freda are
already outside the system of reproductive heteropatriarchy: "Women do
not give her [Erzulie] food unless they tend towards the hermaphrodite or

are elderly women who are widows or have abandoned the hope of mating" (1990, 122).

McCarthy Brown reports on the widespread speculation among devotees that Erzulie Dantor is in fact a lover of women:

> Dantò is . . . a frequent participant in marriages with vivan-yo (the living). . . . When gossip is the mode, people in Alourdes's community admit that some of these marriages are with women. Thus the portrait emerges of an independent, childbearing woman with an unconventional sexuality that, on several counts, flouts the authority of the patriarchal family. (1991, 228–29)

Further complicating the rumors of Erzulie's sexual inclination toward women, McCarthy Brown (1991, 228) reports on popular tales that say that Ti-Jan Petwo, her son, is also her lover. With her characterization as a *madevinez*—the Haitian Kreyòl word for women-loving women—and her presentation as an incestuous pedophile, Dantor's status as a non-heteronormative divinity becomes readily apparent.

Narrating Possession

What accounts for these cross-gendered identifications and same-sex desires, even when they are veiled in codedness and tragedy, is the transcorporeal representation of the body of Vodou in which the immaterial aspect of the self, the gwobonanj, can be substituted with the lwa during trance possession. In these narratives, the descriptions of this evacuation and replacement of the self during the experience of trance possession circulate around the metaphors of ridership, loss, travel, surrender, drowning, ecstasy, and ravishment. The withdrawal of the ego resulting from trance possession is a sought-after experience that acquires sexual connotations in most of these metaphors. The very fact that these possessions are presented as a form of human sacramental copulation with the divine renders them nonheteronormative and therefore capable of generating a radical politics of alterity.

Most of these female-authored ethnographic Vodou accounts begin with an explanation of the horse and rider metaphor for trance possession, move through an initiatory journey in the middle chapters, and end with the near or full possession of the female author by the lwa. As the title of her autoethnography suggests, Maya Deren describes the initiate as a horse that surrenders its will to a riding lwa: "The metaphor is drawn from a horse and his rider and the actions and events which result are the expression of the will of the rider" (1970, 29). Similarly, the title of Zora Neale Hurston's account is also evocative of the horse and rider metaphor. Hurston provides an explanation of the title of her book toward the end of the journey to close the narrative frame. In this illustration of the title, she explains how the community must relay to the entranced initiate the words that the lwa has spoken regarding him or her: "'Parlay Cheval Ou' (Tell My Horse), [is the signal that] the loa begins to dictate through the lips of his mount and goes on and on" (Hurston 1990, 221). It is significant that all the female ethnographers have chosen the horse and rider metaphor as a foundational mode for understanding embodiment and possession, and it seems only fitting that a critical feminist reading of this corpus of Vodou scholarship should reveal the gender of the equine as feminine through the figure of the mare invoked in the title of this chapter. The concavity of the saddle, the vessel-like quality of the horse, and the synergy between the horse and its rider evoke a receptacularity that is distinctly female and laden with sexual connotations that present trance as a mystical union and foreshadow the important image of the *femme cheval* discussed in chapter 4.[3]

In complementary fashion, Mimerose Beaubrun describes possession as a state of sleep and dreaming, a metaphor that she deploys beginning from the very title, *Nan Dòmi*—literally "In Sleep [State/Mode]." Beaubrun describes feeling her eyes heavy, dancing without conscious control, having a sense of falling into a deep sleep, yet not being asleep. She then explains how her limbs swayed without subjective control, as she saw yellow and then white. Using the language of fainting, she finds herself dancing, not knowing how to stop (Beaubrun 2013, 47). Experiencing something akin to lucid dreaming, Beaubrun feels drowsy, yet awake and unable to talk (48). Paradoxically, dreaming implies closing one's eyelids, and it is only in this state that one acquires enviable vision: "Entrer Nan dòmi, c'est avoir la capacité de voir ce que les autres ne perçoivent pas" (Beaubrun 2010, 238); "Nan Dòmi is to have the capacity to see what others do not perceive" (Beaubrun 2013, 227).

Maya Deren also evokes dreaming as a foundational image for the trance possession experience with which her narrative culminates:

> As sometimes in dreams, so here I can observe myself, can note with pleasure how the full hem of my white skirt plays with the rhythms, can watch, as if in a mirror, how the smile begins with a softening of

the lips, spreads imperceptibly into a radiance which, surely, is lovelier than any I have ever seen. It is when I turn, as if to a neighbor, to say, "Look! See how lovely that is!" and see that the others are removed to a distance, withdrawn to a circle which is already watching, that I realize, like a shaft of terror struck through me, that it is no longer myself whom I watch. Yet it *is* myself, for as that terror strikes, we two are made one again, joined by and upon the point of the left leg which is as if rooted to the earth. (1970, 258–59)

In this passage, which is the climax and ending of her book, Deren's description of her trance uses the images of the dream to convey an image of her self doubling, refracting as she experiences a deep sense of depersonalization prior to the temporary evacuation of her ego. Evoking some of the great mystics of Christianity—St. Theresa of Avila and St. John of the Cross come to mind—Deren presents this union with the divine as ecstasy. This orgasmic sentiment is echoed by Beaubrun when she declares, "Je me plaisais dans cet état entre deux eaux: profondément endormie et pleinement consciente de moi-même" (2010, 48); "I experienced pleasure in that state between two waters: profoundly asleep and fully conscious of myself" (2013, 48). Along these lines, I read Deren's mystical union with Erzulie as homoerotic:

> The white darkness moves up the veins of my left leg like a swift tide rising, rising; is a great force which I cannot sustain, or contain, which, surely, will burst my skin. It is too much, too bright, too white for me; this is darkness. "Mercy!" I scream within me. I hear it echoed by the voices, shrill and unearthly: "Erzulie!" The bright darkness floods up through my body, reaches my head, engulfs me. I am sucked down and exploded upward at once. That is all. (1970, 260)

As presented in this extended quote from Deren, devotees who experience trance often feel a surge of power rising through their bodies. When the power reaches the head, they experience a sense of drowning and then black out. McCarthy Brown confirms the widespread nature of this experience when she reports on Alourdes's description of what it is like to enter into trance:

> When the spirits come into your head, you feel light, light like a piece of paper . . . very light in your head. You feel dizzy in your head. Then after, you pass out. But the spirit come, and he talk to people, and he look at the table you make for him . . . you know. . . . Then he leaves . . .

and you come very, very, very far. But when the spirit in your body, in your head, you don't know nothing. They have to tell you what the spirit say, what message he leave for you. (1991, 353)

As she narrates her first possession experience, Alourdes's daughter, Maggie, reverberates her mother's and Maya Deren's focus on their heads just prior to lending their bodies to the lwas: "I started to be Miss Invisible—The Invisible Woman! . . . I'm losing my foot. . . . I'm losing my arm. . . . I'm losing my body, and it's just going. . . . Once it hits your head, that's it! It's black, and then I don't know nothing. Nothing!" (McCarthy Brown 1991, 353). It is important to note in both experiences here cited as well as in others in *Mama Lola*, a language of corporeal loss, of feet not touching the ground, of water running over the body, of high blood pressure and a sense of floating. What proceeds from trance is invariably experienced by the initiate as a state of unconsciousness followed by amnesia. Alourdes's experience of return from travel after the departure of the lwa is also echoed by Beaubrun when she discusses "la transe qui fait voyager dans les régions lointaines mais consciemment, celle que l'on appelle la transe de l'extase" (2010, 237); the "trance of ecstasy . . . in which one travels to faraway lands, but in a state of consciousness" in which one's "voyages resemble dreams, but dreams experienced in a wakened state" (2013, 227).

The experience of trance possession is such a staple of the female-authored Vodou ethnography that four out of the five anthropologists studied here experience and include it as the pivotal and culminating scene of their accounts. Only Katherine Dunham is left with the disappointment of not having gone into trance for her lwa, Dambala: "After my marriage to Damballa I longed for some inkling, some indication of 'possession'" (1969, 228). Dunham never formally experienced possession (Aschenbrenner 2002, 81), yet her company's dancers would often go into trance in New York during practices, and it was she who would have to teach the dancers how to remain in full control of their bodies during choreographies based on ritual dances (78). Yet even in this narrative in which the author fails to go into trance, she includes, as if in proxy for her own missing account, the observed description of her friend Julien's trance for Dambala:

Flat on the ground, his hands clasped behind his back, he advanced; smiling and undulating, he advanced toward the offering. His body rippled, his neck became elongated, his tongue darted rapidly in and out between his open lips, and the familiar ric-a-tic of the serpent god filled the improvised tent. (Dunham 1969, 233)

Of Dreams and Night Mares 47

Here Dunham reminds us that for the forlorn and destitute, there always remain the vicarious pleasures of the voyeur.

An aerial view of the field of anthropology of Haitian Vodou reveals a distinct line of inquiry that is characterized by female-authored accounts in which scholars fully integrate themselves into Vodou communities as initiates. These ethnographers have harnessed the unique transcorporeal nature of the body of Vodou in which the gwobonanj can be temporarily replaced by a lwa to open up possibilities for cross-gender identifications, non-heteronormative associations, and queer desires in their accounts. The initiatory journeys of their authors culminate in trance possession experiences described in the final pages of the accounts. In this way, the ethnographies become the tangible textual corporeality of their authors, subjectifying their literate audiences as divine, scanning their way from the feet to the crown, from introduction to conclusion, until the final merger, the closing of the book, the blacking out, the postegoic bliss to be enjoyed prior to hearing the revelations—the reviews, the critical analyses—that the divine readers, as riders, will certainly convey to their dreaming horses.

HECTOR HYPPOLITE ÈL MÊME

Between Queer Fetishization and Vodou Self-Portraiture

Hector Hyppolite mouri!	Hector Hyppolite died!
Hyppolite mouri!	Hyppolite died!
Popo mouri!	Popo died!
Mes z'amis! ga'dez z'yés li . . .	My friends, see his eyes . . .
Gadez chivé'l	See his hair
Gadez mains'l	See his hands
Hector Hyppolite mouri!	Hector Hyppolite died!
Qui coté ous quittez pinceaux	Where did you leave the stencils
Coté ous quittez bateau-a?	Where did you leave the boat?
Oh! ça n-a di Magritte?	Oh! Magritte did not say that?
Hector Hyppolite mouri! . . .	Hector Hyppolite died! . . .

—FÉLIX MORISSEAU-LEROY (1948),
in Serge St. Jean, *Hector Hyppolite: Une Somme*

Hyppolite mouri . . .	Hyppolite died . . .
Popo té grand	Hyppolite was big
Popo te be	Hyppolite was beautiful

Popo te rinmin nous	Popo loved us
Popo fait'n entrer nan Palais	Popo made us enter into the Palace
Popo fait'n entrer nan l'Unesco	Popo made us enter Unesco
Popo fait'n traverser lan mè	Popo made us cross the ocean
Nan "Life," cé Popo	In "Life," that Popo
Nan "Vogue," cé Popo	In "Vogue," that Popo
Et pi, li mouri	And then, he died

—FÉLIX MORISSEAU-LEROY (1948), in Michel-Philippe Lerebours, "À la recherche d'Hector Hyppolite"

Dambala and Aida Wedo, like the Marasa or sacred twins, make up a set of composite divinities that mirror one another in reflective symbiosis within the Vodou pantheon. Dambala is the sacred earthly serpent, having evolved from the Fon Vodun Dan, the divine python revered famously in the port of Ouidah in Benin. Dambala is a masculine terrestrial principle that is married to the serpent in the sky, Aida Wedo, who is represented in the rainbow. The Serpent and the Rainbow or Laserpan Arkansyel articulate in Haiti what their originating West African Vodou belief system conceived through MawuLisa, the twinning of the archetypal feminine (Mawu) and masculine (Lisa) principles.

This concept and its related imagery also find expression in Levantine and European symbology through the caduceus staff and in more recent scientific advancements through the discovery of the structure of DNA. Centuries prior to the discovery of the DNA molecule in 1953 by James D. Watson, Francis Crick, and Maurice Wilkins, African thought was already positing that living beings owed their very existence to two twinning, twirling coils of metainformation. In the Haitian Vodou religious-poetic rendition of this germ of life, Dambala and Aida Wedo are the double helix whose copulating contortions engender and sustain all life.

While most of the affect surrounding the representation of Dambala and Aida Wedo is generative, that of two serpents encircling each other as lovers, in this chapter, I would like to explore the fracturing and asphyxiating qualities of the snake embrace. Functioning as a leitmotif in this chapter, I argue that the Vodou divinities of Dambala and Aida Wedo emblematize the uneasy rapport and engagement between queer Vodou practitioners and the white queer ethnographers who have traditionally dominated the discursive representation of Vodou and its adherents. More particularly, I want to demonstrate how this stranglehold of love is a dominant emotive structure in the interaction between a queer Haitian artist, Hector Hyppolite, and two white queer ethnographers, the French Pierre Verger and the German Hubert Fichte.

Hector Hyppolite's life is full of myth, uncertainty, and the marvelous real. He was born September 15, 1891, probably in Rivière Froide, not far from Port-au-Prince. Both his father and grandfather appeared to be oungans. He is a possible relative of President Florvil Hyppolite (1889–96), but as he lived most of his life in abject poverty, he enjoyed none of the material benefits of having a prominent relative. At twelve years old and after attending only primary school, he became a cobbler. He began to make art to make ends meet, painting greeting cards copied from calendar images and selling reproductions of postcards to American marines. In 1945, Philippe Thoby-Marcelin and DeWitt Peters approached him in Saint Marc after seeing the façade of a bar he painted in Montrouis. The name of the bar, Ici La Renaissance, was full of significance for Haitian art's development at the time. As an oungan, he had an ounfò at Port-au-Prince, where he lived next to the sea on the Rue St. Honoré, between la Grand-Rue and La rue du Quais. After three brief years in the spotlight of the art world, Hyppolite died June 9, 1948, a famous man. In this short time, he produced an unbelievable amount of work. He left behind three hundred paintings and fourteen vèvè drawings: "Hector Hyppolite créa son oeuvre en l'espace de quelques années, dans un sorte de possession, dans une fièvre furieuse et exultante, jusqu'à sa mort en 1948" (Le Clézio 2011, 5; Hector Hyppolite created his work in the space of a few years in a sort of possession, in a furious and exultant fever until his death in 1948). Rodman (1948, 8) underscores the obsession and compulsivity that characterize these years in Port-au-Prince in religious terms as well by highlighting how painting for Hyppolite was an act of religious possession. Poupeye also says, "He claimed to work in a state of possession" (1998, 82). His achievement has been recognized by the Haitian nation: "Le gouvernement haïtien ayant décrété une 'année Hector Hyppolite' allant du 9 juin 2008 au 9 juin 2009" (Comité Hector Hyppolite 2011, 14; The Haitian government having decreed a year in honor of Hector Hyppolite from June 9, 2008, to June 9, 2009). The year of his remembrance began with the inauguration of Place Hector Hyppolite in Port-au-Prince, which includes an effigy of the artist by Ludovic Booz.

German anthropologist Hubert Fichte recognizes the important connection of Hector Hyppolite's art to a wider Caribbean network of artists—he mentions Hyppolite's connections to Lam, an artist studied in chapter 4— and to European aesthetic trends:

1943 kam der Holländer deWitt Peters, ein Englischlehrer, aus dem USA nach Haiti. Er entdeckte die Maler Hector Hyppolire [*sic*] und Philomé Obin. In 1945 eröffnet Peters das heute noch bestehende *Centre d'Art*, wo den haitianischen "Naiven" die technischen "Naiven" die technischen Grundlagen der Tafelmalerei beigebracht werden sollen.

Wilfredo [*sic*] Lam, aus Kuba, holt den Surrealistenpapst André Breton herbei und der erklärt, daß Hyppolite den Gang der europaischen Malerei hätte verändern könen. (Ein billiges und paternalistisches Statement—die Afrikaner hatten gerade ihr wichtiges zur Entwicklung des analystischen Kubismus getan!) (Fichte 1979, 19)

In 1943, the Dutchman DeWitt Peters, an English teacher, came from the United States to Haiti. He discovered the painters Hector Hyppolire [*sic*] and Philomé Obin. In 1945, Peters opens the Centre d'Art, which still exists, where the Haitian "naive" artists are to be taught the technical "naive," the basic techniques of painting on canvas.

Wilfredo [*sic*] Lam, from Cuba, brings over the pope of surrealism, André Breton, and declares that Hyppolite could have changed the course of European painting. (A cheap and paternalistic statement— the Africans had just made important contributions to the development of analytical Cubism!)

Breton did, in fact, notice the importance of Haitian art and of Hyppolite's position within this moment: "As far as I am aware, Hector Hyppolite's paintings are the first ever to record actual voodoo [*sic*] scenes and divinities, and in this respect alone as primitive religious paintings, they would carry considerable importance" (2002, 311). Breton saw the literary movement of negritude and Haitan art as ways of reinvigorating European surrealism. His introduction to Césaire's *Cahier d'un retour au pays natal* reveals this motivation. Moreover, Breton, after buying five of Hyppolite's paintings in 1946, reportedly said, "Ils apporteront du neuf à la peinture française. Elle en a besoin" (St. Jean 1973, 1; they will bring something new to French painting. It needs it), or "this . . . should revolutionize French painting; it needs a revolution" (Rodman 1948, 62). More poignantly, Fichte's quote reveals his awareness of the tendency of white foreign intellectuals to patronize Caribbean artists. He sees it in the work of Peters and Breton, but we wonder, then, how Fichte can himself at times, and certainly early in his involvement with Haiti and Vodou, participate in this same reductive and fetizishing project in spite of all the various other merits that his work might possess. His inability to fully divorce himself from a European perspective when analyzing

Afro-diasporic art is clearly seen in statements such as "Afroamerikanische Kunst ist religiös. . . . Es gibt eine Ästhetik des Faktischen—Ready Made und Objet trouvé" (Fichte 1979, 18; African American Art is religious. . . . There is an aesthetics of the factual—ready-made and objet trouvé).

This element of ethnographic distortion is a particularly problematic aspect of Caribbean representation given the region's inclination toward the marvelous real. In keeping with this indistinguishability between the factual and the fantastical, there is often doubt as to how Hyppolite chose to present himself versus the actual events of his life. For example, selling postcards to marines seems anachronistic or apocryphal, for he also reported having spent the same time period in Cuba as a sugarcane worker (Lerebours 2011, 25). Yet Hyppolite denies having learned to paint while there: "Il nie cependant avoir appris à peindre à Cuba et y avoir fait des tableaux" (26; He nevertheless denies having learned to paint in Cuba and having made paintings there). The narrative that Hyppolite constructed about his life is full of the same magical realism that also characterizes his paintings:

> Et ce fut la grande aventure grâce à mille dollars donnés par une amie du nom de Magritte, une danseuse africaine qui avait gagné à la loterie. Ensemble, ils partent pour New York et de là, s'embarquent pour l'Afrique où ils visitent le Dahomey avant de se rendere en Éthiopie. Le voyage dure en tout cinq ans. Voyage pour le moins surprenant surtout si on le situe au cours de la Première Guerre mondiale, à ce moment où la traversée de l'Atlantique est aussi difficile et aléatoire que les déplacements à l'intérieur de l'Afrique. (Lerebours 2011, 26)

> And this was a great adventure thanks to a thousand dollars given by a friend whose name was Magritte, an African dancer who won the lottery. Together, they leave for New York and from there embark for Africa, where they visit Dahomey before going to Ethiopia. In all, the trip lasts five years. This trip is surprising, especially when one places it in the context of the First World War, a moment in which transatlantic crossings were as difficult and unpredictable as traveling in the African interior.

Most critics see Hyppolite's return to Africa as a critical moment in his spiritual awakening: "Ses récits de cinq ans de randonnées en Afrique sont le signe de sa soif de connaître le pays de ses origines raciales et spirituelles" (Stebich 1978, 160; His accounts of five years of meanderings in Africa are a sign of his thirst to know the land of his racial and spiritual origins). During a seven-year stay in Dahomey, "Hector Hyppolite had in fact undergone just such an initiation" (Breton 2002, 310). "Hyppolite . . . rêve de retour en Éthiopie, au pays du Ras Tafari" (Le Clézio 2011, 5; Hyppolite . . . dreams of returning to Africa, to the country of Ras Tafari). Might this voyage have been invented? To start, his stories about benefactors and patrons during these voyages appear fancifully fictional:

> S'il faut en croire l'artiste, une femme lui aurait donné mille dollars, grâce auxquels, en compagnie d'un peintre nommé Echeberry, il aurait gagné New York et de là, l'Afrique pour se transporter au hasard, du Dahomey en Ethiopie jusqu'en 1920, date de son retour en Haiti. (St. Jean 1973, 11)

> If one is to believe the artist, a woman gave him one thousand dollars, with which, and in the company of a painter named Echeberry, he was to have reached New York and, from there, Africa in order to travel from Dahomey to Ethiopia until 1920, the date of his return to Haiti.

His biographer doubts such trips ever took place:

> It is entirely possible that Hyppolite never traveled to Africa, that the experience took shape first in his mind, partly as an escape from the frustrations of a life in Haiti that offered no rewards to his aesthetic ambitions, and partly as the fulfillment of a wish, an effort to identify himself more closely with ancestral religions and artistic images. (Rodman 1948, 70)

Supporting Rodman's doubts, the geographical imaginary of Hyppolite seems to defy reason: "On se souvient de cet amour qu'il aurait partagé avec une femme nommée Marguerite Jackenson dans l'île africaine de Caradjine que personne n'a jamais pu situer sur aucune carte" (Alexis 2004, 140; We remember that love that he is to have shared with a woman named Marguerite Jackenson on the African island of Caradjine, which no one was ever able to place on any map). Rodman and Alexis are not the only ones who express such doubts: "Je ne t'ai rien dit,—n'en ayant pas les preuves—, de tous les voyages dont il parlait. Etait-ce plaisanterie ou désir? A l'en croire il aurait été en Afrique, même de l'Est" (Paillière 1975, 11; I never told you—not having any proof—of all the trips of which he spoke. Were these a joke or wishful thinking? To believe him, he is supposed to have been to Africa, even East Africa).

The concurrence of the real and the marvelous in Hyppolite's narration of his own life should not surprise us given Alejo Carpentier's elaboration on the inextricable quality of the two in Caribbean discourse in his seminal essays

"On the Marvelous Real in America" and "The Baroque and the Marvelous Real." The *retour au pays natal* is one trope that links Hyppolite's narrative to a wider Caribbean experience that has been elaborated upon by Aimé Cesaire and many others, and which, according to Carpentier, deploys the tactical, progressive politics that differentiate this marvelous real from European surrealism.[1] As I hope will become apparent throughout the chapter, this marvelous real autopresentation is entwined around the discourse of queer white ethnographers in a serpentine wrestling match with metaphysical connotations.

This marvelous real-life narration and self-portraiture exist in a continuum with fanciful descriptions of Hyppolite's appearance. Most seem to highlight a queer self-performance that helps to explain the metaphysical androgyny of his artistic self-portraiture. Rodman (1948, 66) in *Renaissance in Haiti* describes him in a mannerist, Greco-esque manner as "tall, almost emaciated," with long hair. He comments on Hyppolite's racial hybridity to emphasize his femininity: "He is very black, but his features seem more Indian than African—the nose aquiline, the cheekbones high and sharp, the mouth rather compressed" (Rodman 1948, 66). Breton also felt obliged to comment on the grace of his countenance: "He was less than fifty years old, black skinned, fine featured, of typical attractive Guinean appearance" (2002, 310). In similar fashion, "Plusieurs de ceux qui l'ont connu pensent qu'il avait du sang amérindien. Ses pommettes quelque saillantes et sa chevelure pourraient porter à le croire" (Lerebours 2011, 20; Many of those who knew him thought that he had Amerindian blood. His prominent cheekbones and his full head of hair would have lent some credence to this). Making more direct inferences between Hyppolite's appearance and his gender and sexual identification, Lerebours uses coded language that relies on the discourse of effeminacy in order to convey Hyppolite's queerness:

> Présence réelle et obsédante, tant au Centre d'art qu'au Foyer des arts plastiques. On me l'avait tant de fois décrit que l'on s'attendait à le voir surgir à n'importe quel moment. Assez bel homme. De ce type que chez nous on appelle marabout. De taille moyenne, mince et svelte. Très foncé de peau. Une chevelure de jais; lise et soigneuse; touffue et assez longu; rabattue en arrière. Il dit lui-même, à Philippe Thoby-Marchelin: "... et comme j'étais un très beau garçon, les femmes me couraient après." Son visage quelque peu marqué par l'âge et par la vie rude qu'il avait connue jusqu'à son arrivée au Centre d'art, reflétait une certaine candeur et une discrète confiance en soi. Élégant et même

un peu coquet, portant presque toujours un costume de "drill" blanc, des chaussures blanches, souvent coiffé d'un chapeau panama, il avait, à n'en point douter, des manières d'aristocrate. De toute sa personne émanait une forte impression de dignité, laquelle se retrouvait dans chacune de ses paroles, dans chacun de ses actes et en imposait respect. Certains le disaient doté d'un formidable charisma. Tel était le portrait de l'homme que plus d'un trouvait poétique et attachant. (Lerebours 2011, 20)

A real and haunting presence, both in the Centre d'Art as well as in the Plastic Arts Centre. He had been so often described to me that we expected to see him appear at any moment. Quite handsome, of the type we call marabout. Medium height, slender and slim. Very dark skin. Jet-black hair, straight and well kept, bushy and pretty long, tied in the back. He himself told Philippe Thoby-Marchelin ". . . and since I was a beautiful boy, the women ran after me." His face was somewhat marked by age and by the hard life he had known until his arrival at the Art Center. It reflected a certain innocence and discreet self-confidence. Stylish and even a little flirtatious, yet almost always wearing a white suit, white shoes, often wearing a Panama hat, he had, without a doubt, aristocratic manners. From his whole person there emanated a strong sense of dignity, which was reflected in his every word, in every action, and elicited respect. Some said he was gifted with a great charisma. This was the portrait of the man whom more than one person found poetic and endearing.

Lerebours's presentation of Hyppolite as being "coquettish" and having certain mannerisms are code for his queerness. Using standard references to homosexuality from the Western literary canon, his presentation of Hyppolite is Wildean, and his extended youthfulness renders him akin to that author's hero, Dorian Gray. Let us also notice how his description of Hyppolite matches the domain of his two main tutelary deities. Evoking the iconography of Gédé, Lerebours describes Hyppolite as dressed in white from head to toe, often wearing a hat. The highlighting of his stunning physical appearance, especially as it conforms to an idealized type of feminine beauty in Haiti—the marabout, a tall, slender, and very dark-skinned woman with loose hair and purple gums—presents him as decidedly androgynous, as if he were supernaturally merging with the Haitian Vodou lwa Erzulie.

The work of several other critics continues the association of Hyppolite with Vodou lwas, especially Gédé. Pierre Verger stayed in Haiti almost seven

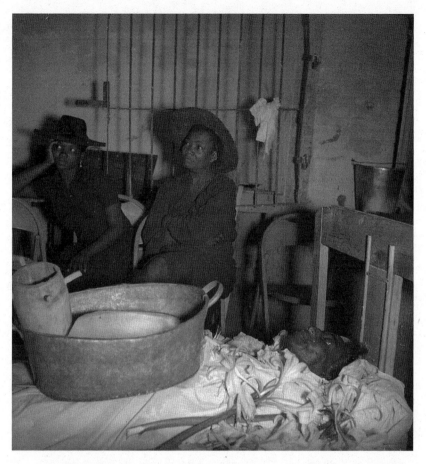

FIG. 2.1. Funerary photo of Hector Hyppolite, evoking Guédé Nibo, one of his tutelary lwas. The pail and skinless drum also suggest a transcendental receptacular corporeality. Photograph by Pierre Verger. Used by permission of Fundação Pierre Verger.

weeks in 1948, during which he took photos of the famous pilgrimage water-
falls of Saut d'Eau and of Mambo Lorgina Delorge. Serendipitously, Verger
happened to be in Haiti on June 9, the day of Hyppolite's death, and recorded
this event by taking a series of important photographs, one of which was
published in his collection *Le Messager* (Verger 1993, photo 127 [figures 2.1
and 2.2]). Also adding to the coincidence of notable Vodou personalities
at the wake and funeral, Alfred Métraux (1978, 268) records in *Itinéraires*
how Verger took this deathbed photograph and how Seilly molded the death
mask. Métraux remarks that they covered all of Hyppolite's body, except his
head, in a white sheet, and it is likely that Métraux understood how the

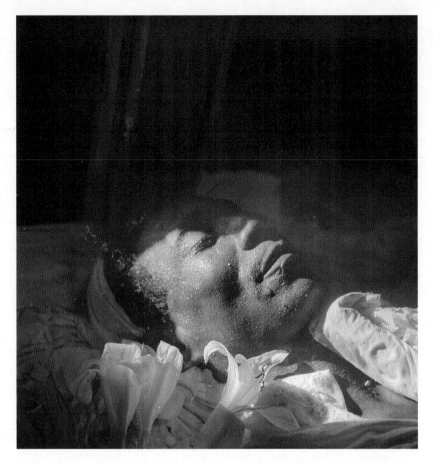

FIG. 2.2. Hector Hyppolite lying in state. Photograph by Pierre Verger. Used by permission of Fundação Pierre Verger.

painter's dead body uncannily resembled Géde Nibo in this state, one of his titulary lwas, the subject of many of his paintings, and the source of his self-presentation. Paillière had met Hyppolite at a costume ball given by DeWitt Peters on the eve of the Touissant, Halloween to Americans. Hyppolite had gone dressed as Baron Samedi, one of the avatars of Gédé. Discursively, Paillère (1975, 7) superimposed this image on that of a dead Hyppolite.

In the deathbed photograph in figure 2.2, Verger captures how Hyppolite's body, even after it has given up the ghost, continues to project an aura of sensuality, even seduction. The upper half of the portrait is dark, an impenetrable night that descends upon the face of the painter. In the lower part of the portrait, white lilies and a shirt cushion the painter's face and glow in a metaphysical manner that imbues Hyppolite with a spectral, ecclesiastical aura. Here, Hyppolite is seen reclining in a fluffy white coffin, heavily made up, his head resting on a flattering head scarf that doubles as a pillow. The light, as if filtered through gothic church windows, emphasizes the makeup, revealing how his skin and lips crackle under the foundation, like dry and parched land. As a central aspect of the composition, a mole under the lower lip protrudes provocatively beside his signature high cheekbones. The mole and its shadow direct us toward Hyppolite's open shirt, which exposes his very long and elegant neck in an almost necrophilic manner. Here in this last portrait of Hyppolite, Verger seems to finally reveal the grandeur of the painter's lineage in his resemblance to Akhenaten, lean and androgynous, the pharaoh responsible for the renaissance of art in Egypt.

The fetishism in Verger's photographs is similar to that found in many early writings of Fichte because the two queer white ethnographers form a nearly unified front that valorizes, while at the same time essentializes, Caribbean artists, especially when these Caribbean artists are queer. Fichte himself appears to be aware of his continuation of Verger's perspective as he includes a fictional Verger as an alter ego in his novels. Katschthaler (2005, 202) writes,

> Im zweiten Teil macht Fichte, vermittelt durch Jäcki, deutlich, dass er es für nötig hält, sexuelle Erlebnisse mitzuteilen. Jäcki unterhält sich oft mit dem alten Ethnologen Pierre Verger, doch erst ab einem gewissen Zeitpunkt beginnt er ihn auch sexuell wahrzunehmen. Unmittelbar darauf heißt es:
> Seinen Roman über den alten Ethnologen und den jungen, der sich aufdrängt und alles durcheinanderbringt konnte er sich nicht vorstellen ohne Sex.
> Jäcki würde darstellen müssen, wie der junge übrigens deutsche Ethnologe bei Professora Norma beginnt einen der Trommler wie wahnsinnig zu begehren. (*Explosion*, S. 168)

Mediated through Jäcki in the second part, Fichte makes it clear that he considers it necessary to communicate sexual experiences. Jäcki talks often with the old anthropologist Pierre Verger, but only at a certain point does he begin to perceive him sexually. Immediately afterward, he states he could not imagine his novel, about the old anthropologist and the young one who imposes himself and makes everything messy, without sex.

Jäcki would have to portray how the young German ethnologist at Professor Norma's begins to madly covet one of the drummers.

Das Sexualität nicht nur Gegenstand des Romans, sondern auch der Ethnologie ist, das lässt Fichte Jäcki klar aussprechen. Es geht wieder um Verger, und die Wahrnehmung seines Sexualabend durch Jäcki. (Katschthaler 2005, 202)

Fichte has Jäcki clearly express that sexuality is a subject not only of the novel but of ethnology. Once more it is about Verger and the perception of his sexual decline through Jäcki.

The inclusion of Verger and the black character, Jäcki, in the narrative allows Fichte to experience, impersonate, and speak doubly as an anthropologist and as an informant, to converse with Verger as a fellow anthropologist and as an informant lover. In so doing, we see the struggle for identity between self and other, which is the foundation of the twining of Dambala and Aida Wedo, inscribed within Fichte's narrative as a way to understand his own mixed-race ancestry—as German and Jew—and as a bisexual man. Already a composite of selves, Fichte's plural self-presentation is further complicated by its perceived extension of the life of Verger. Adding yet another layer to this serpentine duality, both ethnographers are engaged in the battle for cultural representation through and against Hyppolite via a sexually fetishistic desire.

Yet the ethnographers do not have the last word in their cold, limbless, and scaly wrestling match with the painter. The deathbed photograph of Hyppolite by Verger contrasts sharply with the artistic self-presentation of the painter. Instead of the darkness dominating the upper half of Verger's photograph, Hyppolite's face is the commanding presence in the analogous section of his self-portrait. Even though, in his *Autoportrait*, Hyppolite also associates himself with Gédé Nibo—a lwa whose domain is death—through his white hat and cream jacket, the painting overflows with life and color. The element of sensuality remains strong due to the multicolored flowers, which, unlike the monochromatic and pallid ones in the Verger photograph, remain attached to the verdant stem, uncut, and rooted to an imaginary soil on the lower left-hand side of the frame. In fact, the trunk of the artist is drawn as an extension of this living stem. The pink tie playfully references Erzulie Freda, the lwa of love and sensuality in the Vodou pantheon. The commingling of both divinities in the self-portrait augments the power of the composition in its philosophical emblematization of the universal Eros

FIG. 2.3. The black male body through the homoerotic photographic gaze of Pierre Verger. Photograph by Pierre Verger. Used by permission of Fundação Pierre Verger.

and Thanatos motif. If darkness is gaining ground over the light in the Verger photograph, the aura emanating from the bust of the painter's artistic reflection seems to repel the ultimately failed approach of night.

The eroticism in both works acquires different valences just as they differ in their representations of the life-and-death motif. The eroticization of the dead body of Hyppolite, who cannot see, yet is seen by Verger, is part of an overall structure of fetishization of black Caribbean queer artists by white European queer critics. Let us note how this fetishization continues in the work of Fichte:

> Schon gar nicht bei Ausländern, weil da das Seelische, die seelische Bindung völlig fehlt.

FIG. 2.4. Hector Hyppolite's self-presentation as Erzulie. The moustaches on several of the deity's ladies-in-waiting reveal the regendering of the initiate as a salient feature of Hyppolite's transcorporeality. Hector Hyppolite, *Ezili and Her Earthly Court*, ca. 1946. Oil on board, 23 × 29½ in. (58.42 × 74.93 cm). Milwaukee Art Museum, gift of Richard and Ema Flagg, M1991.128. Photograph by Efraim Lev-er.

Ich habe ein Erektion dann, wenn ich also mit einem Deutsche zusammen bin. . . . Aber bei den Ausländern ist die Faszination der Jugend in Verbindung mit Potenz . . . der also vor Potenz und Geilheit zuckt. (Fichte 2007, 48)

Certainly not with foreigners, because there the spiritual, the spiritual bond is missing altogether.

I have an erection then, when I am together with a German man. . . . But with the foreigners the fascination of youth is connected to virility . . . which thus flinches in the face of virility and lust.

In *Explosion* kann Fichte also plötzlich auch die sexuellen Begegnungen beschreiben, ohne in Gefahr zu geraten, sich zum Sexabenteurer zu stilisieren und dem Exotismus zu frönen. Warum is das erst jetzt möglich und warum konnte das in *Xango* und *Petersilie* nicht geschehen?

Einen ersten Hinweis auf die Beantwortung dieser Fragen kann folgende Stelle aus *Explosion* geben. Nachdem beschrieben wurde, wie Jäcki von einem Neger mit einem Messer bedroht wird und dann mit ihm verkehrt. (Katschthaler 2005, 201)

In *Explosion*, then, Fichte can suddenly describe sexual encounters as well without danger of stylizing himself as a sex adventurer indulging in the exotic. Why is it only now possible and why could it not happen in *Xango* or *Petersilie*? The following passage from *Explosion* can provide a first indication of this question's answer. Afterward is a description of how Jäcki is threatened by a Negro with a knife and then has intercourse with him.

Alongside these essentialistic representations of the southern erotic/exotic, this fetishization functions as a type of escapist utopia for Fichte:

Auch theoretisch kann die Sexualität des Ethnologen natürlich eine Rolle spielen. Fichtes ethnologische These von Bikontinentalität und Bisexualität, die er schon in *Xango* und *Petersilie*, wie ich gezeigt habe, relativiert hat, taucht in *Explosion* wieder auf, wird aber auch hier als eskapistische Utopie entlarvt. Einer Stelle, an der es um die afroamerikanische Utopie geht, folgt der Bericht über den mord an einem Homosexuellen (*Explosion*, S. 12 und S. 19), oder die Utopie von Bisexualität und Bikontinentalität wird ironisch als fixe Idée Jäcki dargestellt (*Explosion*, S. 92 f.). Den ganzen Roman durchzieht, wie schon gezeigt, das Thema der Folter an Homosexuellen in Brasilien. Schließlich sind die Schwulen am Ende des Romans nicht etwa im afroamerikanischen Raum, sondern in Europa, in Portugal plötzlich frei geworden. (Katschthaler 2005, 203–4)

The sexuality of the ethnologist can of course play a role theoretically as well. Fichte's anthropological thesis of bicontinentality and bisexuality, which he had already related in *Xango* and *Petersilie*, as I have shown, resurfaces again in *Explosion*, but here, too, is exposed as an escapist utopia. One section concerning the African American utopia follows the report of a homosexual's murder (*Explosion*, p. 12 and p. 19), and the utopia of bisexuality and bicontinentality is depicted ironically as Jäcki's idée fixe (*Explosion*, pp. 92 ff.). What runs through the entire novel, as already shown, is the issue of torture of homosexuals in Brazil. Finally, at the end of the novel the gays are not in an African American space, but in Europe, in Portugal having suddenly become free.

The double helix of interplay between Brazil and Portugal and their operation as multivalent zones of freedom and repression twist and invert received notions of space. Europeans go to Brazil to find fulfillment, and Brazilians find freedom in Europe. This black European utopia is Fichte's unique vision, for, according to Hyppolite, Africa, which he articulates via the mythical island of Caradjine, is the ultimate utopia. Within and perhaps as a result of the fetishization of black men in his work, Fichte also manages to depict the manner in which black queer men are alienated from the possibility of building links of solidarity with others:

> Jäcki begegnete auf der Grindelalle einem dicken Neger.
> —Plunschmul, dachte Jäcki:
> —Wurde meine Oma sagen.
> Mitten in dem wundartigen Mund
> —Schwarz wie Kohle
> Vom Scheitel bis zur Sohle
> Ist der Neger Jim
> Seine beste
> Weiße Weste
> Trägt er nur zum Swing!
> Flamte etwas Rosarotes auf-wenn er sich über die Lippen leckte und die innere Haut zum Vorschein kam.
> —Pupillen—Glasmarmeln, Schwarz, eine kleine Lampe brennt an jeder Seite.
> Das Augenweiß blitzte Jäcki wütend an.
> Die Handë des dicken Negers schienen Jäcki wie die Äste von Bäumen der Kindheit.
> Der dicke Neger versteckte sie in den Hosentaschen, als er merkte, daß Jäcki ihn beobachtete. (Fichte 1988, 65)

> Jäcki met a big Negro on Grindelallee.
> —*Plunschmul*, thought Jäcki:
> —My grandmother would say.
> In the middle of the sore-like mouth
> —Black as Coal
> From head to toe
> Is the Negro Jim
> His best
> White vest
> He wears only for Swing!

Blazing something pink-red when he licked across his lips and the inner skin came to the fore.

—Pupil. Glass marbles Black, a small lamp burning on each side.

The whites of his eyes flashed angrily at Jäcki.

The hands of the big Negro seemed to Jäcki like the branches of trees in his childhood.

The big Negro hid them in his pockets when he realized Jäcki was watching him.

The continuum of fetishization seen in Verger and Fichte is also evident in Jean Genet, whom Fichte interviews and with whom he displays a solidarity that relies on the othering of men of color:

H.F. You spoke a moment ago about the end of your sexual life, did your fascination, your desire not go any further with the Black Panthers?

J.G. What they asked of me was really very, very difficult. I was still taking Nembutal, since I had to sleep. These were young guys, from eighteen to twenty-five years old, maybe twenty-eight. David was twenty-eight, he had an extraordinary energy. He would wake me up at two in the morning. I'd have to give a press conference, at two in the morning, and I had to be awake and ready to respond to the questions. Believe me, I wasn't thinking about making love. And then there was another phenomenon, which is that I didn't make any distinctions between the Panthers, I loved them all, I wasn't attracted by one rather than another. I loved the phenomenon of the Black Panthers. I was in love with that.

H.F. So you weren't imposing on yourself an erotic abstinence that in a more liberal world you would not have accepted?

J.G. Not at all. To the point that Bobby Seale had sent me a letter asking me to write an article on homosexuality. . . . I answered saying, "If you attack homosexuals, I'll attack the Blacks." The next week I received a copy of the newspaper. Newton himself had written an article in which he said it was absolutely necessary to be on the side of the homosexuals, that it was necessary to defend them, that they were a minority group, and that it was necessary to accept their help in defending the Panthers and at the same time to accept defending them. (Genet 2004, 149–50)

Like Fichte, Jean Genet's works display a fetishistic desire for the black body. One only need recall *Un Chant d'amour*, as poem and film, his play *Les Nègres* and *Querelle de Brest*, as novel and as a film by Fassbinder, to make the connection with Verger and Fichte visible. The entire interview is fetishistic of men of color—Middle Easterners (Moroccans, Syrians, Pakistanis) and blacks. It is pederastic, infantilizing, and paternalistic. And it contains a disclosure of blackmail. Yet there is deep awareness of race and sexuality as mutually imbricated, interconnected, and coarticulated. However, blackness seems not to be an object of study for itself, only a stand-in and metaphor for understanding the marginality of queerness. Herein lies the way in which the fetishism of European queer male critics operates as a strategy of co-optation to understand their own marginality via the bodies of subordinate, ultramarine queer artists of color. These white critics achieve subjectification through the subjugation of black artists through the mechanism of desire and the optical techniques of photographic and textual representation. At least in the case of Fichte, the scrutinizing study of Afro-diasporic religion is motivated by a desire to achive a perspective from which he can understand, or perhaps homogenize and neutralize, his own alterity in Europe as a bisexual German Jew.

Yet artists like Hyppolite transcend this fetishization through self-portraiture, often with the inclusion of textuality in their tableaux. Framed within the leaves of the composite human-vegetable chimera reminiscent of Wifredo Lam's paintings, we have a curious text that has drawn the attention of some critics but without full elucidation:

> Le lendemain quand je revins, il avait ajouté au bas: HECTOR HYPPO-
> LITE PAR EL MEME. Mais une main qui s'est crue pieuse a, plus tard,
> corrigé la génial faute de français et à écrit "PAR LUI MEME." Comme
> si cette prevue pouvait être annulée . . . d'un implicite et séculaire bail-
> lon sur l'échantillon d'une majorité nationale! Mais qu'avais-je à me
> plaindre! LA PEINTURE D'HECTOR HYPPOLITE ECLATE, en dépit tout, et
> son expression ne se peut comprimer par les lois d'aucune grammaire!
> (Paillière 1975, 19)

> The next day when I returned, he had added at the bottom: HECTOR
> HYPPOLITE BY HE-SELF.[2] But a hand that thought itself devout later
> corrected the brilliant mistake in French and wrote "BY HIMSELF" As
> if his intention could be erased . . . an implicit and secular gag on the
> representation of the national majority! But of what had I to complain!

THE PAINTING OF HECTOR HYPPOLITE BURSTS, despite everything, and its expression cannot be constrained by the laws of any grammar!

> Initialment, dit-on, on pouvait lire, "Hector Hyppolite par el même." On voit en effet qu'une correction a été apportée pour mettre "lui-même." Mais plus que cela, il est peu probable, encore une fois, qu'Hyppolite ait lui-même inscrit ce titre dans son tableau. (Alexis 2011, 111)

> Initially, it is said that one could read "Hector Hyppolite by he-self." We see that in reality a correction was introduced to add "himself." But more than that, it is highly unlikely that Hyppolite himself wrote this title on his painting.

The major point of contention here is the gender pronoun: *èl* is neither French, where it would have been either *lui* or *il*, nor Kreyòl, where it would have been *li*. Can it be the Spanish masculine article orthographically *el* or perhaps, phonetically, the French feminine article *elle*? I discard the option that he was trying to write in Spanish, his trip to Cuba and the accent over the pronoun vowel notwithstanding. The orientation of the grave accent instead of the Spanish tilde seems to tell us that he was using French conventions.

Paillière also further hypercorrects the title by transcribing it in all caps and by continuing a tradition that further Frenchifies the title by adding the preposition *par* when there is clearly no space for it to have ever been a part of the original or the subsequently amended title. In a manner similar to what critics do with the painting popularly referred to as *La Dauration de l'amour*, art critics are not faithful to the author's intentions or mistakes for that matter. They are inconsistent in their attempt to correct perceived misspellings by the artist. The text in the painting clearly says "La Dauration de l'armor." Critics don't correct the first noun phrase—in standard French it would read "L'adoration"—but do correct the second one. The transcriptions by critics add yet another level of meaning, which seems to indicate that this writing, just like his paintings, is receptive and adaptable to the preconceptions and desires of viewers and readers, according to their reading and language proficiencies. As jocular one-eyed winking Gédé, Hyppolite seems to smile and mutter from the grave, "You corrected one mistake but didn't catch the other!" He encourages even the most educated of audiences to read him more closely and not to presume that even those with the most sophisticated intellectual abilities are incapable of glossing over evident linguistic and perhaps deliberate traps.

FIG. 2.5. "Hector Hyppolite èl Même" at bottom center of painting, from the cover of the sole book devoted exclusively to this painter. Hector Hyppolite, *Auto-portrait*. Musée d'Art Haïtien. Comité Hector Hyppolite, eds., *Hector Hyppolite* (Paris: Éditions de Capri, 2011).

Is "Hector Hyppolite èl même" a result of his illiteracy? Did someone else write this and other titles for him? As noted by Alexis, "Hyppolite étant analphabète, le titre a peut-être été écrit par quelqu'un d'autre" (2011, 103; Hyppolite being illiterate, the title was perhaps written by someone else). Was he writing in what he thought was French? Certainly "même" is French; it would have been "mem" or "memn" in Kreyòl. If he indeed meant it in French, did he intend to write "il," the nominative masculine article, which would have been in the incorrect grammatical case in standard French? Or did he think "èl" was the masculine accusative article instead of "lui"? Or, if indeed trying to write in French, could he have intended to use the phonetic version of the feminine accusative article "elle" to refer to himself? What would the implications of this grammatical regendering imply for a writer who never married, who identified spiritually with a female sea divinity, and

FIG. 2.6. Hector Hyppolite, *La Dauration de l'Armor* (*L'Adoration de l'amour*; intentional misspelling?), 1946–48. Oil on cardboard, 29½ × 23½ in. (74.93 × 59.69 cm). Milwaukee Art Museum, gift of Mr. and Mrs. Richard B. Flagg, M1978.123. Photograph by Larry Sanders.

who feminized his self-presentation? Is this queer disclosure? Is this male and female grammatical gendering a way of representing the androgynous ideal of his possession by Lasirèn? Moreover, if he had been trying to write in Kreyòl, why did he alter the vowel and transpose the consonant as he did in the vévé titles: "èl" instead of "li"? Was it a deliberate act by Hyppolite?

Hyppolite's text prompts us to see the queer potential in dyslexia, as a non-normative and challenging intellectual reinterpretation that disorients the reader with its serpentine and circuitous switchbacks.

Let us unravel, layer by layer, how this palimpsestic regendering and standardization of the self occurs orthographically in the *Autoportrait*. Someone changed "èl" to "lui" by using yellow paint over the original white letters. The first change involved adding an *l* before "èl," the second an exchange of *e* for *u*, and the third transforming the final *l* to an *i* by coloring the base of the letter and adding a dot on top. All of these changes leave the grave accent intact, an error in either French or Kreyòl orthography. Likewise, the Frenchification remains an incomplete project due to the inability to add the preposition "par" due to lack of space. The correction of Hyppolite's *Autoportrait* remains therefore unaccomplished.

Alexis assumes someone else corrected the pronoun but fails to see that the handwriting appears to be the same, which might lead us to believe that even if it weren't Hyppolite who was writing, at least it was always the same person writing and correcting. Whether Hyppolite wrote and corrected it himself or a second person wrote the title and either Hyppolite or that person changed it, the point remains that language calls the painter's gender identity into question in this *Autoportrait*. In fact, the text in the painting fully diplays the multiply articulated nature of the artist's identity, as modulated by color, social class, education, language, gender, and sexuality. The *Autoportrait* indeed reminds us that identity is produced by and through language.

Returning to the image with which we began this chapter, the conversation between these two contrapuntal representations of Hector Hyppolite allegorizes the mythical interaction between Dambala and Aida Wedo. Like two serpents twining around each other, the ethnographer and the informant struggle for the right and power to create an account with a claim of truth. Their struggle, in the case of Hyppolite versus Verger and Fichte, is the proverbial battle between life and death. For Hyppolite, it was a lethal encounter, but one that allowed the palimpsestic words of his testament to resound more loudly and allow him the last word in the match. The struggle between painting and photography also coils around the clash of reason and emotion, ideas that have for centuries been antinomically ascribed to the West and the Rest. Yet the struggle between Verger-Fichte and Hyppolite is productive, seductive, and erotic. There is a passion that honors, desires, and, multivalently, appropriates the Other. While this problematic aspect is certainly evident in the work of Verger, we must avoid the temptation of

FIG. 2.7. The body of the entranced as container, receptacle, support platform, saddle, and transportation vessel for the divine. Hector Hyppolite, *Black Magic* (*Magique Noir*), ca. 1946–47. Oil on board, 25½ × 37½ in. (64.77 × 95.25 cm). Milwaukee Art Museum, gift of Richard and Ema Flagg, M1991.127. Photograph by Efraim Lev-er.

dismissing it without evaluating possible concurrent positive aspects within it. Verger's gaze is sexually fetishistic, yet valorizing and memorializing. From Hyppolite, on the other hand, there is a queer self-portraiture that rechannels and works with, through, and against these fetishistic projections from the white queer ethnographer. In a climactic moment in the encounter, Hyppolite delivers the sole textual moment of the struggle as he screams in a garbled, enigmatic voice we must decode, as if written in hieroglyphics. The passion, whether in its injurious or pleasurable aspects, refuses easy moral categorizations and calls only for the serpentine embrace of its actuality. The fact that the metaphysical and pluralistic notion of being presents itself in both tableaux as representation and self-portraiture—in the performance of the artist as a lwa—furthers the notion of transcorporeality expounded in this book and calls us to scan the long horizon of its implications where the realm of the ritual merges with the aesthetic. More than being contained within the context of religious possession, transcorporeality is a performative strategy for subjective representation found across the various arenas of existence in which humans are allowed a certain measure of volunteeristic definition in association with the divine.

In sharp contrast to the widespread knowledge of the work of Pierre Verger in the academy, as well as within certain circles of religious practitioners, the work of Hubert Fichte remains relatively unknown, especially outside the German-speaking world, in spite of its outstanding contributions to the field of Afro-Atlantic studies. Alongside Pierre Verger and Lydia Cabrera, Hubert Fichte is among the first generation of white scholars of elite social background to study African religions in the Americas. All are queer, but Fichte distinguishes himself from Cabrera and Verger by discussing sexual orientation openly and at length in his treatises. Perhaps due to the untranslated state of many of his works or their strong poetic quality, his groundbreaking insight into queer performance in Afro-Atlantic religions has gone unreferenced in Anglophone work dealing with this topic, and the present chapter seeks to begin redressing these omissions.

Hubert Fichte was among the first to document and to try to understand the common noncorrespondence of traditional gender/sex pairings in Afro-Atlantic religions. His idea of bicontinentality offers the first theoretical instrument through which to understand the fluid functioning of gender in neo-African religions:

> Das ist unter den Gläubigen der Yoruba, Ewe, Fon, in der Neuen Welt, in Brasilien und Haiti zum bespiel, anders. . . . Für die Gläubigen der afrobrasilienischen Religionen kann Bisexualität als Verhaltenskonstante angenommen werden. Wie diese Bipolarität des afroamericanikanischen Sexualverhaltens entsteht, die der Bikontinentalität der afroamerikanischen Kultur entspricht, bleiben zu erforschen. (Fichte 1976, 56)

> Among the faithful of the Yoruba, Ewe, Fon, in the New World, in Brazil and Haiti for example, this is different. . . . For the believers of Afro-Brazilian religions, bisexuality can be assumed a constant of behavior. How this bipolarity of Afro-American sexual behavior develops and how it corresponds to the bicontinentality of American culture remains to be investigated.

The recurrence of the prefix "bi-" in reference to location, desire, and behavior is important as it underscores how the unique sexual manifestations that these religions allow are grounded in the scattering of their population on both sides of the Atlantic. In Fichte's provocative prefixed term, the Americas and Africa function as genders, lovers, and continents of desire. I acknowledge Fichte's bicontinentality as a precursor to my own usage of the idea of transcorporeality in this volume and as one of the inspirations for the invocation of Aida and Dambala Wedo as the spiritual and structural guides for this discussion.

While Anglophone criticism has remained oblivious to his work, German critics have noted both the contributions and limitations of Hubert Fichte's writing to the understanding of Afro-diasporic religions. At least one seems to have focused on the suffixation of desire formulated by Fichte:

[Die] Titel der Trilogie sind Siglen des Forschungsprogramms von Hubert Fichte und Leonore Mau. Xango ist der Name des brasilianischen Donnergottes, dem auch das Merkmal der Bisexualität zugeschrieben wird. So steht er sowohl für das Interesse an den afroamerikanischen Religionen wie auch für die sexuellen Verhaltensweisen, die Fichte erforschen will. (Cramer 1999, 50)

The titles of the trilogy are acronyms for the research program of Hubert Fichte and Leonore Mau. Xango is the name of the Brazilian Thunder God, to which the quality of bisexuality is also attributed. He is likewise of interest in the Afro-American religions as well as for the sexual behaviors Fichte wants to explore.

Fichte is also among the first ethnographers to situate the workings of Vodou gender and sexuality within its larger society. He avoids the temptation to project generalizations from Vodou onto Haiti at large and eloquently presents the evolution of his thought on this topic in the following passage:

Vielleicht ist es umgekehrt:
Viellicht ist die haitianische Gesellschaft gar nicht so tolerant, dass sogar die Vaudoupriester homosexuell sein dürfen—vielleicht is diese Gesellschaft so intolerant, dass nur die Vaudoupriester homosexuell sein dürfen. (Fichte 1976, 198)

Maybe it's the other way around:
Maybe Haitian society is not so tolerant that even the Vodou priests may be gay—maybe this society is so intolerant that only the Vodou priest may be homosexual.

Vodou functions as a queer space in an otherwise intolerant society. The patriarchal nature of the Haitian nation-state contrasts sharply with the plethora of gendered options visible in Haitian Vodou ceremeonies, which is here described in an impressionistic manner by Fichte:

Geschlechtslose—die Loas sind geschlechtlos—, Bisexuelle, Männer, Frauen, männliche Homosexuelle, active Boundaliers, passive Massissi, weibliche Homosexuelle. (Fichte 1976, 215)

Genderless—the lwas are genderless—bisexuals, men, women, male homosexuals, active boundaliers or sexual "tops," passive *masisi*, female homosexuals.

In this initial recorded observation, Fichte sees Vodou lwas as not having a gender, a questionable statement that we may forgive a novice spectator to the religion. What redeems his usage of "genderless" is that Fichte is noting that Vodou spirits bypass heteronormative prescriptions in their representation and ritual incarnations. He is commendable in his usage of the local term for men-loving men (masisi, also *makomé*). His usage of the local term for women-loving women (*madevinez*) does not appear until his later works on the topic, attesting to his growth and development as an ethnographer.

In order to shed light on the Haitian Vodou lwas most visibly presented in the Verger photograph and the Hyppolite *Autoportrait*, Hubert Fichte devotes particular attention to the role of Gédé Nibo and Erzulie Freda in his work:

In Haiti gibt es den phallischen Totengott Guédé Nibo, der homosexuell ist; die haitianische Liebesgöttin Erzulie wird als Göttin der Prostituierten und der Schwulen verehrt. (Fichte 1976, 58)

In Haiti there is the phallic god of death Gédé Nibo, who is homosexual; the Haitian love goddess Erzulie is worshiped as the goddess of prostitutes and gays.

Fichte quickly notices that these two particular deities have strong associations with queer Vodou practitioners as he underscores how Haitian homosexuals pray to Gédé Nibo Massissi and to Erzulie Freda (Fichte 1996, 369). Gédé Nibo's personality explains the association witnessed by Fichte and helps to complete his partial elaborations. In Vodou lore, Gédé Nibo is a young man who was killed violently. Therefore, he has a particular association with those who die young. Once in the spirit realm, Bawon Samedi and Gran Brigit adopt him. In demeanor he is comical, lascivious, witty, and effeminate. In appearance, he is a dandy. From a gay Euro–North American perspective it is difficult not to draw a parallel, at least subconsciously, with Oscar Wilde. Hence the reason for Fichte's persistence about the function of Gédé Nibo in his ethnographic interviews:

Ich frage:

—Ist Guédé Nibo Massissi? Schwul?

André antwortet:

—Das ist falsch. Die Götter . . . aus zwei Teilen bestehen. (Fichte 1976, 182)

I ask:

—Is Guédé Nibo masisi? Gay?

André answers:

—This is wrong. The gods . . . are composed of two parts.

Gédé Nibo forces Fichte to face the noncorrespondence of Western categories of sexual alterity with nonheternormative identities elsewhere. Local informants refute and refine Fichte's assumption. Fichte's documentation of his own evolution, rather than delivering a streamlined product, displays a rare and admirable humility. His growth, however, happens in fits and starts, for we observe a tendency for him to devolve into Western categories to explain Haitian realities:

> Es gibt einen schwulen Totengott, Guédé Nibo, und Anfang November singt das ganze Land, jeder haitianische Bauer die Hymnen auf die Schwulen—"Massissi"—und die ruralen Familienväter vollführen ambivalente Gesten vorne und hinten an ihrer Hose. Bei den Heilkuren gegen magische, "übernatürliche" Erkraunkungen werden die Totengöter angerufen. (Fichte 1976, 143)

> There is a gay god of death, Guédé Nibo, and in early November the whole country, every Haitian peasant, sings hymns to the gays— "masisi"—and rural family fathers perform ambivalent gestures at the front and back of their pants. The gods of the dead are invoked in the cures for magic and "supernatural" illnesses.

> Die Bauern singen von Zozo und Coco und fassen sich an den Schlitz. Guédé Nibo wird angesungen und die Schwulen. (Fichte 1976, 166)

> The peasants sing of Zozo and Coco and touch their own / each others' slits. Guédé Nibo is sung to, as are the gays.

Even though he persists in erroneously saying that Gédé Nibo is "Schwul" (the German word for gay), his observations that fathers are dancing lascivious homoerotic dances with each other evinces that his usage of Western terms is inaccurate for the understanding of sexual alterity in Haiti. Schwul and gay identities are, popularly, almost completely antithetically opposed to the idea of paternity in both German and Anglophone contexts. Yet Fichte notes that the male-on-male phallic dance is performed by those who have carried out their reproductive imperative. Fichte elaborates on the bicontinentality of this bisexuality:

> Das Holzschneiden ist volkstümlich an beiden Stränden des Atlantik; auf Haiti hat es die gleichen riesigen Holzphalli hervorgebracht, wie in Benin oder Togo—hier werden sie von den Totengöttern präsentiert, von dem schrecklichen, schwulen Gude [sic] Nibo. (Fichte 1979, 18)

> Woodcarving is a folk tradition on both shores of the Atlantic. In Haiti, it has produced the same giant wooden phalluses as in Benin and Togo. Here they represent the gods of the dead, the terrible, gay Gude [sic] Nibo.

In a passage that recalls the character of Yassigui'ndja in René Maran's novel *Batouala* and Josephine Baker's Banana Dance at the Folies Bergère, and in what constitutes one of the first ethnographic accounts of the practice, Fichte notes that men are not the only ones performing a homoerotic dance: women too assume the phallus and dance suggestively with each other: "The gods of the dead, Guédés, in Haiti are like Osiris, phallic. On or around November 2, groups of Haitian women run through the countryside and cities bearing a large, wooden phallus, their faces painted white, dressed in purple, and wearing dark sunglasses" (Fichte 1996, 370).

The continuum of eroticism that spans the domains of Gédé Nibo and Erzulie Freda is fully exhibited in the iconography of Hector Hyppolite. The eroticism present in the open shirt of the Verger photo and in the pink tie of the *Autoportrait* is explained through Hubert Fichte's application of pressure on the Haitian Vodou lwa of love, which has such great importance to queer Vodou devotees. On the special connection between Erzulie and queer men in Vodou, Hubert Fichte writes,

> Erzulie ist die Göttin der Schönheit, der Koketterie, der Liebe. Die Prostituierten und die Homosexuellen verehren sie besonders. Reispuder, Parfüms, Champagner warden ihr geopfert. Sie liebt die Verschwendung. (Fichte 1976, 142)

Erzulie is the goddess of beauty, of coquetry, of love. The prostitutes and homosexuals particularly adore her. Rice powder, perfume, champagne are sacrificed to her. She loves extravagance.

Sie geniert sich und ist stolz, dass der Homosexuelle sie erwählt hat. (Fichte 1976, 165)

She is embarrassed and proud that the homosexual has chosen her.

Erzulie Freda and Gédé Nibo represent extravangance, decadence, and pleasure in distinct female and male versions. They offer Vodouisants the ability to access ritual and quotidian identities and practices for which secular Haitian dominant gender narratives have little space. While there is some small overlap between the lwas and Haitian revolutionaries, none of the leaders of the revolution is presented as queer. While the nation-state is grounded on militant virility (Jean-Jacques Dessalines, Toussaint L'Ouverture) and a supportive femininity (Cécile Fatiman, Catherine Flon), the pantheon of Haitian Vodou, on the other hand, includes salient nonheteronormative figures. This split is also reinforced by the fact that Haitian political institutions are modeled on those of Europe—even the Haitian Revolution was simultaneous with the French Revolution—and that the religion of the Haitian masses, beneath the thin veneer of Roman Catholicism, is African through and through. Its precolonial African roots and worldview account for Vodou's openness to sexual diversity as opposed to the constraints of gendered national narratives elaborated during a revolutionary moment of emergency, which allow for little more than hierarchical binary options of sexual expression. Fichte is captivated by the contrast and seeks to explore the full potential of this openness in Vodou. Before it was noted by other major anthropologists, Fichte documented how the fluidity of gender in Afro-Atlantic religions produces the unique notion of mystic marriages:

Nicht weit von Port-au-Prince, der Haupstadt von Haiti, findet man zwischen Wohnhäusern und Heiligenhütten ein besonderes Haus für Göttin oder Gott, mit säuberlich hergerichtetem Bett, Pantoffeln, Altären, Kerzen.

Hier übernachtet der Gott am ihm heiligen Tag.

Er verbringt die Nacht mit einem ihm angetrauten Priester.

Ich kenne zwei solcher Schlafzimmer—eines für die schöne, eitle "Liebesgöttin" Erzulie Freda, das andere für den Schlangengott Damballah Ouedo. (Von ehelichen Schlafzimmern anderer Götter ist mir nie berichtet worden.)

Wie bei Herodot ist diese Götterverbindung, Götterehe etwas Besonderes; es können Männer mit dem Schlangengott Damballah verheiratet werden—vielleicht bleibt dessen Geschlecht amphibisch ambivalent—, es werden Frauen mit Erzulie verheiratet: Massissi und Madevinaise, Schwuler und Kesmus sind dem haitianischen Glaubenssystem nicht fremd.

Die haitianischen Götter-Ehepartner sind nicht ihr ganzes Leben an Keuschheitsgelübde gebunden, sie dürfen nur am heiligen Tag des Gottes keinen unruhigen Umgang mit Sterblichen haben. (Fichte 1987, 416)

Not far from Port-au-Prince, the capital of Haiti, one finds, nestled between residences and small religious huts, a house built specifically for a goddess or god, complete with a freshly made bed, slippers, altars, and candles. The god sleeps here on the night and day of his holy day. He spends the night with a trusted priest. I know of two such bedrooms—one for the beautiful and vain "goddess of love," Erzulie Freda, the other for the snake god Damballah Ouedo. (I have never heard of bedrooms for married gods.) Just as in Herodotus, sexual relations, or marriage, between gods is something out of the ordinary; men may be wed to the snake god Damballah Ouedo—though the latter seems amphibious with respect to gender—and women may be married to Erzulie Freda: masisi and madevinaise [sic]—male and female gays, respectively—are hardly foreign to Haitian religious beliefs. Those who do marry gods are not bound to remain chaste their entire lives; they must refrain from intercourse with mortals only on the god's holy day. (Fichte 1996, 368)

It might be easy for us to dismiss the Herodotus allusions in the text and title of Fichte's work as Eurocentric and anachronistic baggage, but his references to the fifth-century historian from Asia Minor who recorded sacramental sexuality in the ancient Near East reveal the universal—that is, nonaberrant—quality of this practice, which is also found in Haitian Vodou. However, the allusion to Herodotus seems to frustrate and derail some German critics from understanding how mystic marriages in Vodou operate:

Aber auch von Fichte werden nicht erfahren, warum kultische Sexualität oft neurotisch und unpraktisch ist, obwohl diese Frage zentral ist, für die von ihm gezogenen Verbindungen zwischen Homosexualität, Ritualistik und Literatur. (Hauschild 2002, 299)

Nor does one learn from Fichte why cultic sexuality is often neurotic and impractical, even though this question is central to the connections drawn by him between homosexuality, ritual, and literature.

This Eurocentric projection can be said to have been inadvertently inspired by Fichte: "wenn man die Liebesgöttin der Griechen nicht eine athenische Erzulie nennen will, vielleicht als eine haitianische Aphrodite bezeichnet werden könnte" (Fichte 1987, 417); "I would hesitate to call Athena a Greek Erzulie, but Erzulie might be thought of as a Haitian Aphrodite" (Fichte 1996, 369). The mystic marriages that captured Fichte's fascination speak to a sacramental sexuality that defies heteronormative prescriptions, in which men and women may marry—that is, enter into partial cohabitation contractual agreements, sleeping together weekly, with—divinities of their own gender. For example, and as predicted by the formula noted by Fichte, female devotees might reserve one day a week to sleep with Erzulie, even if they are already married or cohabitating with another human being, even a man. Fichte here continues to use the local term "masisi" and starts using the term "madevinez," but equates them with gay and lesbian, even though the repertoire of these Western identities does not encompass sleeping with immaterial beings of any kind.

Hyppolite himself entered into such mystic marriages. Several scholars note the fact that Hyppolite never married because he claimed to be in a mystical marriage to Lasirèn, the goddess of the sea (Barnitz 2001, 124; Congdon and Hallmark 2002, 108; Cosentino 1995b, 198). Hyppolite was an oungan, a Vodou priest who knew he "had an important message to communicate, that he was the guardian of a secret" (Breton 2002, 309). Hector Hyppolite communicated this supernatural message through his painting, which was in turn inspired through his spiritual life as a Vodou priest, devoted to the lwa and united in mystic marriage to Lasirèn. In "A Visit with Hector Hyppolite," Selden Rodman records Hyppolite's thoughts on the matter:

> I am married, you know to my protective spirit, so I can't marry anyone else. When I was a child, my grandfather, a great priest of vaodou, married me to La Sirène, and she has always been my mystic wife. But I have three mistresses. That's not very many. Usually I have seven. But lately I've been getting disgusted with women. They are always getting into trouble. So I have only three now. They live together. They are not jealous. Why should they be? It's a great advantage to them to be my mistresses, after all. . . . They eat regularly, sleep regularly, and I'm an expert in love matters. So altogether they have little to complain about. I have several children outside, but they're all grown up now; they're

FIG. 2.8. The divine feminine spirit as bird regendering the artist and model. Hector Hyppolite, *Mistress Siren* (*Le Metrés Sirène*), 1946. Oil on board, 19½ × 16 in. (49.53 × 40.64 cm). Milwaukee Art Museum, gift of Richard and Ema Flagg, M1991.130. Photograph by John R. Glembin.

big and they're ambitious and they're just waiting for me to die so they can inherit from me. But my new baby, ah, she's different. I shall bring her up in my own way. Her name signifies love. So when she's a grown woman and a man calls her by her name, he will be saying to her: You are my love. (Rodman 1948, 67)

The queerness in the passage remains unanalyzed by Rodman. Hyppolite's description of his sexual life is unabashedly nonheteronormative: He has a spiritual reason for remaining a bachelor. He acknowledges a growing repulsion toward women. Nevertheless, he has mistresses. He is polygamous and has children outside of wedlock by different women. He passes no judgment on utilitarianism in his sexual unions and his relationship to his children. His allegorically named daughter appears to function as a fictive construct, as she renders him the parent of Love, the main attribute of the Haitian Vodou lwa Erzulie Freda. St. Jean (1973, 10) confirms that he had no marriages of record, but lists the birth of only one daughter: Ermite. The noncorrespondence of this name with the one given by Hyppolite seems to endorse the possibility that he was speaking of family in metaphorical and allegorical terms. Supporting my interpretation is the fact that this daughter does not fit the chronology of Hyppolite's life as she would have been conceived and born while he was out of the country. How could he have fathered a Haitian child while away? He left in 1909 for Cuba, returned in 1920, and Ermite was born in 1916 (St. Jean 1973, 4–5). Ermite married the painter Rigaud Benoit (Comité Hector Hyppolite 2011, 10), who was codedly described as Hyppolite's "inseparable companion" (Rodman 1948, 68) and as the "compère et ami intime d'Hector Hyppolite" (St. Jean 1973, 4; the compère and intimate friend of Hector Hyppolite). Given the magical realism that characterized Hyppolite's life and work, it would not be unlikely that Hyppolite would use the lexicon of biological issue to articulate mystical Vodou concepts. It also seems likely that he would refer to his *ounsis* through the trope of children, as Philippe Thoby-Marcelin "avait trouvé la demeure d'Hector Hyppolite, prête de vaudou, vivant dans le dénuement le plus abject, au milieu de ses hounsis" (St. Jean 1973, 11; had found the domicile of Hector Hyppolite, Vodou priest, living in the most abject poverty among his initiates). Similarly, when he discusses keeping several women, he may not have been referring to real mistresses. As many of his paintings evoke Erzulie Dantor, we see that he is associated with three female lwas—Lasirèn, Dantor, and Freda. Are these the three mistresses to whom he is referring? As familial metaphors are common for referencing interpersonal links within Vodou communities, Hyppolite has the opportunity here to queer the discourse of reproductive heterosexuality to describe sexuality and relationships that are in many ways antinomical to the dominant script.

It is my contention that his mystic marriages to Lasirèn and Erzulie Dantor allowed him a public expression of a substratum female persona that, combined with his own maleness, produced the idealized androgyny that suffuses many of his paintings. Hyppolite's female subjects are crafted as a feminized version of himself; they are feminine self-portraits, drawn in his own likeness. "La femme reste au coeur de l'oeuvre d'Hyppolite, lwa ou simple mortelle. Toujours vécue dans une douce obsession" (Lerebours 2011, 30; The woman remains at the heart of the work of Hyppolite, a lwa or a mere mortal, always lived as a sweet obsession), but this woman is not an other-object to Hyppolite but a self-subject. Let us consider some images that reveal this androgynous transcorporeal symbiosis of authorial self-representation and female lwa. In some photos we notice Hyppolite has a preference for pink ties. His carefully arranged hair and air of distinction reveal attributes of Erzulie. There is a strong resemblance between his photos and his representations of Erzulie. The portraits of the artist as lwa (figures 2.4 and

FIG. 2.9. Portrait of the artist as female lwa. Hector Hyppolite, *The Siren* (*Lasuréne* [*La Sirène*]), 1946. Oil on Masonite, 24 × 30 in. (60.96 × 76.2 cm). Milwaukee Art Museum, gift of Richard and Ema Flagg, M1991.131. Photograph by Efraim Lev-er.

2.8–2.11) are reminiscent of another important queer Caribbean self-portrait, Audre Lorde's *Zami: A New Spelling of My Name*. The epigraph to *Queering Black Atlantic Religions* recounts how the evolution of the autobiographical protagonist of Lorde's biomythography culminates in her merger with the West African Vodou sea deity, Afrekete, a counterpart of the Haitian Vodou lwa Lasirèn. Further, the portraits catalogued as *Maitresse Erzulie* and *Erzulie auf einem Delphin*, among many others, present Erzulie as a feminized version of the painter.[3] Both paintings present the commingling of zoological and human attributes and are counterparts to Wifredo Lam's chimeras, which, as discussed in chapter 4, articulate the phenomenon of possession. But which element represents the divine: the animal or the human? In Hyppolite's hieroglyphic tableaux, the relationally supracorporeal image functions as the external, divine *kajou nut* to an earthly sweet and pulpous vessel. The bird and the woman with loose hair are divinities, while the dolphin and the woman with the pink ribbon are initiates. Let us notice how the woman with loose hair rides the dolphin. Functioning transcorporeally, the dolphin is her concave vessel. The species is not an indicator of the metaphysical identification of the persona. Rather, it is the hierarchical spatial ordering within the relationship that reveals the identity. In figure 2.10, *Woman with a Ribbon*, a feminized and divinized version of the artist serves as the foundation for the representation of Erzulie. This is a somewhat androgynous figure. Her hiding her breasts is more than modesty, as it makes her gender more difficult to discern. Nevertheless, in her androgyny, she appears to be slightly pregnant. Is this Hyppolite's Vodou translation of the Annunciation? The birds do seem to function as a type of Holy Ghost and angel Gabriel. This is a queer union of the divine and human. All birds are paired with other birds, yet the central couple, the human-divine composite being, defies boundaries of expected biological monodimensional pairing. Hyppolite here seems to say that ritual possession produces a spiritual androgyny that refracts heterosexual pairing.

Generally, biographers of Hyppolite have discussed his queerness through a code mirroring the artist's own: "En tant de labeur ne lui fit vivre que maigrement d'une vie toujours précaire et dans une solitude dangereuse, à laquelle il n'échappe qu'au cabaret ou au nirvana" (St. Jean 1973, 10; His labor only allowed him to live meagerly and precariously in a dangerous loneliness, which he escaped only at the cabaret or through nirvana). The reference to the cabaret functions in the language of its day as a marker of a decadent lifestyle of nighttime escapades and implies same-sex behavior. Building on this, Ute Stebich decribes Hyppolite in a coded language of effeminacy: "tall and extremely thin, he moved with imperial dignity and grace; a mane of shoulder-length hair surrounded his fine features" and he "enjoyed exploring the ambigous nature of female spirits" (1978, 160–61). This aesthetic self-presentation of the artist is confirmed by L. G. Hoffman, who furthers the language of effeminacy in describing the painter:

> As he approached we noticed the nobility of his carriage and the serene and luminous expression of his face. His jet black hair with its innumerable small waves was parted in the middle and worn long to the shoulders. . . . Greeting us with a poised and ceremonial curtsey, he told us our visit was no surprise. He had known of it long before from a vision he had in a dream. (1985, 69)

More recently and directly, Randy Conner and David Sparks (2004, 275–76), in *Queering the Creole Spriritual Traditions*, say Haitian anthropologists, art

FIG. 2.10. Transcorporeal self-portraiture: The profile of Maitresse Erzulie bears an uncanny physical resemblance to that of its painter. Hector Hyppolite, *Woman with a Ribbon* (*Femme aux fleurs et aux oiseaux*), 1948. Oil on cardboard, 86 × 57 cm. Musée d'Art Haïtien.

historians, and filmmakers confirmed that Hyppolite was known to be "a homosexual" or "bisexual."

As one snake twists over the other, we perceive how the sensual self-protraiture of Hyppolite contrasts with the sexual fetishization of the black body found in Fichte. In Fichte's early literature, set within a European context, desire for the black body is presented as an extension and outgrowth of gay men's leather paraphilia. The conflation between black leather and dark skin becomes evident in his interviews with Hans Eppendorfer in *Ledermann*:

> Hattest du Federn?
> Hatten die Stämme Haut?
> Und wie rochen sie?

—Nach Körper. Viel zu groß. Sie hatten Pulsschlag, etwas Vibrier-
endes. Manchmal hatte man das Gefühl, es waren riesige aufgerichtete
Schwänze, deren Eicheln bis rauf, ganz weit, ganz zum Mond ragten.

Weiß oder Schwarz?
—Schwarz. Alles Schwarz. Schwarz. Schwarz.
Du ziehst dich gerne hübsch an? (Eppendorfer 1977, 126–27)

Did you have feathers?
Did the tribes have skin?
And how did they smell?
—Of body odor. Much too large. They had a pulsing beat, something
vibrant. Sometimes it felt like there were huge erect cocks with their
glandes up almost reaching the moon.

White or black?
—Black. All black. Black. Black.
You like to dress up pretty?

Here Fichte displays his deployment of the gay white male gaze onto black
men and how his desire for men of color is akin to and a substitute for
leather fetishism. For Fichte, the love of black leather is nearly synonymous
with dark skin, graphically replicating the most dangerous zoologizing tendencies of colonialism. More specifically, however, for our current study, the
conflation of black skin and black leather repeats and extends the eroticizing
of the dead queer black male body captured by Verger in his photograph of
Hyppolite. For both, and in Fichte in particular, this objectification achieves
a paternalism with strong elements of Orientalism:

Hast du etwas wie eine Lederszene in Ägypten angetroffen?
—Nein. Uberhaupt nicht.

Und du hast sehr gut ohne leben könen?
—Ich war fasziniert von den Menschen. Ich fand die einfach fabel-
haft und ich habe zwei Studenten, mit denen ich mich anfreundete,
die haben mich standing überall hin begleitet. Wir haben über alle
Sachen gesprochen, auch außerhalb von Kairo. . . . Natürlich habe
ich für die bezahlt, weil die einfach nicht viel hatten. Die holten mich
schon frühmorgens aus dem Hotel ab und dann fuhren wir einfach
rum und bis spät in die Nacht und dann bezahlte ich ihnen natürlich
zum Schluß das Geld, was ich noch in ägyptischen Pfunden da hatte,

das gelassen. Selbstverständlich. Ich habe ihnen ein Dauerstipendium am Goetheinstitut besorgt, den beiden, mit völliger Lehrmittelfreiheit und ich habe dafür gesorgt, daß sie Schreibpapier zur Verfügung haben. Ich habe ihnen auch Bücher und Hefte und Schreibblocks und Materialien gekauft. (Eppendorfer 1997, 166)

Have you encountered something like a leather scene in Egypt?
—No. Not at all.

And you have been able to live well without one?
—I was fascinated by the people. I found the people absolutely fabulous and I have two students whom I befriended, who accompanied me everywhere. We talked about all manner of things, aside from Cairo as well. . . . Of course I had to pay for them, because they did not have much. They picked me up in the early morning from the hotel, and then we just drove around until late into the night, and then I paid them the money, of course, afterward, whatever I had left in Egyptian pounds, without a fuss. Naturally. I got them a permanent scholarship at the Goethe Institute, both of them, including all teaching materials, and I made sure that they had writing paper available. I also bought them books and notebooks and writing pads and materials.

Aber du konntest in Ägypten leben und erotische Erlebnisse genießen ohne die Heavier Scenes der Lederwelt?
—Aber Ja! (Eppendorfer 1997, 166)

But you could live in Egypt and enjoy erotic experiences without the heavier scenes of the leather world?
—Of course!

The question assumes the nonexistence of a leather scene in Egypt, which has a certain basis in truth when one considers that most queer leather fetishist communities are in so-called Western, predominantly white countries. Using Fichte to explain this geographical distribution of the leather scene, we can surmise that the preponderance of leather sexualities in Euro–North America is communally and unconsciously driven by an objectification of the ethnic other, who is desired, impersonated, and abjected in a ritualistic fashion in these communities. If Fichte is able to do without the gay leather scene in Egypt, it is because there he already has access to dark skin, which he is, in fact, purchasing through gifts, scholarships, and other educational materials and benefits to his younger liaisons. The transmutability and substitutition of black leather via dark skins further underscores the thingification of queers of color through white gay men's technological optics of desire. Moreover, Fichte's questions and his dialogue with other gay white men—Genet, Eppendorfer—reveal his fetishistic desire for men of color as well as his awareness of the exploitative nature of his relationships with black and brown men. There is also the fetishization of Vodou that curiously works with and against the dangerous and prevalent misrepresentations of the religion. And this queer reification of Vodou and black men is what Hyppolite's self-portraiture comments upon and seeks to transcend by providing a lived, direct account of the religion and its initiates, the *Auto-portrait* of Vodou. This fetishization of the black body in Fichte diminishes greatly as he carries out his ethnographic work in Haiti and provides spaces for queer Vodouisants to express themselves in their own words through interviews. Perhaps as a way of understanding and atoning for his own opportunistic monetary exchange for sexual favors, Fichte becomes very concerned with the topic of queer sex work among Vodouisants:

—Ich bin in einem Milieu von Homosexuellen geboren. In der Nähe des Bicentenaire. Ich bin homosexuell. Der Homosexueller ist ein Mann, der einen Mann liebt. Der Homosexuelle ist der Mann. Auf dem Lande gibt es viele. Aber da die anderen darüber lachen, machen sie es heimlich. In der Stadt ist es einfacher. Seit ich 19 bin, bin ich homosexuell. Vorher habe ich es mit Mädchen gemacht. Seit 10, 11. Aber ich mag es nicht. Ich liebe Männer mehr als Frauen. Ich wurde als Homosexueller in einem Viertel von Homosexuellen geboren. Ich war daran gewöhnt.

—Es gibt Götter, die die Homosexueller verachten, und andere, die sie lieben.

—Ogum verachtet sie.

—Agassou, Attiassou, Damballah, Erzulie lieben die Homosexuellen.

—Hier ist es sehr einfach, Männer zu finden. Ich bezahle sie. Ich gebe 10, 15 Dollar, wenn ich sie sehr liebe, sonst 2 bis 4 Dollar. Aber wenn es Liebe ist, gebe ich sehr viel aus. Ich habe nie mit jemandem geschlafen, ohne zu bezahlen; das Geld gewinnt die Männer.

—Ich nehme den Mann wie eine Frau.

—Ich lasse mich nicht nehmen. Ich bin ein Boundalier.

—Ich fasse ihn auch an.

—Ich mache es ihm auch mit dem Mund und er mir. Das ekelt mich nicht.

—Ich habe viele große Passionen gehabt.

—Ich stecke ihm die Zunge in die Ohren, in die Nase, in den Mund und ich nehme die Zunge und berühre seinen ganzen Körper. Ich schlafe jeden Tag in der Woche mit einem Jungen. (Fichte 1976, 194).

—I was born in a milieu of homosexuals. Near the bicentennial. I'm homosexual. A homosexual is a man who loves a man. A homosexual is a man. In the countryside, there are many. But as the others laugh about it, they do it secretly. In the city, it's easier. Since I was nineteen, I've been homosexual. Previously I had done it with girls. Since ten, eleven. But I do not like it. I love men more than women. I was born as a homosexual in a homosexuals' quarter. I was used to it.

—There are gods who despise homosexuals, and others who love them.

—Ogum despises them.

—Agassou, Attiassou, Damballah, Erzulie love homosexuals.

—Here it is very easy to find men. I'll pay. I spend ten, fifteen dollars if I love them very much, otherwise two to four dollars. But if it's love, I spend a lot. I've never slept with someone without paying. The money wins over the men.

—I'll take the man as a woman.

—I do not let them take me. I'm a *boundalier*, a "top."

—I touch him, too.

—I also do it to him with my mouth, and he me. It does not disgust me.

—I have had many great passions.

—I stick my tongue in his ears, in the nose, in the mouth and I take the tongue and touch his whole body. I sleep every day of the week with a boy.

Seneca kommt auf eine Coca-Cola mit.

Er sagt:

—Auf dem Lande glauben die Leute, die Homosexuellen seien vom Teufel geschickt.

—In der Haupstadt gibt es viele.

—Die Vaudoupriester sind zu neunzig Prozent Massissi.

—Viele Priesterinnen sind lesbisch.

—Es gibt kein Gesetz gegen Homosexualität. Vor der Polizei braucht man sich nicht zu fürchten.

—Wenn man wegen unsittlicher. Handlungen oder so verhaftet wird, prügelt einen die Polizei nur durch und man kann wieder gehen.

—Mein Vater würde mich verstossen, wenn er es wüsste.

—Mein Bruder nennt mich manchmal "Alte Tante."

—Ich glaube, mein Mutter konnte mich früher nicht ausstehen. Sie fing erst an, mich zu lieben, als ich mit Männern ging.

—Ich habe seit meinem achten Jahr was mit Mädchen gemacht, wie alle hier. Mit 12 habe ich zuerst mit einem Mann. Dann habe ich vier Jahre gar nichts gemacht—nur gebetet.

—Jetzt fürchte ich, dass ich überhaupt nie mehr mit Frauen kann.

—Ich bin homosexuell geworden—aus Übersättigung glaube ich.

Heute nachmittag hat Seneca einen Vierjährigen gesehen, der mit einem Mädchen scherzte. Seneca hat ihn verprügelt.

Wenig spatter überraschte er den Vierjährigen mit einem Jungen. Seneca erzählt alles dem Bruder des Kleinen, damit der ihn ordentlich bestraft. (Fichte 1976, 197)

Seneca comes for a Coca-Cola.

He says:

—In the country, people believe that homosexuals were sent by the devil.

—In the capital there are many.

—The Vodou priests are 90 percent masisi.

—Many female priests are lesbian.

—There is no law against homosexuality. One does not have to be afraid of the police.

—If one is arrested because of immoral actions, the police only beat you up and then you can go again.

—My father would disown me if he knew.

—My brother sometimes calls me "Old Aunt."

—I think my mother could not stand me before. She only started to love me when I started going with men.

—Since I was eight years old, I've done things with girls, like everyone here. At twelve, I first did something with a man. Then I didn't do anything for four years but pray.

—Now I fear that I may never ever be able to do anything with women.

—I became homosexual from saturation I think.

This afternoon Seneca saw a four-year-old joking with a girl. Seneca beat him up.

A little later, he surprised the four-year-old with a boy. Seneca tells everything to his brother, so he punishes him properly.

The redeeming aspect of Fichte's work is embedded within these interviews because they reveal to Fichte and his readers a world of sexual alterity that does not conform to the gay and lesbian paradigms of Euro–North America. While he does lapse into some of these imported terms—"lesbisch," for example—his alternation between local and foreign terms serves to demonstrate the instability of these culturally constructed categories. The most widespread popular religion of the country of study being open to same-sex desire is a novelty to ethnographers coming from the nominally Christian West. Payment for sex in this context is part of an age-differentiated system of patronage more than a form of work. Fichte seems motivated to underline this system of sexual-monetary patronage in order to explain and exculpate himself for his previous participation in it throughout parts of the global South. As far as his informants are concerned, their self-expression of queer Vodou identities in Fichte's interviews contrasts sharply with Fichte's early fetishistic representation of the black body. More saliently, this self-expression in Fichte's Haitian interviews approximates the self-portraiture of Hyppolite, in that they both frustrate Western attemps to impose imported, dominant categories of sexual alterity and promote distinct and local subjectivities that are unproblematically queer, Caribbean, and spiritual.

Fichte is transformed by his contact with Vodou, which is reflected not only in the transformation of his portrayal of the black body but also in his writing style.

Eine Tonsur wird geschnitten.
Haare ins Einweihungsgefäß—Pot de Tête.
Kabbalistische Einweihungsformeln, die den rebellischen Geist einweihen. (Fichte 1985, 236)

A tonsure is cut.
Hair into the initiate receptacle—Pot de Tête.
Kabbalistic initiation formulas that initiate the rebellious spirit.

The pòtet of Vodou are often made of dried-out calabash gourds, or *kwi*. This explains the subconscious slippage between "calabash" and "kabbalah," and the articulation of both mystical traditions reveals the almost surrealistic automatic writing under which Fichte appears to be operating. Once in Haiti, he develops a distinctive ethnopoetic style that is characterized by a unique blend of anthropological content narrated as and within poetic versification. This ethnopoesis is uniquely musical, improvisational, spiralist, and dominated by stream of consciousness. Like Lydia Cabrera's (1995) *El Monte*, it would appear to be composed of directly transcribed and minimally edited fieldnotes. Advancing the argument of this book, I wish to call this style, in which the ethnographer transcribes raw field notes, thus giving the text a mystical, transcendental, and disorienting quality, *transcripturality*. The writing used by Cabrera and Fichte forces the reader to enter into the maze, or thicket—another word for "el monte"—of the tropics and of trance. For this reason, this transcorporeal style displays in its construction and evokes in its reception the disorientation of the self as it is overataken by the orisha or lwa during the Afro-diasporic religious ritual. This transcorporeal textuality in both Fichte and Cabrera performs the trance state in which the information was presumably given by the informant, recorded by the anthropologist, and, ultimately, ideally received by the reader.

It can be argued that this transcripturality constitutes the foundation of spiralism, a literary movement tracing back to the late 1960s and whose main figures are the Haitian writers René Philoctète, Jean-Claude Fignolé, and Frankétienne. According to them, spiralism centers on the idea that the universe is interconnected, unpredictable, and governed by chaos. These are all emotions that characterize the trance possession experience as described by Vodou initiates. Hector Hyppolite's written textuality in his tableaux seems to display the same disorienting qualities as this spiralism in its cryptic orthography. Certainly the multilayered semantic potentialities of "Hector Hyppolite èl même" in the *Autoportrait* and the enigmatic title "La Dauration l'armor" generate a kind of linguistic disorientation that challenges critics to question commonly held assumptions and binarisms such as French/Kreyòl, written/oral, literacy/illiteracy, and education/naïveté. The explosion of these binarisms in the textuality of Hector Hyppolite propels us toward a realm beyond the structural dualities of language. The transcorporeal style is bewitching, infectious. I write, "Hissssssss! I peer through the fangs and see the forked tongues render the coiling serpents mute but I free myself from their suffocating embrace, regaining my breath just in time to deliver this important message to you. Listen . . ." This post-Saussurean realm of the monad, à la Leibniz, is the perspectival space that is ultimately depicted in the self-portraiture of Hyppolite: the space in which and from which the entranced viewer might obtain the enlightened *konesans* that makes visible the commingling of the divine, human, plant, and animal—the oneness of all life and the indistinguishabilty of this life from the so-called inanimate world.

According to Lerebours, "Hector Hyppolite, à son arrivée au Centre d'art, savait à peine lire et écrire" (2011, 24–25; Upon his arrival at the Art Center, Hector Hyppolite could barely read and write). His apparent inability to read and write contrasts with Alexis's interpretation of the female subject of his paintings: "La femme qu'il a peinte est souvent lascive, la femme bourgeoise. . . . La femme est lettrée" (2004, 139; The woman he painted is often lascivious, the bourgeois woman. . . . The woman is literate). If we are to accept the literate quality of the female subject in Hyppolite's paintings, we might also wish to see her as a Hegelian contrapuntal dialectical partner to the painter whereby the binarisms woman/man and subject/object are substructurally generated via the underlying opposition of literacy/illiteracy.

If limited writing abilities provide us with difficulty in ascertaining the intended meaning of Hyppolite's textuality, there likewise remains the diglossic phenomenon in the relationship between Kreyòl and French in Haiti. Breton himself remarked on Hyppolite's limited fluency in French: "His extreme reserve, coupled with the great difficulty he had in expressing himself in French, ultimately made a coherent conversation almost impossible. When I learnt, a few months ago, of his death I regretted all the more that it had proved impossible for me to draw from him an explanation of his motivations" (2002, 310).

Further complicating Hyppolite's possible near illiteracy is the playful usage of acronyms in his paintings. Initials of words and names are anagramized and oftentimes transposed through a type of metathesis. His usage recalls the abbreviation and circumlocution of the name of the Hebrew divinity through the tetragrammaton: YHWH. Was Hyppolite using these enigmatic, transposed initials because he was illiterate? Did they constitute a type of shorthand for spatial limitations in the paintings? Célius sees in them a transcendental function:

> De toute evidence, il en appelle à ces lettres pour ajouter un peu de mystère, pour conférer un caractère ésotérique, renforcé . . . à la symbolique franc-maçone que rappellent d'ailleurs également l'usage de mots abréges réduits en lettres séparées par des points. . . . Et par le jeu sur la signature, Hyppolite se place au coeur même de sa creation. (2011, 97)

> Obviously, he appeals to these letters to add a bit of mystery, to impart a reinforced esoteric character . . . in the symbolic Freemason manner

that recalls the use of abbreviated words separated by periods. . . . And through the game of the signature, Hyppolite locates himself in the very heart of his creation.

The relationship between the orthography and the images in the paintings presents us with an alternative form of textuality, whose enigma bears an important relation to the painter's gendered self-performance, an overall strategy of queer representation begging to be decoded by critics. There is in Hyppolite's use of initials a queer discourse which is sexual and orthographic and that demands the elaboration of a unique decoding strategy.

La concomitance entre les deux mouvements de rehabilitation du créole et de renaissance artistique, dans les années 1940, ne saurait être fortuite aux yeux de l'historien, pour lequel il s'agit de deux voies d'accès ouvertes à la culture populaire haïtiene jusque-là tenue en bride et pour ainsi inhibée: la naissance du créole comme langue écrite reconnue et l'émergence de la peinture naïve haïtienne (les primitifs) comme expressions simultanées d'un nouveau langage populaire. En résumé, il s'agissait de deux responses à un même besoin: le besoin de renouvellement culturel par ressourcement, en débridant et, pour ainsi dire, en libérant (c'est le mot juste) l'expression artistique du peuple haïtien à même, désormais, d'exploiter plus aisément à travers ces nouvelles forms d'expression toute la richesse alors à peine soupçonnée d'une authentique culture populaire. (Manigat 2011, 119)

The coincidence between the two movements, the rehabilitation of Kreyòl and the artistic renaissance of the 1940s, cannot be trivial in the eyes of the historian since it deals with two open access roads to Haitian popular culture until then held in check and thus inhibited: the birth of Kreyòl as a recognized written language and the emergence of Haitian naive (primitive) painting as simultaneous expressions of a new vernacular. In summary, these were two responses to the same need: the need for cultural renewal through healing, unleashing, and, so to speak, liberating (that's the right word) the artistic expression of the Haitian people, exploiting more easily through these new forms of expression all the scarcely suspected wealth of a genuine popular culture.

Here, Manigat most aptly captures the interconnectedness between the rise of the acceptance of Kreyòl as a bona-fide language and the intensification of Haitian artistic production. This is a point that is also similarly articulated about the connection between the end of the official suppression of Vodou and the rise of Haitian art:

> Even though Vaudou plays an important role in Haitian life as the traditional religion of the Creole-speaking masses, it was repressed by the ruling class, culminating in the anti-superstitious campaign of 1942–43. Its practice was finally legalized in 1946, which helps to explain why Vaudou-related art came to prominence in the late forties. (Poupeye 1998, 81)

As simultaneous expressions of Haitian cultural emancipation from Western impositions and constraints, Manigat and Poupeye help us to make sense of the imbricated nature of art, language, and religion in Hyppolite's tableaux. Hyppolite's work seems to respond to the charge of illiteracy by saying it is the art critics and viewers who need to expand their reading abilities so as not to miss the deeper, transcendental messages in his paintings. And this ability to read can only be accessed through a broadening of the concept of the self and of the ways in which it can represent itself. This is a strong tenet in the philosophy of Vodou aesthetics and one which Hyppolite's art foments in its viewers, an epiphanic moment of rapture and trance leading to the sublime knowledge of the self-in-and-as-the-cosmos.

This is the moment of life and death in the dance between the serpents. The metaphysics of Hyppolite's paintings buck against the drive to box and fix Vodou solely into the realm of the local. This is the initial impetus of most white queer ethnographers, including Fichte, at least during the entry phase into the worldview of diasporic African religions. In response to this, transcorporeality, the conceptualization of the body as a vessel for the divine, becomes for Hyppolite a technique of self-portraiture that challenges white queer ethnographic fetishization. It is noteworthy that in a preliminary fashion and without making the connection to trance possession, Breton had noticed the usage of receptacularity of the human body in the work of Hyppolite: "One only has to study his *Maritravo*, for instance, to observe the perfect balance established between the vase and the human figure on the right, both equally pot bellied" (2002, 312). Perhaps in its clearest manner, the deployment of this transcorporeality in the work of Hyppolite achieves maximum expression in an untitled painting, in which the representation of a boat conveys the idea of the metaphysical vessel. The boat in the painting had a material referent. Just before his death, Hyppolite was obsessed with the construction of a boat (Lerebours 2011, 36). This task consumed Hyppolite's attention and finances:

FIG. 2.11. The lwa rides the initiate during trance as the passenger does the boat in this allegorical painting. Hector Hyppolite, *Promenade sur Mer*, 1946–48. 41 × 61 cm. Musée d'Art Haitïen.

Pendant tout un temps, les revenus que lui rapportait sa peinture passaient dans la construction d'un bateau. Le Centre d'Art dû, à maintes reprises, consenter à des avances pour permettre à Hyppolite d'acheter les matériaux nécessaires à ce projet, ambitieux pour le moins. Ce bateau, en effet, il voulait le construire pour amener, à Saint Marc, tous ses amis. (Alexis 2004, 136)

For a time, the income that he earned from his painting was spent on building a boat. The Art Centre had repeatedly agreed to advance payments to allow Hyppolite to buy the materials needed for this project, ambitious to say the least. In fact, he wanted to build the boat to bring all his friends to Saint Marc.

The selflessness of the boat construction enterprise allows us to see how the communal and *kounbit* aspect of Vodou philosophy thoroughly suffuses Hyppolite's work ethic.[4] He built the boat to share it with his friends, among them notable intellectuals and artists. Métraux writes, "Avec Verger et l'artiste américaine (Irma Cavat), nous montons sur le pont du bateau d'Hyppolite. La nuit est orageuse, c'est à peine si nous distinguons quelques lumières du côté de Léogane" (1978, 268–69; With Verger and an American artist (Irma Cavat), we went aboard Hyppolite's boat. The night was tempestuous, and it was with difficulty that we discerned some lights in the direction of Leogane). He also claimed to use the boat as a way to connect with the lwa of the sea: "La Sirène l'accompagnera, le protégera. Il se fera, raconte-t-on, construire un bateau où il ira régulièrement peindre car là, il entendait mieux la voix du lwa qui lui dictait son oeuvre" (Lerebours 2011, 28; Lasirèn will accompany him, will protect him. It is said he had a boat built where he would go to paint regularly because there he could better hear the voice of the lwa who dictated his work). The communion between the boat and the pilot is akin to the state of trance in which the lwa rides and guides the human initiate. It would seem that Hyppolite would perform this communion with Lasirèn through meditative and entranced sea voyages. Given the death of Hyppolite shortly after the completion of the boat, it is difficult not to see these spiritually motivated trips as prophetic intimations of his upcoming passage to the afterlife. In this sense, the boat also serves as a kind of coffin that is replicated in the photos taken by Verger of Hyppolite's wake and funeral procession. It would seem that Alexis may have hinted at this when addressing the attributes of the boat as it was painted by Hyppolite: "Il ne s'agit pas ici de voiliers de cabotage mais d'un bateau à coque d'acier, avec moteur. La cheminée est là pour le prouver. C'est donc un bateau qui peut aller loin. Hyppolite aurait peut-être voulu embarquer sur un tel bateau. Il disait avoir beaucoup voyagé" (2004, 137; It is not a question here of sailboats but of a steel-hulled boat with an engine. The exhaust pipe is there to prove it. This is a boat that can go far. Hyppolite might have wanted to embark on such a boat. He said he had traveled extensively). The sense of urgency in its contruction might certainly be interpreted as being motivated by a premonition of death.

Though the painting remains officially untitled, it is variously referred to as *Fisherman in a Cove, Man in a Speedboat,* or *La Chaloupe* and curiously reproduced in a mirror image orientation. LeGrace Benson provides a most apt description of the painting:

A speeding motorboat cuts a circle through the waves into the calm waves of a bay. The swooshing wake stretches a comet's tail behind a man with his face set ferociously forward. He could be a tourist letting go of his sedate boardroom manners in a sea that cannot vote "no," or a bandit fleeing the coast patrol, or a mission doctor on an emergency call to the next settlement down the shore. Hector Hyppolite captures

FIG. 2.12. The relationship between the lwa and its *serviteur* is presented through the vessel-and-captain symbiosis of this painting. Hector Hyppolite, *La Chaloupe* (*Man in a Speedboat*), 1946–48. 31 × 46 cm. Musée d'Art Haitïen.

an event in mid-course, its beginning and its end indeterminate, its momentary trajectory arrested on a little piece of cardboard 12 by 18 inches. Its resonant impact remains in motion after 60 years. (2011, 131)

If Benson presents us with possible motivations for the trip portrayed, it is because this remains a cryptic element of the narrative. However, the sense of urgency remains clear. There is visible stress on the face of the pilot. He seems sad, anguished, and worried, perhaps pondering the ephemerality of life. If read from left to right, the boat is leaving. It is a departure. Twilight marks the hour, but is it morning or evening? We recall Césaire's first lines in his *Cahier* as he stares out to sea: "Au bout du petit matin" (1983, 7; At the end of daybreak). A gateway between this world and the next is opened within this liminal space of disorientation and surrealistic creativity. We might surmise that the sun is setting, for in the west-facing coastline of Saint Marc and Port-au-Prince, this is the perspective of seeing the sun set over the waters. We feel the anxiety of leaving the safety of the cove for an uncertain destination as the light is growing dim. The horizon is the same color as the land, implying that we experience our existence only within a thin part of the full spectrum of reality and that supra- and infradimensional wavelengths exist as points of departure and arrival on the journey of life. In this life transition, in this crossing over, we imagine Hyppolite going to his imagined island of Caradjine, his own mythical Africa/Guinen, which in Kreyòl is referred to as *Lotbolanme-a* (The other side of the sea). Like many of his paintings, this is also a self-portrait. The graphic H. H. at the bottom of the painting is both signature and title, as the painting seems to say, "This is my life" and "Life is a journey."

Lwa Mèt Awe Tawoyo is husband to Lasirèn. In this painting as in his death, we see Hyppolite fully marrying Lasirèn. In this composition, Hyppolite represents himself as Awe with his boat, Imamou. The cardboard upon which the image has been recorded implies the recycled nature of existence and the philosophy of reincarnation espoused by the West African religion of Ifá. This painting further presents how the concept of transcorporeality is present in Hyppolite's work. In this boat/captain pairing, we see the relationship between the corpus and its anima, which is also analogous to that of the initiate and lwa during trance possession. The concavity of the boat allegorizes the receptacular nature of the body of the initiate who allows himself to be maneuvered by the divine and taken to unexpected destinations. As an iteration of the horse-and-rider metaphor, which is most widely disseminated in the Ogou/St. Jacques Majeur/Senjakmajé iconographical tradition, the vessel/captain image seems like the idealized representation of the ecstasy of the mystical marriage of Awe to Lasirèn.

Hubert Fichte, conversant in the widest spectrum of African diasporic religions, is among the first to record the survival and adaptation of Vodou from Dahomey to the north coast of Brazil. The change of spelling from Awe to Agbé in this new location is a small one when one considers the queer re-gendering of this deity from male to female and the consequent absorption by this Brazilian deity of the siren motif.

> Agbé
> Deni:
> Eine Tochter.
> Das sechste und letzte Kind Sobos
> Sie spricht.
> Meerstern.
> Halb ein Fisch.
> Alle ihre Gerichte sind salzlos.
> Wir stellen sie ihr auf kleinen Tellern hin.
> Die Fahne Agbés wurde nur zum Fest der Bezahlung
> Herausgeholt.

Celeste:

Applikationsarbeit.

Blau mit kleinen weißen Fischen darauf und Wellenlinien.

Deni:

Sie ist eine Sirene.

Ihre Mission ist das Wasser.

Das Salzwasser ausnahmsweise.

Celeste:

Gegen Ende tritt sie an die Stelle Sepazimus und wird
bei jedem Fest wie eine Königin geehrt.

Sie sammelt die Gegenstände zum Schluß ein.

Agbé wird von den anderen Vodun Muroko
genannt.

(Fichte 1989, 195–96)

Agbé

Deni:

A daughter.

The sixth and last child of Sobo

She speaks.

Star of the Sea.

Half a fish.

All her dishes are unsalted.

We put them out for her on small plates.

The Agbé's flag was only brought out
for a feast of payment.

Celeste:

Appliqué work.

Blue with small white fish on it and wavy lines.

Deni:

She is a siren.

Her mission is water.

Saltwater as an exception.

Celeste:

Toward the end she takes the place of Sepazimus and is
honored at every celebration like a queen.

She collects the items at the end.

Agbé is called Muroko by the other Vodou.

And so we return once more to the religious Afro-diasporic concept of twin-ning and twining, doubling and marriages between deities with which this chapter began, and which we saw reflected in the relationship of Hector Hyppolite and his lwa and in the exchange between Hyppolite and white queer ethnographers Hubert Fichte and Pierre Verger. Like Dambala and Aida Wedo in Haitian Vodou, Awe and Lasirèn have twirled around each other since their inception in West Africa. Then, the Sea marries the Siren in Brazil, where they blend into one divinity, Agbé. Reading Hyppolite along-side Fichte would seem to indicate that Brazil is the direction in which Hyp-polite's boat is moving, to the realm where the mystic marriage is finally consummated. As one of the versions of the dirge in the epigraph cited at the beginning of the chapter proclaims: "Popo fait'n traverser lan mè" (Popo made us cross the ocean). This time, it is not a voyage of return so much as a continuation in the direction of full communion with being. After all, Hyppolite did say he built the boat with the intention of bringing his friends together. A mystical oungan like Hyppolite could not have been referring only to his earthly friends when he uttered that statement. "Coté ous quit-tez bateau-a?" (Where did you leave the boat?) cries another version of the dirge. I dare say he left his boat in a new and unexpected land where the Vodous of Dahomey, their spiritual spouses and their devotees, in conjunc-tion with critics and intellectuals, exist indistinguishably from one another as Being "èl même," the distinction between self and other having dissolved after the engulfing, strangling embrace of the snake has wrung out their last breath.

PART II

LUCUMÍ/SANTERÍA

A CHRONOLOGY OF QUEER LUCUMÍ SCHOLARSHIP
Degeneracy, Ambivalence, Transcorporeality

The duality in the title of the 1993 Cuban film *Fresa y Chocolate*, directed by
Tomás Gutiérrez Alea and Juan Carlos Tabío, has been widely understood
in terms of homosexual and heterosexual preferences. After all, the film begins and ends with the protagonists eating different flavors of ice cream in
scenes full of sexual innuendo. The film can easily be seen as a reconciliation
between straight and gay desire, as well as liberal and conservative politics,
by contrasting the opening scene, in which Diego tries to convince David
that strawberry is the best flavor, and the ending of the movie, in which the
characters reach an understanding that there are different strokes for different folks. Are there other ways in which the film might be affirming this *à
chacun son goût* ideology? I would like to propose that *Fresa y Chocolate* is
as much about religion as it is about sexual orientation and that, in fact, it
stands as a pivotal moment in the coarticulation of sexual desire and forms
of spirituality. *Fresa y Chocolate*'s system of oppositions is richly stratified as
it connotes a series of binarisms in Cuban culture that the film seeks to resolve through a syncretic strategy: strawberry/chocolate, foreign/local, gay/

straight, white/black, bourgeois/working class, and, most importantly for our present study, the rapport between the religious discourses of Roman Catholicism and Lucumí. My objective in this chapter is to make evident the existence of a queer Lucumí tradition of scholarship by anthropologists from Cuba, the US, and France and to trace the evolution of this research trajectory in three distinct thematic phases—degeneracy, ambivalence, and transcorporeality—through the release of the movie *Fresa y Chocolate*, which I see as marking a pivotal moment in the chronology of this line of inquiry. This tradition begins in earnest with the publication of Fernando Ortiz's *Los negros brujos* in 1906. In this, his first published book, Ortiz, the premier scholar and pioneer of Afro-Cuban culture during the first half of the twentieth century, anticipates his coinage and usage of the term "transculturation" when he states:

> La raza blanca influyó en el hampa cubana mediante los vicios europeos, modificados y agravados bajo ciertos aspectos por factores sociales hijos del ambiente. La raza negra aportó sus supersticiones, su sensualismo, su impulsividad, en fin, su psiquis africana. La raza amarilla trajo la embriaguez por el opio, sus vicios homosexuales y otras refinadas corrupciones de su secular civilización. (1973, 19)

> The white race influenced the Cuban underworld with its European vices, modified and worsened in some ways by social factors derived from the environment. The black race contributed its superstitions, its sensuality, its impulsivity, in essence its African psyche. The yellow race brought its opium intoxication, its homosexual vices and other refined corruptions of its secular civilization.

Ortiz's essentialist language deserves to be contextualized within an early twentieth-century discourse in order to be fully appreciated as the seminal and influential work that it is for queer Lucumí scholarship. Ortiz's work comes directly out of the scientific racism of modernism prevalent from the 1880s to the 1930s. Heavily influenced by the writings of Havelock Ellis's work on criminality, early sexology, and racial typology, Ortiz's particular strand of scientific racism, however, displays a broader type of Caribbean race anthropology than has yet to be studied alongside folkloric and pseudo-anthropological works from the Caribbean such as Charles Davenport's *Race Crossing in Jamaica* (1929), a eugenicist work that makes statistical arguments that biological and cultural degradation followed white and black genetic mixture. It is also important to note that such essentialist ideas

FIG. 3.1. Diego manages to make David take off his shirt by accidentally spilling coffee on it. Enveloping him in such a yellow towel would be understood by Lucumí adepts as an embrace by Oshún, as this is the deity's favorite color. Film still from *Fresa y Chocolate*, Miramax Films.

were also absorbed and reinterpreted by black peoples during the period, especially in the case of the negritude writers who transformed these pejorative stereotypes into the ennobling distinctive trademarks of Afro-diasporic peoples. It is significant that Ortiz only discussed homosexuality in his first work and then only as vice and degeneracy. The conflation of racial and sexual othering is significant in the categorization of Asians as homosexuals, articulating the feminization of nineteenth-century Chinese labor in Cuba, and is also relevant for the discussion of gender and Wifredo Lam, the subject of chapter 4. The Orientalization of homosexuality is typical of the essentialistic scientific racism of the period, as informed by Sir Francis Burton's pseudo-geographical concept of the Sotadic Zone, a region of the world in which homosexuality was widely practiced. While Africans are presented as hypersexual, it is with a highly heterosexual and prolifically reproductive sexuality. This furthers the myth of Africa as devoid of homosexuality, as discussed in the introduction. In spite of its essentialism and its associations of homosexuality with Asians, Ortiz's work paves the way for a line of investigation that addresses same-sex desire as a culturally relative practice and one that might be validated by the ideological frameworks of non-European immigrants to the island of Cuba.

In another important passage, Ortiz continues his essentialistic discourse, with a keen eye for the religious practices of Africans:

No es raro que los negros sudorosos se despojen de la camisa, mostrando sus bustos lustrosos y sus bronceados brazos, que ciñen con febril abrazo el cuerpo de la bailadora. Llegados a este momento, los bailadores se alocan por la irritación sexual, el *chequeteque*, la música, la danza, etc., y lo orgía corona frecuentemente la festividad religiosa. . . . El baile suele terminar en una escena puramente religiosa, libre de todo carácter externo de erotismo; tal es el acceso epiléptico que ataca a algún concurrente y que recibe el nombre de *dar el santo* o *subirse el santo a la cabeza*, aludiendo a los fenómenos parecidos que produce la embriaguez o el hecho de subirse el alcohol *a la cabeza*, como se dice vulgarmente. (1973, 83)

It is not unusual for the sweat-drenched blacks to shed their shirts, displaying their shiny chests and their bronzed arms with which they embrace the body of the dancer. Having arrived at that moment, the dancers become crazed with sexual excitement, the rhythmic noises, the music, the dancing, etc., and the orgiastic frequently crowns the religious festivity. . . . The dance often ends in a purely religious scene, free from all external erotic character. Such is the epileptic seizure that attacks some attendees and which is called *being given the saint* or *putting the saint on the head*, alluding to the similar phenomena produced by drunkenness or the rising of alcohol to the head, as it is referred to in vulgar fashion.

The ambivalent language regarding sexuality originates from a moralistic and judgmental observer who renders Africans as libidinous people in their religious rituals. In this discourse, Africans are rendered as hypersexual degenerates. The sexual metaphor for trance possession and the presentation of the religious ceremony as an orgiastic event contribute to the presentation of Africans as hypersexual beasts unable to compartmentalize their emotions and behavior according to established models of comportment that decently partition the religious from the erotic. The pathological metaphor for trance possession, which he compares to epilepsy, presents Africans as members of a sick culture. The erroneous analogizing of intoxication and vice with trance possession—through the association with alcohol—presents Africans as driven by unchecked impulses and incapable of rational restraint. The frenzied representation of the black body is almost negritude-like in its depiction, and as such it is reminiscent of Leon Gontran Damas's poetic rendition of African ceremonial scenes. However, in spite of and through his exoticism, Ortiz is redeemable for tracing a lineage that coarticulates dissident sexuality and African religions in Cuba.

This early period in which same-sex desire is synonymous with degeneracy is also characterized by wide gaps in the trajectory of publication on the topic. Deferring the discussion of Lydia Cabrera's 1968 opus *El Monte* to chapter 4, the next important work to address same-sex desire in Lucumí is Joseph Murphy's 1988 work *Santería: African Spirits in the Americas*. Murphy introduces into the conversation the notion of sacramental regendering when he presents the Yorùbá social and religious term *iyawo*:

> For five days, the *iyawo* is kept in prenatal isolation, usually at the home of her godmother, preparing her head for the great rebirth of new life. Against these five days of private transformation are three public ones during which the santería community witnesses the new birth. The *iyawo* is shown to be a new person before the community, who give praise to the *orisha* for a new vehichle of *ashe*. (1988, 87)

Murphy's work stands as one of the first explanations of initiation, revealing the secrets of Lucumí initiation by clearly outlining what happens in each of the steps toward the reception of a new member into a leadership role in the spiritual community. Murphy's presentation of the initiate's seclusion as a form of communal gestation and her exiting and inclusion in the fold as a form of birth align Lucumí with the near-universal religious tropes of life, death, and rebirth. The three public days—Día de coronación (installment of orisha on the head and stones), Día del Medio (presented in state, receiving visitors), and Día del Itá (*dilogún* reading, oracle)—are particularly helpful in revealing the metaphors of royalty that dominate the initiation process. However, he is most original in his presentation of the term "iyawo." Even though it remains undeveloped and untranslated in Murphy's work, this term would cause the most heated debate in African diasporic religions during the 1990s and 2000s. A rough translation of the Yorùbá word would be "bride," and as such the term, sacramentally, has the potential to masculinize the orishas and feminize the initiates, adding a polemic spiritual layer to the biological sex and sociocultural construction of gender. Murphy offers the first hints of regendering as an important component of possession and sacramentalization of the devotee. This evinces the concern for Yorùbá terminology that permeates the Anglophone tradition in the US academy. This focus on terminology occupies a much more minor position in Cuban scholarship. A possible reason for this is that while US academics tend to see Lucumí as an African religion in the Caribbean, Cubans tend to see the religion as an autochthonous and creolized aspect of Cuban culture, oftentimes downplaying its African roots.

FIG. 3.2. Diego's rage is enhanced by Changó's double ax in the background. Changó is the orisha of passion and virility. Film still from *Fresa y Chocolate*, Miramax Films.

In 1992, Lachatañeré took an important step by presenting the most important early work acknowledging the large number of queer initiates in Lucumí:

> Quizás esta tendencia a la homosexualidad de los "hijos" de Yemayá y Obatalá en la línea masculina y femenina, respectivamente, tenga una explicación posible en el hermafroditismo que presentan ambas deidades; el cual se explica desde el punto de vista que la primera, o sea, la Virgen de Regla, unas veces aparece como una mujer suave y melosa, llena de mundanales extravíos, y otras, cuando viene por el "camino" de Olokun, se convierte en un santo guerrero muy "fuerte." En lo que respecta a Obatalá, a pesar de ser una deidad que "por la delicadeza de su espíritu hace muy sufrida la vida de sus hijos," cuando viene por el "camino" de Osanquiriyan se presenta dando fuertes sacudidas al receptor, apareciendo como un personaje hombruno con caracteres masculinos bien diferenciados. (1992, 224)

> Maybe the tendency for the children of Yemayá and Obatalá to be homosexual along the masculine and feminine lines, respectively, has an explanation in the hermaphroditism that both deities display. This can be explained as follows: the first, or the Virgin of Regla, sometimes appears as a soft and smooth woman, full of worldly temptations, and at other times, when she comes through the avatar of Olokun, she be-

comes a very strong warrior deity. Regarding Obatalá, even though he is a deity who, through his delicate nature, makes the lives of his children difficult, when he comes through the avatar of Osanquiriyan, he shakes his host violently as he arrives, appearing as a manly persona with clearly delineated masculine characteristics.

While Lachateñeré's use of sexually anomalous pathological language (hermafroditismo) to discuss queerness continues a problematic trajectory that begins with Ortiz, this is greatly diminished in comparison with the early writer's work and is compensated for by the pioneering nature of his work. His is an important discussion of cross-gender identifications in the syncretism of deities and how this affects initiates' gender. His use of trance possession to discuss the performance of gender in deities and initiates is an element that other writers develop at future stages of a queer Lucumí scholarship.

Lachateñeré continues with some very important passing comments on the phenomenon of cross-gender identifications in trance possession that deserve some critical attention for their invocation of psychoanalysis:

Y como la tendencia es que las personas de sexo masculino caigan en éxtasis bajo la Yemayá "hembra," quien se aparece con un carcajada ancha y limpia, contoneando su cuerpo en requiebros femeninos; y, por lo contrario, las "hijas" de Obatalá, al pasar por el éxtasis, retumban el piso con sus pisadas hombrunas y gastan energías que no son del uso femenino, quizá que influencia en el subconsciente pueda ejercer este fenómeno. A fin de cuentas, éste es un buen material para una especulación freudiana, en la cual no estamos interesados. Lo más importante es que estos casos se presentan como excepciones que no afectan, en lo absoluto, el funcionamiento normal de los cultos, si éstos se quieren mirar desde el punto de vista sexual. (1992, 224)

And since the tendency is that people of the male sex fall into ecstasy under Yemayá "female," who appears with a wide and clean outburst of laughter, shaking her body with feminine movements, and by contrast the "daughters" of Obatalá who, upon passing through ecstasy, shake the floor with manly steps and expend energy that is not feminine in nature, one wonders what influence this might have on the subconscious. In the end, this is good material for a Freudian speculation in which we are not interested. The most important thing is that these cases lend themselves as exceptions that do not affect at all the normal functioning of the cults, if one wishes to see them from a sexual point of view.

It is important to note that Lachatañeré insists that this type of gender-transgressive possession is infrequent, depends on rigid gender divisions, and in no way disrupts heterosexuality, which he troublingly presents as a desirable norm. His appraisal is dependent on an outmoded discourse of effeminacy and *marimachismo*. His comment on the subconscious is recoverable, however, as it hints at the fact that these possessions may function as more than carnivalesque moments, and their effects could spill over into the everyday life of initiates. Most importantly, his comment in passing is helpful in bringing to light how cross-gender trance possessions prove the authenticity of trance in ways that possession of an initiate by a same-gender deity could not, as the temporary regendering of the body presents an irrefutable change in the persona of the sacramental body. One can only wonder about Lachatañeré's rejection of Freudianism, especially when later in the text he approves of psychoanalysis as a methodological tool for the understanding of these possessions:

> Nosotros, ocasionalmente, hablamos de hermafroditismo al referirnos a una de las características de un culto que funciona en la ciudad de La Habana, y expresamos que tal hermafroditismo se podía reconocer en la forma externa de los *santos*, o sea, en sus manifestaciones a través del éxtasis, ya que algunas deidades vienen por *caminos femeninos y caminos masculinos*, pero atribuimos el hermafroditismo a una reacción psicológica del individuo, como una vía posible para interpretar un fenómeno biológico. (1992, 264)

> We occasionally speak of hermaphroditism when we refer to one of the characteristics of a cult that functions in the city of Havana, and we express how such hermaphroditism could be recognized in the external form of the saints, in other words, in their manifestations through ecstasy, since some deities come through masculine and feminine paths, but we attribute the hermaphroditism to a psychological reaction of the individual in order to provide a possible way to interpret a biological phenomenon.

In this passage, we also observe the continuation of outmoded discourses of sexology and sexual taxonomization, which afford the author a medical language to discuss the erotics of possession. The ambivalent usage of Freudian language displays the ability of psychoanalysis to explain the phenom-

FIG. 3.3. Diego channels the Virgin of the Caridad del Cobre, the Catholic representation of Oshún, the coquettish orisha of sensuality and love. Film still from *Fresa y Chocolate*, Miramax Films.

enon of trance possession without need of acknowledging a possible spiritual cause. Moreover, Lachatañeré's passage helps us see that cross-gender identifications break down the barriers between a number of binarisms in Lucumí. First, cross-gender identifications are evident in the syncretism of orisha-saint. They are also apparent in differently gendered avatars of one deity. Furthermore, these cross-gender identifications occur between deities and initiates of different genders. It would appear that by "biological" Lachatañeré means that these cross-gender possessions do not subvert male and female sexual corporealities. In that sense, this Cuban author continues a strong heteronormative interpretation of an evidently transgressive occurrence.

The following passage presents Lachatañeré's complete rejection of a non-heteronormative interpretation for these cross-gender possessions:

> Mas, al llegar al punto donde se ha de explicar la identidad entre un orisha varón y una deidad o santo católico en la línea femenina, se ha de rechazar la dualidad del sexo como un agente actuante en tal identificación. En primer término, en este tipo de identidades se han utilizado, en casos como el mencionado, los caracteres o agentes de coincidencia entre las dos divinidades puestas en comparación; el carácter de guerrera de Santa Bárbara—de acuerdo con la concepción del esclavo—y el carácter de guerrero de Shangó; el poder que sobre el

trueno y el rayo tiene este orisha y el mismo poder que tiene la santa, y así sucesivamente, sin que haya meditado seriamente en la diferencia de sexo. (1992, 264)

But when we arrive at the point in which we must explain the identity between a male orisha and a deity or a Catholic saint along the feminine line, we should reject the duality of sex as an agent acting upon such an identification. In the first instance, in this type of identification, the elements of similarity between both divinities being compared have been used, in cases such as the aforementioned; the warrior personalities of Saint Barbara—in accordance with the slave's conception—and the warrior personality of Shangó; the power that this orisha and saint have over lightning and thunder and so on, without the slave having meditated seriously over the difference of sex.

For Lachatañeré, the fact that the syncretic coupling between the African and Roman Catholic religious personae was based on shared attributes seems to imply, troublingly, that Africans were blind to gender. His rejection of the non-heteronormative effects of the possessions displays a chauvinism that couples with racism when he presents slaves as unthinking subjects.

A pivotal moment in this historization of Lucumí in Cuban cultural representation takes place in 1993 with the release of *Fresa y Chocolate*, a film that itself alludes to an earlier and significant juncture coarticulating sexuality, religion, and politics in Cuban society during the 1970s. The narrative centers on David, a somewhat homophobic revolutionary university student whose Manichean outlook is challenged by his friendship with Diego, a forty-something homosexual artist and bon vivant. In spite of its setting in a pervasively male chauvinistic social context, the movie revolves around the relationship between these two men and the progression of their relationship from antagonism to admiration and tolerance. One day, David eats chocolate ice cream and is interrupted by Diego, who tries to convince him that his taste for strawberry ice cream is superior. Diego flirts with David and persuades him to come to his apartment under the pretext of finding some photos he took of David when he played the character Torvald in Ibsen's *A Doll's House*. Once in the apartment, David is struck by Diego's library, full of foreign and forbidden literature. Diego's cultural interests are also evident in his large religious art collection and his plans to put together an art exhibit with the aid of a foreign embassy, a counterrevolutionary act that David condemns. One of David's friends, Miguel, convinces him to collect more information and evidence to accuse Diego of subversive and unpatriotic behavior. However, these visits transform their relationship, and a strong bond of friendship between the two men develops. Yet this bond is not strong enough to overpower the political apparatus, which forces Diego to flee Cuba and find refuge in a more tolerant society abroad.

Most of the criticism of the movie has focused on the evolution of the interplay between the politics of the Marxist state and queer sexuality. As important as it is, this critique ignores the important role that Lucumí philosophy and cultural aesthetics play in the movie. It is noteworthy that one of the most important articles on the movie by queer studies scholar David William Foster (2003), "Negociaciones queer en *Fresa y Chocolate*: Ideología y homoerotismo," does not mention Lucumí at all. In the same vein, José Quiroga offers nothing on Lucumí in his important analysis of the movie. He only focuses on revolution, gender roles, and the silence imposed on critiques of the film: "Since it has been hailed as opening up the complex issue of homosexuals in Cuba, any critique of the film has been accused of being blind to the very real problems entailed in making a film like this in Cuba" (Quiroga 2000, 133). While he is astute in overcoming this silence by pointing out how the movie can be read as "a sentimental tale that can only end with the banishment of the suffering homosexual" (132), it is important to point out that his critique is similarly silent on the equally important religious thematics and iconography.

The only critic who has acknowledged the role of Lucumí in the movie has done so merely in passing and relegates the religion to a secondary role, as a simple backdrop to echo and frame the main idea of reconciliation and peaceful coexistence:

> Creemos que la función global que desempeña el tema de la santería, aparte de mostrar aspectos de la cotidianeidad de la isla (con su punto de exotismo y color local también), tiene que ver con la propuesta integradora que caracteriza al filme en su conjunto. Si se quiere hacer una apuesta por una patria cubana integradora y sin exclusiones, qué mayor ejemplo de integración que el sincretismo religioso tal y como se manifiesta en la santería. (Campa Marcé 2002, 127)

> We believe that the global function that Santería plays, besides showing quotidian aspects of the island (with some exoticism and local color, too), has to do with the integrationist proposal that characterizes the film in its totality. If the purpose is to bid for an integrationist Cuban nation with no exclusions, what better example of integration than religious syncretism just as it is manifested in Santería.

The coarticulation of religion and revolution has its own difficult history, as Matibag reminds us:

> In the first decade and a half of the Revolution, however, the official culture chose to see in that religion's subculture an alternate or competing economic activity that negated the centralized planned economy of the state. Afro-Cuban religious practice was therefore actively discouraged. Intolerance ceded to a tolerance toward the end of the 1970s, when the cultural ministries decided that if they couldn't beat Afro-Cuban religion, they could at least in a sense invite it to join them. Under these circumstances, Afro-Cuban religion became a governmentally approved "folklore." Yet the promotion of folklore as the alternative to outright prohibition entailed subtle and not-so-subtle forms of negation since folklorization not only consisted of a process of simplifying and secularizing religious expression but also subjected Afro-Cuban religious values to a materialist critique. This strategy of containment—for that is what it amounted to—resulted in the assessment of Afro-Cuban religion as an irrational, barbaric, and mystifying, although admittedly beautiful and colorful, body of antisocial tendencies. (1996, 227)

The official atheist policy of the first years of the revolution yielded to a more open view regarding religious expressions that troublingly solidified Lucumí, as Matibag reminds us, as a type of *religión popular*, that is, co-opted by the nation for folkloric purposes. However, the tracing of the coarticulation of sexuality and religion has not been as evident in scholarship, and it is my aim to remedy this deficiency in this chapter. In spite of the notable absence of discussion on the religious theme of the movie, the release of *Fresa y Chocolate* marks an important moment of openness for the coarticulation of queer desire and Lucumí cultural practices in scholarly and aesthetic discourse. In fact, *Fresa y Chocolate* is as much about Lucumí as it is about queerness. One of the few critics who has commented in passing on the role of Lucumí in the film presents a parallel, explicatory subtext that demonstrates the syncretic strategy of survival through adaptation, which characterizes this religion and, we should note, queerness:

> When we were shown Fresa y Chocolate at the CONJUNTO 94, I was sitting next to Teresa Cárdenas, a black Cuban dancer from Matanzas who had already seen the film several times. We had become friends at a ceremony for Santa Barbara/Changó, and she kindly translated some of the dialogue and musical references for me, while always hitting me

FIG. 3.4. Nancy prays and takes a ritual bath to Santa Barbara/Changó to secure the love of David. Film still from *Fresa y Chocolate*, Miramax Films.

with her elbow whenever there was another one of the many visual allusions to the cultural practice of Santería, which would have otherwise remained obscure to me. (Birringer 1996b, 117–18)

Birringer here addresses how the important role of the informant as a liminal conveyor of subaltern knowledges to erudite audiences and as coauthor of the testimonial ethnographical genre is the hallmark of works on Afro-diasporic religions. The anthropologist needs the native collaborator to explain to him the existence and meaning of that which the exploited classes have hidden and encrypted from the dominant. Interestingly, in this case, the ethnographer only avows his privileged access to the source of information without caring to actually elaborate on the informant or on the information she provides. It is possible, however, to utilize this passing reference to Lucumí in the movie to present how the religion's aesthetics operate in multiple registers to diverse audiences, allowing it to fly over the heads of some (the bird of the Yorùbá) and swim at unreachable depths (*anbadlo*) when it needs to remain concealed from threats to its continuity. In a manner similar to the way in which the planter and priest were fooled by the slave's devotion to images of Roman Catholic saints, which enabled a secretive continuation of African religious rituals during the colonial period, the untrained audiences of the movie remain unaware of its religious elements, until and unless these are revealed by someone with insider status. Just as the binarism of saint/orisha allows for the continuation of African religion under a thin veneer of Christianity, so do gayness and art function as the visible part of oppositional pairs that have Yorùbá religious customs as their invisible underwater iceberg-like base. In such a way, we may redeem the aloofness of the ethnographer, for he helps us to see what the popular interpretation of the movie is or should be and forces us to ask how the discourse of queerness in the movie uses, erases, or promotes African religions. I propose that it enacts all three of these verbal discursive modes for queerness and religion and that these are inseparable aspects of the narrative of the movie.

Diego, the *maricón* of the film, is by far its most complex character. He performs himself in accordance with the symbolic repertoire of four Lucumí orishas. In his initial advances toward David, Diego adopts a caring, almost maternal stance and cloaks himself in the guise of Yemayá, the sea goddess, by wearing a blue kimono for their first conversation at Diego's apartment. Coming into his own a bit later on, Diego embodies Ochún, the goddess of love, through his seductive nature, often associated with the color yellow, a distinguishing color of the orisha.[1] More vividly, Diego is strategically positioned in front of an altar to La Caridad del Cobre, which he decorates with yellow sunflower offerings. After deliberately spilling coffee on David's shirt to force him to take it off, he graciously hands him a yellow towel, enveloping him, as it were, in the charm of the orisha's sexual play. Through his aggressive virility, Diego also embodies Changó. At a rare moment of masculine rage in the movie, Diego's face is presented with Changó's red double ax in the background. When his rage bubbles over, the symbol framing his face is Ogun's horseshoe. In all these scenes, Diego wears monochromatic garments so as to make the association with the orishas legible to initiates and a mere source of aesthetic stimulation for the lay viewer. The statues and accessories of the saints and orishas are placed behind, around, and above Diego's face, as if suggesting the channeling of these deities in a receptacular fashion. Through the performing of these various situational personalities, Diego functions as a transcorporeal body, providing transport for a variety of spiritual subjectivities, which are transient, removable, and modular. The gay man is presented as the ideal transcorporeal body since his liminal gendered status references the confluence of realms and his assumed sexually passive status marks him as a receptive body in carnal and spiritual ways. In counterpoint to Diego's pluri-receptacular body, David does not embody as many orishas. He is the *hombre nuevo* of the revolution whose heterosexuality makes him impenetrable, inviolable, and impermeable to material and metaphysical externalities.

FIG. 3.5. Oshún, goddess of love, unites Yemayá (blue) in the effeminate Diego (*left*) and Obatalá (white) in the studious David. Film still from *Fresa y Chocolate*, Miramax Films.

Passive gay men share representational receptacularity with women in Lucumí, a religion that allows both privileged status as the ideal vessels for the orishas. In the film, Nancy is also associated with the orisha Changó. Let us keep in mind that Changó is not restricted to maleness per se and encompasses masculinity broadly:

> When we limit the understanding of Sàngó to mere "masculine traits," his duality is never fully explored. Despite the fact that male and female initiates of Sàngó have been taught that Sàngó is the womanizer of the goddesses of Yorùbá tradition, he is truly the lover of women. This restricted understanding diminishes the depth of the potential relationship that we can have as we participate in Sàngó's energy internally and communally. The nature-based force Sàngó cannot be adequately interpreted through these distorted notions of gender. (Olomo 2009, 321)

Changó's sacramental masculinity is, therefore, able to be superimposed onto femininity and femaleness, rendering Nancy's character transcorporeal. Masculine Changó, in his association with Santa Barbara, performs an important cross-gender identification that has been noted by some as a form of spiritual cross-dressing: "el transvestismo de Shangó y la transformación de 'género' que sufre éste al pasar del panteón yorubá al cristiano" (Vadillo 2002, 78; The transvestitism of Shangó and the transformation of "gender" that he suffers when moving from the Yorùbá to the Christian pantheon).

Changó's color is red like his, and Nancy's, volatile temper. Nancy wears red dresses. Nancy receives and gives red flowers to David. She takes a ritual bath in front of the statue of Santa Barbara. She is associated with blood as she cuts her veins in a suicide attempt that also speaks to the tempestuous quality of Changó. It is hinted that she is a *jinetera*, a Cuban sex worker; she is oversexed, like Changó. The jinetera is queer in that she is a prostitute: a non-heteronormative woman enacting permeability, ritual femaleness, and profane wifeliness. The second film based on a story by Senel Paz, *Adorables mentiras* (*Adorable Lies*), directed by Gerardo Chijona, included the character of Nancy from *Fresa y Chocolate*, played by the same actor, Mirtha Ibarra, as a prostitute (Santí 1998, 411). In asking for a hug, Diego remarks, "Pensaba que al abrazarte me iba a sentir más limpio" (I thought that by hugging you I was going to feel cleaner), words that echo pointedly Nancy's earlier statement before the *santero* about her own planned disclosure to David regarding her past as a prostitute: "Dentro de mí [*sic*] hay una cosa limpia que nadie ha podido ensuciar" (Santí 1998, 421; Inside of me there is something clean that no one has been able to mar). Nancy's identification with Changó is overdetermined in her non-heteronormative sex worker status and in her seemingly contradictory affirmation of heterosexual standards by providing a romantic and sexual outlet for David, thus preventing him from becoming Diego's lover. However, Nancy does not figure in the original story by Senel Paz. One effect of Nancy's inclusion is to "frame the gay action within a hetero narrative" (Smith 1994, 31). In fact, it can be claimed that Nancy rescues David from a homosexual relationship. While the character of Nancy heterosexualizes the narrative by her condition as a straight woman, it expands the subversiveness of the film by including sex work as a component of queerness. The heterosexuality of the sex worker prevents the easy perception of her queer political implications, a syncretic strategy of double meanings that is the distinguishing trademark of the orisha-saint binarism.

My emphasis on the confluence of subaltern religions and dissident sexualities is important given the superfluous ways in which the ethnographer and actor address this deeply profound matter. Here, Perugorría, the straight actor playing the gay character of Diego, responds to the ethnographer's poignant question:

BIRRINGER: Is the connection between homosexuality and religion subversive?

PERUGORRÍA: No, but it is noteworthy that many gays—something I've seen all my life—seek refuge in religion. (Birringer 1996a, 69)

Perugorría enacts a series of denials in this interview. There is a denial of the counterdiscursive quality of queerness. His assertion of his heterosexuality throughout the interview is a troubling claim to privilege. His presentation of religion as the proverbial popular opiate is unoriginal within a Marxist state. More important for the present study, his dismissal of Lucumí in his appeal to universal religion is regrettable.

However, the coarticulation of gender, sex, and race in Perugorría's divine avatar, Oshún/Ochún, is more visible to other critics. In reference to the status of Oshún as a libidinous subject, cultural critic Cachita foregrounds the way in which her sexual nature is fueled by her representation as a mixed-race woman:

> Ochún in Cuba is most popularly imaged as a *mulata*, a woman of mixed race who lives between the worlds of black and white, at once both and neither. Her liminal status gives her great power and great sorrow for she is at once beyond some of the restrictions of social categories while at the same time without their identity and security. Perhaps it is with reference to her image as a mulata that Ochún is conceived as a flirt, courtesan, or prostitute. Mixed-race women occupied a peculiar niche in colonial Cuban society where they might achieve a level of social prominence, financial independence, and upward mobility for their children if they became official mistresses of wealthy Cuban white men. This [made them the objects] of desire and scorn. The love of such women could never be self-determining and so their gracious and flirtatious manner could never be free of their desperate need to defend themselves and their children. The arts of the coquette concealed ulterior motives. (2001, 95–96)

While the actor who plays Diego, Perugorría, is not visibly of mixed race, his queer performative status affords him a gendered liminality that is also evident in his performance of Oshún. The *blanco* Cuban racial status of the actor, however, does not prevent him from problematically performing blackness by singing "Todos los negros tomamos café" (All of us blacks drink coffee). The actor has repeatedly affirmed his heterosexuality in interviews, and this seems to compromise the purported liberatory aspects of this movie, in which the only people shown in sexual contexts in bed are straight characters. Gesturing toward an answer to an earlier question, the movie seems to advance a queer politics at the expense of real queers and nonwhites. Queers and blacks are subjects with rights as long as the dominant classes do not have to be in their presence. In fact, the only recognizably black character in the movie is that of a santero whom Nancy briefly consults regarding her love life. In his oracular role,

> el sacerdote de *Regla de Ocha* es además adivino. Ellos usan various tipos de oráculos en su función adivinatoria. Los más conocidos son: los cocos, el Diloggun [*sic*], el Tablero de Ifá y el Ekuele. Todos los sacerdotes pueden usar los dos primeros, pero los últimos sólo pueden ser manejados por los *babalaos*. Los oráculos son utilizados en todo momento para diagnosticar una enfermedad, para descubrir a un enemigo que está perjudicando al cliente, para averiguar quien es el *eleda* de éste, etc. (Cros Sandoval 1975, 64)

> the priest of *Regla de Ocha* is also a diviner. They use various types of oracles in their divinatory function. The best known are the coconuts, the Diloggún, the Ifá board and the Ekuele. All priests can use the two first methods, but the last two can only be used by the *babalaos*. The oracles are used to diagnose illness, to uncover an enemy who is injuring a client, to investigate who is his *eleda*, etc.[2]

Constituting an elision of blackness, a present absence, the black santero in the movie is silent, not uttering a word, which is uncharacteristic for an oracular consultation. His muteness when Nancy asks him to reveal the oracular predictions of the dilogún imbues him with an ominous nature, a thorough negativity. Evoking Spivak, "Can the santero speak?" What would he have said? What did he want to say to Nancy in the movie? Or, more poignantly, what might he have wanted to say about the movie? His foreboding glance speaks to the representation of black people as bad news who should not be allowed to speak, but whose culture nevertheless is co-opted by governmental and gender-progressive projects, which, to their shame, have not quite yet managed to shed their racism. It is the same inability to handle multiple subjectivities that has prevented critics from seeing how a film that is largely about sexuality could not also be a film about race, how a film about queer representation could not also be a film about black culture. This erasure of blackness is predicated on a problematic mono-identitarianism that my project seeks to overcome by presenting the always already gendered and racialized nature of religious life and practice.

How can we consider this a politically progressive film when, as a queer film, it is actually framed within a heteronarrative? When it presents gay men as stereotypical effeminate predators? When it banishes the homosexual at the end of film? When there is no presentation of same-sex eroticism

FIG. 3.6. Can the santero speak? The santero remains silent as he reads the dilogún oracle for Nancy. Film still from *Fresa y Chocolate*, Miramax Films.

but two erotic scenes in which David is in bed with women? When it abjects the black santero? These questions allow us to see the incompleteness of the coarticulated sexual-racial-religious progressive politics in the film and preface works that narrow these gaps.

The work of Fernández Robaina provides us with one of the clearest examples of the progression of the discourse on cross-gender possession after the release of *Fresa y Chocolate*. His stance on the discourses of same-sex desire in Lucumí moves from anxiety to recognition to a critique on discrimination. Just a year after the release of the movie, in 1994, he expressed outrage over queer-positive interpretations of traditional liturgical stories. He dismissed the possibility that a traditional story of a deity's transvestism could encompass a queer dimension. To him, this implies an unacceptable heresy. He cannot abide the idea that deities could afford special protection to gays. His use of the somewhat derogatory term *afeminado* is troubling, yet he claims there is no discrimination. There is a fair amount of doublespeak and utilization of universalist discourse to silence voices from the margins. The emphasis on punishment of queers who do not serve orishas properly is clearly homophobic:

> Y a veces inventan cada cosa imposible de creer o de aceptar, como asegurar que Changó protege a los afeminados porque hay un camino de Changó donde este orisha se viste de mujer. Eso es falsear la historia, interpretar arbitrariamente los *pataquines* de los orishas. . . . El

A Chronology of Queer Lucumí Scholarship 121

hecho de que Changó proteja a los afeminados no es algo particular; todos los orishas protegen a todos los seres humanos; nuestra religión no discrimina a nadie por cuestiones de gustos sexuales.... Claro, que cuando, afeminado o no, se aparta del camino del santo, del respeto que se tiene que observar a la Regla de Ocha, se tiene que esperar el castigo, para que otros comprendan que la ley del santo hay que cumplirla. (Fernández Robaina 1994, 74)

And sometimes they invent all sorts of impossible things to believe or accept, such as maintaining that Changó protects effeminate men because there is a story in which he dresses himself as a woman. This falsifies the story, arbitrarily interpreting the *pataquines* [Yorùbá mythological story] of the orishas. The fact that Changó protects effeminate men is nothing special since all the orishas protect all human beings; our religion does not discriminate against anyone because of sexual preference. However, whether effeminate or not, out of the respect one must observe toward the Regla de Ocha, one must expect punishment if one deviates from the saint's path, so that others understand that the saint's laws must be obeyed.

But the evolution of his thought shows development, and later publications display less defensiveness and invite questions and empirical work that would explain the gender component of trance possession. In 1996, he writes,

The involvement of women and homosexuals requires socioeconomic, sociocultural and psychological studies that can reveal more about common, highly visible events, such as the possession of believers by orisha spirits. Such research might explain why women and homosexuals tend to be possessed by male and female *orishas*, whereas men are rarely possessed by female *orishas*, at least in current times. (Fernández Robaina 1996, 207)

Here, Fernández Robaina poses a most important question regarding gender and possession. This is the first time the question is posed publicly in academic records, and it spawns a series of important works. The categorization of women and homosexual men in opposition to heterosexual men is important. The idea here is that women and passive homosexual men represent receptacular open bodies, the epitome and idealized form of the Afrodiasporic sacramental body. There is an element of performance involved that prevents heterosexual or active homosexual men from being penetrated by another being, even a spirit.

FIG. 3.7. A drenched David dressed in blue channels Yemayá, the Virgin of Regla, goddess of the sea. Film still from *Fresa y Chocolate*, Miramax Films.

In his most recent publication, Fernández Robaina acknowledges that there are elements of identification that take precedence over gender. While the idea of contradiction remains troubling as a working term, his acknowlegment of the controversy, polemic, and anxiety generated by these cross-gender possessions elevates the status of the matter to an intellectual sphere:

> Pero cuando el género del orisha es el contrario del caballo podría haber una contradicción, aunque no pocos argumentan la ausencia de esa posible contradicción, puesto que la energía posee a la persona y la hace actuar como lo que esa energía está representando. (Fernández Robaina 2005, 35)

> But when the gender of the orisha is the opposite of the horse's there could be a contradiction, even though those who argue for the absence of this possible contradiction are not few in number, because of the energy that possesses the person and makes them act according to what that energy is representing.

His acknowledgment of misogyny in religion through the subordination of women in certain ritual contexts presents how Lucumí, in spite of the malleability of gender performance, does not constitute a gendered utopia: "[Women] cannot kill 4 legged animals, cannot be oriatés, italeros, babalaos, tocadores de tambor, osainistas. Women can only be apetebí" (Fernández Robaina 1994, 33). His recognition of misogyny yields an acknowledgment of homophobia and heterosexism. He reminds us that "gay men cannot be babalaos, cannot play batá drums and cannot be osainistas" (Fernández Robaina 1994, 34). This time, he exposes the latent heterosexism in canonical texts of the Lucumí oral tradition: "Oddun Offun Obbe: En el se narra una historia en la cual Oyá maldice a una mujer, pronosticándole que su hijo será un addodi, homosexual" (Fernández Robaina 2005, 33; Oddun Offun Obbe: Which details the story in which Oya curses a woman, prophesying that her son will be an addodi, a homosexual). But he presents these homophobic oral narratives alongside others that validate the special bond between same-sex-loving initiates and orishas. As Fernández Robaina explains, homosexuals can receive the "mano de Orula" and have their destiny read through Ifá because this deity is indebted to homosexuals:

> Orula fue atacado por sus enemigos y lanzado medio muerto a un río. Pudo asirse a un tronco que flotaba y, sin conocimiento, fue rescatado de las aguas por unos hombres y llevado a una isla donde sólo vivían hombres que convivían sexualmente entre ellos. Orula fue respetado, curado. En virtud de esta buena acción, Orula decidió demostrar su agradecimiento, otorgándole su ildé para no dejarlos desamparados ante los peligros y la muerte. (Fernández Robaina 2005, 35)[3]

> Orula was attacked by his enemies and thrown half-dead into a river. He was able to grab onto a floating tree trunk and, unconscious, was rescued from the waters by some men and was taken to an island where the only inhabitants were men who had sex with each other. In light of this good deed, Orula decided to demonstrate his gratitude, giving them his ildé [Lucumí beaded bracelet, an amulet of protection] so as to not leave them unprotected against dangers and death.

His queer reading of the literary and liturgical corpus of Ifá is most significant in that it presents gay men as babalaos. This is important given the denial of this tradition among members of the Ifá priesthood.

> En Ogundaketé, uno de los oddun de Ifá se narra que Yemayá se enamoró locamente de un joven homosexual que no le prestaba atención a sus requerimientos, pero ante la insistencia de ella, el joven le puso como condición que él fuera iniciado en Orula. . . . Sin embargo el no cumplió los caprichos de Yemayá. Una vez convertido en babalao, se negó a hacer el amor con ella. . . . Como venganza, Yemayá comenzó a difamar de la hombría del joven. (Fernández Robaina 2005, 35)

Ogundakelé, one of the oddun of Ifá, narrates how Yemayá was madly in love with a young homosexual man who did not pay any attention to her requests, but who, at her insistence, put as a requirement that he be allowed to be initiated into Orula. . . . However, he did not fulfill the wishes of Yemayá. Once having become a babalao, he refused to make love to her. . . . In revenge, Yemayá began to defame the young man's masculinity.

This story remains liberatory even if the homosexual man is presented as deceitful. In fact, this aligns him with Eshu-Elegbara, the divine trickster. So the troubling aspect of this story indeed works to sacramentalize what is seen as marginal.

Also in 1995, Erwan Dianteill, this time writing from the French Academy, presents Lucumí with some troubling associations with the primitive, primeval, and hypersexual. However, his appraisal of the integration of sexuality in the art and religion of Afro-diasporic peoples in contrast to a strict compartmentalization of European frameworks is laudable:

Si la religion est le vecteur sémantique principal de l'art primitif, la sexualité en constitue un second. Elle donne partiellement son sens à l'art des Noirs, non comme exaltation d'une jouissance stérile, mais comme représentation de l'acte sexuel favorisant la fertilité de la nature et des êtres humains. Art, religion et sexualité sont donc étroitement associés dans de nombreux rites propitiatoires. La sexualité dans les arts africains est donc bien présente, mais sous forme figurée et fonctionnelle, alors que les Européens y voient des pratiques orgiaques moralement condamnables. (Dianteill 1995, 68)

If religion is the principal semantic vector of primitive art, sexuality constitutes the second. The latter gives its meaning in part to the arts of blacks, not as an exaltation of a sterile orgasm but as a representation of a sexual act favoring the fertility of nature and human beings. Art, religion and sexuality are therefore closely associated with numerous propitiatory rites. Sexuality in African art is certainly present, but often in a figurative and functional form, where the European sees orgiastic practices deserving moral condemnation.

His revalorization of African epistemology as organic and wholesome in this sense is reminiscent of negritude writers who resignified and embellished what had been damaging stereotypes of black people. The refining of his thought on this matter is evident in his 2000 publication, where his revalorization of sexuality in the arts and religion of the African diaspora helps him seek to understand why gay people seem to be attracted to Lucumí:

> Je n'ai aucune donnée démographique concernant les hommes homosexueles à Cuba. . . . En termes de filiation et d'alliance, les motifs pour lesquels ils s'investissent dans la *santería* restent donc hypothétiques. Nous avons vu plus haut que l'identification à un oricha féminin permet d'assumer—en particulier dans la possession rituelle—un rôle sexuel autrement inaccessible. En outre, l'initiation d'un filleul par un *santero* homosexuel compense symboliquement l'impossibilité d'avoir une descendance biologique. (Dianteill 2000, 96)

> I don't have any demographic information concerning homosexual men in Cuba. . . . In terms of affiliation and alliance, the motives for their participation in Santería remain therefore hypothetical. Above, we have seen that identification with a feminine orisha allows the assumption of a sexual role that would be otherwise inaccessible. Moreover, the initiation of a godchild by a homosexual santero compensates symbolically for the impossibility of having a biological descendant.

Prefacing and inspiring the conclusion that Mary Ann Clark would formulate a few years later, Dianteill presents Lucumí as a feminized and feminizing religious system:

> Il existe un style féminin de la santería et du spiritisme et un style masculin du palo monte et du culte d'Ifá. C'est ce qui permet à des femmes assumant un rôle social masculin de s'investir dans le palo monte, et à des hommes ayant la démarche inverse de se spécialiser dans la santería. La variable féminité/virilité se situe donc sur le plan symbolique, et non strictement organique. (2000, 152)

> There exists a feminine style in Santería and spiritism and a masculine style in Palo Monte and the cult of Ifá. It is this which allows women to assume a masculine social role and to participate in Palo Monte and men with an inverse orientation to specialize in Santería. The variability between femininity and masculinity is thus found in the symbolic plane and is not strictly organic.

In 2005, Clark builds on these statements by Dianteill: "We can, however, suggest that all mediums are gendered female in that all must perform in a wifely

FIG. 3.8. Diego becomes the transcorporeal vehicle for Ogún, orisha of war and metallurgy represented by the horseshoe. Film still from *Fresa y Chocolate*, Miramax Films.

manner in order to complete their transformation into embodied Orisha" because of "the Yoruba idea that the female is the ideal religious type" (Clark 2005, 99, 22). Does her statement not subsume gay men troublingly as a type of woman? Can we go beyond femaleness to speak in a more theoretical manner of the receptacular? What does "wifely" mean here? How are women and passive homosexuals one category? Can we build a categorical, ritual, and political solidarity around the idea(l) of the permeable body? I believe we can discern such a complex theoretical categorization. This is what I call trans-corporeality: the sacramental regendering of material bodies made possible by a conceptualization of the body with an anima like the *nuez de marañón*, external and removable. This unique modular quality of the self enables trance possession, or the moment in which the body of the initiate becomes a re-ceptacular vessel for the orisha, allowing for instances of queer identifications when the orisha and the initiate subscribe to different gendered categories.

In spite of Dianteill advancing the question of sacramental regenderings in Lucumí, one cannot help but question the methodology that yielded such helpful information:

Mon excellente relation avec Selno était très probablement fondée sur un malentendu. Comme les *santeros* de Guanabo, Selno était manife-stement homosexuel. Il n'était pas marié, j'entendis un jour l'un de ses voisins entrer chez lui, en disant "¿Dónde está este [*sic*: ese] maricón?" et tous ses filleuls étaient de jeunes hommes, âgés de dix-huit à vingt-cinq ans. Or, Selno devait penser que Harold et moi étions nous aussi homosexuels. (Dianteill 2000, 50)

My excellent relationship with Selno was probably founded on a misunderstanding. Like other santeros from Guanabo, Selno was obviously homosexual. He was not married. I heard one day one of his neighbors enter his house saying, "Where is that faggot?" and all of his godchildren were young men, ages eighteen to twenty-five years old. Selno must have thought Harold and I were also homosexual.

What are we to think of an ethnographer who passes for gay in order to access the inside knowledge of a community of sexually and ritually dissident subjects? How might such deceit constitute a breach of professional codes of ethics? Dianteill's passing demonstrates a certain characteristic ambivalence and anxiety that also replicates the filmic passing inherent in the character of Diego being played by a nongay actor in *Fresa y Chocolate*.

While the Cuban academic tradition has wrestled with heteropatriarchy, and the French tradition has utilized negritude-like reappraisals of blackness, the Anglophone tradition has focused on language, paying particular attention to one word of special concern. In 2002, Atwood Mason presents this Anglophone concern with the translation of the Yorùbá term "iyawo" as a way to understand the large numbers of gay santeros in Cuba and the diaspora and to clarify the sources of the conflict over homosexual babalaos among the priesthood:

Similarly, homosexual men also occupy an important, if complicated, position within the religious system. Because the religion's initiations repeatedly deploy tropes of birthing, practitioners doubt the efficacy of any man not engaged in active procreation. However, because oricha priests are "taken" by the orichas and because all initiates become the "younger wife" of the orichas, many Cubans and Cuban Americans assume that all oricha priests are gay—and, in reality, many are. This tension surfaces again and again in the discourse of the religion, and babalawos, members of the exclusively male and allegedly straight priesthood of the oricha Orula, often cite this tendency when criticizing oricha priests who threaten them in any way. Gay oricha priests subvert cultural norms about sexuality, but some compensate for their homosexuality's effects on their reputation by becoming severe and rigid about ritual matters. (Atwood Mason 2002, 118)

FIG. 3.9. Gender crossings: David, in blue, is feminine Yemayá and Nancy, with red flowers, is masculine Changó. Film still from *Fresa y Chocolate*, Miramax Films.

In his 2003 work, *Santería Enthroned*, David Brown continues an elaboration of this Yorùbá term when he presents how the wifely status of iyawo enacts a ritual feminization of the initiate that is marked by the assumption of female garments and demeanor:

> In Yorubaland, not only do male initiates wear the dresses of their female deities. In many places, the "wifely" status of the *aworo* (priest) translates into dresses or wraps and female hairstyles for *all* priests of *all* deities. . . . In the Brazilian Candomblé, priests of both genders wear dresses, even for male orixás. . . . Yorubaland and Brazil evidence religious versions of transvestism and gender manipulation not normally found in the Cuban context. (2003, 207)

According to Brown, Cuban Lucumí is the most macho of the religions. In this tradition, male initiates wear male clothes regardless of the gender of the deity, but female initiates wear clothes that reflect the established gender identity of their deity:

> There is a curious double standard, which appears to reflect the sexual mores of Cuban, Cuban-American, and Latino society, rather than strict adherence to the logic of the *oricha*'s ownership of the body. The emphasis upon the subsuming of the initiate's gender by the *oricha*'s gender gives way, it seems, to the vanity of male initiates, males and females who make the unequivocally male *orichas* wear jackets and

bombachas or long pants on the Día del Medio. Females who make female *orichas* wear long gowns. However, males who make female *orichas* do not wear dresses. . . . Male *iyawós* wear male clothes, regardless of their *orichas'* gender. (2003, 206)

Does this allow for a space of subversion of gender categories? If so, do these proscriptions delineate the limits of such progressive and liberatory movements? Rather than merely lending coherence and stability to male bodies, these are proscriptions that seem to impose serious limitations on male bodies. This seems to lend validity to Dianteill's and Clark's idea of Lucumí as a female religion. Along the same line, in 2005, Vidal-Ortiz presents a further limitation on men in Lucumí: "there seems to be an interplay between heterosexual men resisting deity possession while simultaneously assuming that women and 'gays' are better (or prefer) to be mounted, and that this is the role of these 'sexual minorities'" (2005, 140). The answer to Vidal-Ortiz's observation and question lies in the performative receptacularity of passive homosexuals and women in the religion. The ability to be sexually penetrated mirrors the ability to serve as hosts to the orishas in an easier way than the bodies of heterosexual men, allowing the bodies of Diego and Nancy to channel orishas better than David. The representational sexual abilities and preferences of particular bodies function as secular and visible illustration of the sacred proclivities and skills of such bodies.

Also in 2005, Yvonne Daniel presents a real progression in the scholarly articulation of cross-gender possession. In her explanation of an Oyá trance we find a frankness regarding the narration of the regendered body in Lucumí ritual:

The man was now considered "female," since he was incorporating a female *oricha*. Both men and women can alter gender in this way. Women, if they receive male *oricha* energy, manifest maleness and are treated ritually as males. Likewise, males who manifest female oricha energy are treated as women in the ritual setting. (Daniel 2005, 23)

In spite of this advancement, there are current works that return to some of the old prejudiced aspects of Fernando Ortiz's scholarship. In 2008, Cros Sandoval's work evinces that the historical evolution of scholarship is bumpy and full of setbacks:

Normally Santería does not place any moral judgment on a person based on his professional activities, personal characteristics, or sexual orientation. For example, some drug dealers have joined Santería in hopes of obtaining supernatural protection from the authorities and from their enemies. Also, many homosexuals and people whose lifestyle does not conform to the dominant value orientation are initiated as priests, and they enjoy a wide following. This perceived moral ambivalence, in some instances, has damaged the reputation of Santería and its followers. (2008, 364)

The equation of homosexuals with drug dealers returns to the comments made early in the twentieth century by Ortiz regarding his perceived association of queer men and vice. The phrase "damaged the reputation" is troubling, for it revives an old representation of queer people as degenerates.

More recently, in 2010, Fernández Calderón provides probably the most succinct answer to date explaining the high preponderance of queers in the religion:

> Para el caso de la Osha, la visibilidad del grupo homosexual masculino, denominado "addodis" en lengua Yoruba, se calza con una posible mitología que responde a su inclusión. A pesar de existir una arraigada mentalidad machista por la mayoría de los practicantes, tal aspecto no ha impedido el ascenso palpable de homosexuales en los últimos tiempos; la condición de macho, les ha permitido que tengan ventaja por encima de las mujeres heterosexuales que se hallan limitadas por una serie de códigos que las ubica en posiciones subordinadas. (2010, 1–2)

> In the case of Osha, the visibility of the male homosexual group, called "addodis" in the Yorùbá language, is enveloped in a possible mythology related to its inclusion. In spite of the male chauvinist mentality of most of its practitioners, this has not impeded the palpable ascension of homosexuals in recent times. Their male condition has allowed them to have advantages over heterosexual women who are limited by a series of codes which place them in subordinate positions.

Fernández Calderón ascribes the high degree of visibility of queer men in Lucumí to the oral scriptures or *patakís*, which acknowledge the longstanding existence and participation of gay men in the tradition. Through his acknowledgment of machismo, he presents the complex ways in which gay men operate within and outside the privileges of maleness. Indeed, in spite of the prejudice, gay men do possess some access to elevated status in Lucumí. In his exposé, he alludes to the fact that, as in most of chauvinist Cuban society, the leadership of Lucumí is male. However, at the level

FIG. 3.10. Nancy embodies Changó by wearing red earrings and carrying red flowers for David. Film still from *Fresa y Chocolate*, Miramax Films.

of performance and trance possession, it is women who are predominant. Through their maleness and dissident sexuality, gay men can occupy administrative and ritual performative roles, and this duality accords them an undisputed advantage.

Using the movie *Fresa y Chocolate* as a discursive axis, we see a progression in the development and critical evolution of a queer Lucumí scholarly tradition in which same-sex desire moves from degeneracy to ambivalence and to transcorporeality in representation. The association with degeneracy is most clearly evident in the early texts by Fernando Ortiz, which are steeped in scientific racism and nineteenth-century sexology. The ambivalence begins to be seen in authors like Dianteill and Fernández Robaina, who utilize the thematic openness which the movie affords to address same-sex desire in the religion while at the same time maintaining some of the stereotypes of gay men as sexual predators who must be silenced and exiled. This period of ambivalence epitomized by the movie prefaces a more transcorporeal presentation of same-sex-desiring bodies in African religions. This last stage in the development of a queer Lucumí tradition points to the understanding of the bodies of gay men, like the bodies of women, as the ideal mediums through which the deities might express themselves to their devotees. The metaphorical openness of gay men, in sex as in trance, renders them receptacular in nature and thus transcorporeal according to the coinage and usage of the term in the present study.

LUCUMÍ DIASPORIC ETHNOGRAPHY
Fran, Cabrera, Lam

The sea roars behind us as I watch Fran arrange a beautiful altar for Yemayá on the rocks and sand of one of eastern Cuba's beaches. Hundreds have come from the nearby city of Santiago to this ceremony for the female maritime deity. Adorning a large boulder, carefully arranged fabric of different shades of blue simulates the ocean's waves. Atop a smaller rock, a white-and-blue open clay pot full of seawater serves as a sacramental microcosmic ocean, rendering visible the essence of Yemayá. In order to dive into her mystical waters, we must first pass by the master of the threshold, Eleguá, whose stone-and-cowrie shell effigy is surrounded by a wealth of vegetables and fruits that he loves: calabashes, mangoes, plantains. Another deity joins Yemayá and Eleguá in this tableau. Fran's golden beret marks him as a priest of Oshún, the sensuous and opulent deity of romantic love. Oshún looks up from the altars she arranges and looks at me through the eyes of her priest. Manly arms have never moved with such feminine grace as Oshún picks me from the crowd as her special helper. There is desire in her eyes. Enchanted, I succumb to her charm. I will do whatever she requires of me. So, I bring

Fran more ocean water. I tend to the goats and chicken about to be offered to Yemayá. I help him carry a large rectangular blue-and-white cake for the ocean goddess. Why does she want me? What does she want of me? Why does she look at me with such passion?

As the sun sets, once the ecstasy of the ceremony has passed, I experience the anticlimax of Oshún's passion, for there is an element of frustration in this desire. Fran cannot satisfy my craving for knowledge. His answers to some of my questions are oblique and leave me unfulfilled. Whether due to secretiveness or lack of philosophical vocabulary, there is no sweet dessert to this feast. This yearning to define my location, role, and duties within the Lucumí religious tradition propels me to a self-reflective moment of cultural conversion as a scholar of African diaspora religions. As a way of framing the chapter, I return to this element of my cultural conversion in the last paragraph. I would like to use the intervening pages to provide a diasporic ethnography of Lucumí through the work of anthropologist Lydia Cabrera and an extended discussion on the role of the body in the work of Cuban artist Wifredo Lam, as the work of these two cultural producers bears on my informant's personal understanding of his lived Santería practice.

Inasmuch as it is tempting for the ethnographer to select informants to represent the community of study, Fran's life history falls outside the norms of his community and does so most saliently by his emigration to the United States and his subsequent return to Cuba. Fran married a white American female tourist when he was twenty years old, and left for New York with her, only to return nine months later to Santiago. "Yo no me hallaba en Nueva York. No tenía amistades. Me sentía solo y mi único vínculo con el mundo era Fanny (su esposa). Era una presión demasiado pesada para ella. Ella se quejaba también que yo no traía dinero a la casa pero: ¿Cómo trabajar si yo no hablaba inglés?" (I did not feel at home in New York. I had no friends. I felt lonely and my sole link to the world was Fanny [his wife]. It was too much pressure for her. She complained that I did not bring any money home but how could I without speaking any English?) Fran's relationship troubles are also echoed in his inability to find a place for himself in US economic culture: "Al principio yo estaba deslumbrado por los rascacielos y las luces de Times Square pero después yo no entendía ese sistema de anuncios y me deprimía mucho que no podía comprar lo que veía en los comerciales" (At first, I was dazzled by the skyscrapers and the lights in Times Square but later I did not understand that system of advertising and became depressed at not being able to buy the things that I saw advertised). But these proved to be nine important months in the maturation of Fran and his relationship to

Lucumí. Fran's experience in New York City helps to articulate the history of Lucumí in the United States and the need to promote solidarity among migrants and subaltern groups in the face of racism from the dominant group in the host country and competition among various minority groups over resources and status.

In the Cuban diaspora, Lucumí guides amid disorientation, emphasizes past heritage and historical roots, resists assimilation into foreign cultural contexts, relates to mythological and transcendental personae who help migrants in difficult times, and provides familial and kinship ties that are often lost in the process of migration. Sosa explains what Fran means when he says, "Cuando me hice santero ya no me sentía tan solo" (When I became a santero, I stopped feeling so alone):

> As a reaction to the prevalent individualism that characterizes the American style of life, the rites of la Santería provide a means of communitarian activity, which although temporary, seem to help the individual involved overcome his sense of alienation and give him a sense of belonging to an ethnic group that finds itself in a process of adaptation outside of its own sociocultural milieu. (Sosa 2008, 389)

In this map of the Lucumí diaspora, New York City occupies a prominent place. Many important Cuban musicians, for example, encountered and strengthened their devotion to the orishas in New York City:

> Individuals who helped create a receptive environment for the growth of the Regla de Ocha in NYC: Babaláwo Pancho Mora/Ifá Moroti (founding father of Ocha in NYC), Mario Bauza, Pancho Mora, Graciela, Julito Collazo, Katherine Dunham, Mongo Santamaria, Mercedes Nobles, and Luis Bauzo, Lam, links between Dubois and Fernando Ortiz, relationship through students, relationship between Melville Herskovitz and Fernando Ortiz, Herskovitz introduced Dunham to Ortiz, Zora Neale Hurston, Arsenio Rodriguez, Frank "Machito" Grillo, Lydia Cabrera, Chano Pozo, Miguelito Valdez, Tito Puente, Rogelio Martinez y la Sonora Matancera, Celia Cruz, La Lupe, Xiomara Alfaro, Francisco Aguabella. (Moreno Vega 2008, 323–26)

These musicians were drawn to each other to counter the alienation they felt in a new country and used Lucumí as a platform of common cultural motifs for the sake of social cohesion and inspiration for their artistic production. Even Cuban surrealist painter Wifredo Lam was influenced by Lucumí while in New York: "Dunham explained that Lam often attended the Boule

Blanc events at her school" (Moreno Vega 2008, 332). Since these artists fall outside Fran's generational time frame, he only recognizes some of the names but tells me, "Yo puedo muy bien entender por qué ellos se hubieran interesado por la Regla de Ocha cuando estaban en Nueva York. Uno como que necesita salir de Cuba para apreciar lo que es de uno" (I can easily understand why they would have become interested in the Regla de Ocha when they were in New York. We sort of need to get out of Cuba in order to appreciate that which is ours). Fran confesses to me that while he was aware of Lucumí practices all around in his childhood, he did not frequent them very much. His parents' upward mobility pretensions prevented him from investigating Lucumí further. Like these famous musicians, Fran developed a closer relationship with the orishas in New York and became initiated there. This phenomenon of reaffirmation of cultural and national ties through Lucumí is explained by Steven Gregory:

> For Cubans, the experience of migration resulted less in "cognitive dissonance," than in an attenuation of ties to kinship and friendship networks in Cuba which had provided important and culturally-affirming forms of social support and satisfaction. As a result, many Cubans who had not been involved in Santería in Cuba adopted the religion in the United States as a means, in part, of rebuilding these social networks and bracing their identity as *cubanos*. (1999, 98)

During his nine months in New York City, Fran also faced an identity crisis of sorts at being read for the first time as unequivocally black by his surrounding social context. Exhibiting a combination of African and European features, in Cuba Fran is described as *trigueño*, but according to the US one-drop rule, he found himself identified and identifying with African Americans. One of the social contexts in which such identifications were forged was the Lucumí ceremonies he attended in Harlem. Fran's experience here illustrates the important role that New York City occupies for Lucumí because of its function in establishing solidarities among blacks of various nationalities.

> African Americans found in Santería a worldview and kinship based social system that was unambiguously African and whose survival and development in the New World offered proof of the tenacity of African cultures in spite of the horrors of the slave trade and centuries of racial subordination. Through the practice of Yoruba religion, African Americans have defined and exercised an *ethnic* identity that not only

challenges their ascribed status as a "*racial* minority" in American society, but also affirms their historical and cultural commonalities and ties to people of the wider African diaspora. Indeed, the social composition and ritual practices of houses of Ocha increasingly reflect this multiethnic "cosmopolitanism" much as they did during the formative years of the religion in Cuba. (Gregory 1999, 100)

Fran found that being a native-born dark-skinned Cuban provided him almost immediately with a high degree of status among the New York Lucumí houses: "Los Puertorriqueños asumían que yo sabía más que ellos sobre la religión por ser Cubano pero también había riñas entre ellos y yo. Ellos practican la Regla a su manera" (Puerto Ricans assumed that I knew more than they did about the religion since I was Cuban but there were also a lot of fights between them and me. They practice La Regla in their own way). In fact, there are many sources of ethnic conflict in the diasporic Lucumí community of New York. In that multicultural community—largely Cuban, Puerto Rican, and African American—the nationalistic discourse of Cubanismo is unlikely to appeal to other ethnic and racial groups. There is an "unspoken rivalry between Cuban and Puerto Rican musicians" (Moreno Vega 2008, 333). Moreover, the Spanish language, Catholicism, and statues of white saints may present obstacles to many African Americans. African Americans who desire to go back to their roots are at odds with Cubans who emphasize creolization or *mestizaje*. Cubans tend to be secretive about religion in response to historical persecution, but African Americans might want to proclaim it as a response to racism (Cuthrell Curry 1997, 114–15). Moreover, there is Puerto Rican and Cuban racism toward American-born blacks (Hucks 2008, 350). Last, the African American process of Africanization of Lucumí is disturbing to some Cubans (Hucks 2008, 349).

The chronology of US Lucumí largely follows the various waves of Cuban migration to the United States. After the 1959 revolution, there was an increased migration in the 1960s and '70s of white Cuban Lucumí practitioners. In 1979, the Castro government permitted former exiles to visit the island, leading to a renewal of ties, which strengthened Lucumí in the US. The 1980 Mariel boatlift allowed many black Cubans to leave the island, reinvigorating the religion in the United States with members who had direct ancestral ties to the orishas. In 1987, following resentment over mass migrations of poor Cubans, Hollywood responded with a very negative portrayal of Lucumí in the film *The Believers*. In 1990, the loss of Soviet support initiated an openness to tourists, creating the practice of *santurismo*, thereby enabling large numbers of foreigners to enter the country for the purpose of initiation and personal investigation into the religion. The increase in the number of practitioners caused by these various waves of migration and increased travel gave rise to a rapid multiplication of Lucumí houses throughout the country, especially along the East Coast of the US. This expansion was met with widespread suspicion, suppression, and hostility from conservative Christian communities. In 1993, the US Supreme Court ruled in favor of Lucumí, allowing the Lucumí community in Hialeah to perform animal sacrifices to the orishas, in spite of much local hostility to the practice.

Lucumí in New York City has had a strong history of black diasporic religious solidarity, at least since the late 1950s. In 1956, an African American pioneer in black cultural practices, Oseijeman Adefunmi, after a trip to Haiti, established the Order of Damballah Hwedo Ancestor Priests in Greenwich Village (Hucks 2008, 341). After returning from Cuba in 1959, the collaborative effort of a Cuban, Christopher Oliana, and Oseijeman Adefunmi established Harlem's earliest public temple for the practice of orisha traditions on the second floor of 71 East 125th Street, named Shango Temple. "By January 1960, the short-lived Shango Temple had evolved into a Yorùbá Temple with a new location at 28 West 116th Street . . . an important vehicle for creating Great Benin Books" (Hucks 2008, 345). The simultaneous growth of black nationalist movements and the increased migration from Cuba and Puerto Rico created a ripe environment for cross-pollinations among various African diasporic groups, Cubans, initiated Puerto Ricans, and initiated African Americans into the religion. Since its founding in the 1960s, the Yorùbá Temple in Harlem has drawn members from each of these three communities. This Afro-diasporic solidarity has not been without its turbulent moments. For example, Adefunmi debated with Oliana about the representation of the deities. Adefunmi resisted Oliana's recommendation to use a statue of Santa Barbara, a white woman, creating consternation in the community. These initial communities in New York City paved the way for a much larger re-Africanizing project that succeeded in peeling away the thin veneer of Christianity from Lucumí. In 1970, Adefunmi became the founder and first Oba King of Oyontunji African Village in South Carolina. Anecdotally and biographically, these projects attempted to resolve Adefunmi's childhood ethnic turmoil, when his mother "simply told him that Africans had lost their God when they were brought to America during slavery" (Hucks 2008, 341). In his involvement in the New York Lucumí community, Fran felt the influence of Adefunmi in various houses. He reports that his name was mentioned often, especially among African American participants who felt compelled to make their group's contributions to Puerto Rican and Cuban coreligionists visible.

Lydia Cabrera

However, for Fran the most important Lucumí personality is not Adefunmi, but Lydia Cabrera, since in her work he encountered the first written validation of same-sex desire. He knows her books, especially *El Monte*, a copy of which I subsequently gave him as a present, but he does not know very much about her life. Lydia Cabrera (May 20, 1900–September 19, 1991) stands as the most important single ethnographic voice in the study of Lucumí in the twentieth century. Born into a wealthy home, she listened to Yorùbá patakís from her Afro-Cuban nanas.

Privileged, precocious, and gifted, she published her first works in her father's magazine, *Cuba y América*, when she was only fourteen years old. Lydia Cabrera's personal and professional life was marked profoundly by her relationships with two women: María Teresa de Rojas, with whom she moved to Miami in 1960, and Venezuelan writer Teresa de la Parra.

Cabrera met de la Parra in Havana in 1924 or 1925, around the time when de la Parra published her landmark feminist novel *Ifigenia*, originally written at the suggestion of her older lover Emilia de Barrios and subsequently considered immoral in Venezuela and banned by the Catholic Church. Three years later, Cabrera began a romantic relationship with de la Parra far from Cuba, in Paris. In 1932, de la Parra was diagnosed with tuberculosis, and Cabrera spent two years with her in a sanatorium in Leysin, Switzerland. When de la Parra died in 1936, Cabrera inherited de la Parra's manuscripts, her library, and her emerald ring. Cabrera wrote her first professional excursion into Afro-Cuban folklore, *Cuentos negros de Cuba*, to entertain de la Parra during her illness. José Quiroga (2000, 83) sees in *Cuentos negros de Cuba* and in *Ifigenia* a type of queer commissioning that allows a romantic relationship to pass as a pedagogical one: "these relationships were coded as the meeting between acolyte and mentor," he writes. The success of this book began Cabrera's prolific career as an ethnographer of the African religions of Cuba. Among her most important works on Lucumí are *El Monte: Igbo Finda* (1968), *Anagó: Vocabulario Lucumí* (1970), *Yemayá y Ochún* (1980), and *Los animales en el folklore y la magia de Cuba* (1988). These works mark

FIG. 4.1. Lydia Cabrera with her informants. Photograph by Pierre Verger. Used by permission of Fundação Pierre Verger.

the passage from orality to scripture as they inscribe the oral traditions of the Yorùbá people of Cuba and can now be found on the bookshelves of many Lucumí practitioners.

Cabrera's lesbianism was very much informed by the sexual openness of the 1920s. As part of the educated intelligentsia of Cuba, de la Parra and Cabrera had access to the cosmopolitan transatlantic queer cultural world of the times, and there is a record of this when they discuss the influential German lesbian film *Mädchen in Uniform* and Colette's *Ces Plaisirs*. According to Sylvia Molloy, "Between these two dates [1927 and 1935], seventy-three letters document (onesidedly, to be sure, since Cabrera's letters were presumably destroyed by the Parra family) a complex, intense, and yes, lesbian relationship" (1995, 239). The fact that Molloy's research seeks to uncover codedness and affect through epistolary research in which the writings of only one woman survived renders a deep imbalance in the scholarly understanding of both women. Given the survival of de la Parra's letters to Cabrera, Molloy is able to work through the complex and coded system of sexuality in her letters and define de la Parra as "one who did not identify herself except by denial (her systematic rejection of marriage, of childbearing, of men), by linguistic detour ('auront des amies'), by imperfect familial analogy (like a *second mother*, a *sister*, a *good friend*), or by euphemism (independent, solitary, misfit)" (1995, 246). The fact that the de la Parra family destroyed Cabrera's letters forces Molloy to focus exclusively on the letters written by de la Parra. But how might we unearth Cabrera's desire in the absence of these letters? I propose advancing beyond epistolary research by sifting through her relationship with literary and artistic figures of the time, as well as close readings of her own work, to reconsider Cabrera's queerness and the relationship that her sexual alterity bears to the study of Afro-diasporic religions. This is a question that is already hinted at, but undeveloped, by Molloy when she writes:

> A similar recognition of the marginal, attributable in both cases, I would argue, to the personal experience of margins, that of sexual difference and gender unease, may be observed in Lydia Cabrera's sustained interest in Afro-Cuban lore (*Cuentos Negros de Cuba* was written as a "gift" to Parra during her illness) and in the concern of Gabriela Mistral's poetry with Indians. (1995, 251)

Furthering Molloy's initial comment, Hoffman-Jeep develops the idea that blackness and queerness are coarticulated in Cabrera's work:

> Although perfect silence has surrounded Cabrera's lesbianism in scholarly studies, her sexual orientation informed her creativity, and in part her lifelong identity with Afro-Cuban minority culture. Still, her lesbian identity was a trump card that she never risked playing. Indeed, Cabrera's insider position among the educated Cuban white elite is part masquerade; even where she appears to be an initiate, she is quite frankly an outsider, and where as a white woman, she seems clearly positioned outside of the Black community, she apparently identifies with the marginalized experience and culture of the Cuban Black folk. (2005, 345)

But what precisely is the relationship between queerness and blackness in her work? Based on the fact that she embodies queerness but not a material blackness, I propose that Cabrera articulates her queerness in proxy through a symbolic spiritual blackness. Queer Hispanophone writers who were influenced by her include Cubans José Lezama Lima and Reinaldo Arenas and, most importantly, Spaniard Federico García Lorca, who dedicated a poem to her in 1928 titled "La casada infiel." This poem deserves our close attention, as it displays this coded "vicarious queerness through blackness" that I suggest:

LA CASADA INFIEL

A Lydia Cabrera y a su negrita

Y que yo me la llevé al río
creyendo que era mozuela,
pero tenía marido.

Fue la noche de Santiago

y casi por compromiso.
Se apagaron los faroles
y se encendieron los grillos.
En las últimas esquinas
toqué sus pechos dormidos,
y se me abrieron de pronto
como ramos de jacintos.
El almidón de su enagua
me sonaba en el oído,
como una pieza de seda
rasgada por diez cuchillos.
Sin luz de plata en sus copas
los árboles han crecido,
y un horizonte de perros
ladra muy lejos del río.

Pasadas las zarzamoras,

los juncos y los espinos,
bajo su mata de pelo
hice un hoyo sobre el limo.
Yo me quité la corbata.
Ella se quitó el vestido.
Yo el cinturón con revólver.
Ella sus cuatro corpiños.
Ni nardos ni caracolas

tienen el cutis tan fino,
ni los cristales con luna
relumbran con ese brillo.
Sus muslos se me escapaban
como peces sorprendidos,
la mitad llenos de lumbre,
la mitad llenos de frío.
Aquella noche corrí
el mejor de los caminos,
montado en potra de nácar
sin bridas y sin estribos.
No quiero decir, por hombre,
las cosas que ella me dijo.
La luz del entendimiento
me hace ser muy comedido.
Sucia de besos y arena
yo me la llevé del río.
Con el aire se batían
las espadas de los lirios.

Me porté como quien soy.

Como un gitano legítimo.
Le regalé un costurero
grande de raso pajizo,
y no quise enamorarme
porque teniendo marido
me dijo que era mozuela
cuando la llevaba al río. (García Lorca 1928, 7)

THE UNFAITHFUL WIFE

To Lydia Cabrera and her little black woman

And I took her to down to the river thinking her an unmarried girl,
but she had a husband. It was the night of Saint James as good as on a
promise the lamps were turned off and the crickets turned on. In the
last corners I touched her sleeping breasts, and they opened to me suddenly like hyacinth bouquets. The starch of her skirt sounded in my ear
like a piece of silk torn by ten knives. Without silvery light in their tops
the trees have grown, and a horizon of dogs barks far from the river.

Past the blackberries, the branches and the thorns, under her bush of hair I made a hole over the moss. I took off my tie. She took off her dress. I, the belt with the revolver. She, her four corsets. No nard nor shell has a skin as fine, neither do crystals in the moonlight shine that brightly. Her thighs escaped me like scared fish, half filled with light, half filled with cold. That night I ran the best of the roads, climbing on a mother-of-pearl mare without stirrups, unbridled. I don't want to say, because of my manhood, the things she told me. The light of understanding makes me very restrained. Dirty with kisses and sand, I took her from the river while the lily spears battled with the air.

I behaved as who I am, like a proper gypsy. I gave her a large straw-like satin shawl and I did not want to fall in love since in spite of having a husband she told me she was unmarried when I took her down to the river.

There is a queerness in this poem that begs to be decoded, read as an affirmation of same-sex desire and extended to Cabrera's Afro-Cuban research. The first relationship in the poem is the marginally extratextual one between Lorca and Cabrera. What does it mean for a gay man to dedicate a poem of heterosexual love to a lesbian woman? I see a queer solidarity embedded in this dedication. The following two relationships speak of a mysterious and furtive love. "To Lydia Cabrera and her little black woman." When we consider that the diminutive marker -*ita* can function as a way to qualify small size as well as affection, it is possible to translate the dedication in a more explicit romantic sense: "To Lydia Cabrera and her *dear* black woman. "Who is the *negrita* and what is the nature of Cabrera's relationship to her? When I read the poem to Fran, he eloquently presents the possibility that Lorca may have been alluding to his knowledge of a possible affair between Cabrera and one of her black female informants. This interpretation would certainly allow us to see the problematic way in which Cabrera likely expressed and satisfied her queer desire through the textual and physical vectors of black religions and bodies. Lorca's poem hints at the fact that Cabrera's attraction for black religious culture also includes an erotic desire for the bodies of its practitioners. When Cabrera discusses black subaltern culture in her work, she is speaking of her own sexual marginality. When she discusses queerness in the religion, she is not only referring to others' sexual alterity, she is also speaking about her own. Who is the *gitano*? Is it Cabrera as the pursuer of women or in her embodiment of a nomadic, exiled people? Is it both, and can we see this as an illustration of how "Cabrera's lesbianism aligned her with the Cuban Black person as minority consciousness" (Hoffman-Jeep 2005, 343)? There

FIG. 4.2. Lydia Cabrera with Iyalocha Odedei: Could this be the *negrita* alluded to in García Lorca's poem? Photograph by Pierre Verger. Used by permission of Fundação Pierre Verger.

is certainly an alignment between the negrita and the gitano that speaks to a certain fetishized and sexualized white queer ethnographic gaze on black informants. Who is the *mozuela*? This can certainly be Teresa de la Parra, who, like Iphigenia, defiantly resists the constraints of heterosexual marriage in favor of love outside the norms. While the relationship between the poetic characters and the people in Cabrera's life remains productively ambiguous, what is clear in Lorca's poem is the coarticulation of dissident sexualities and diasporic ethnicities. The key to unlocking the cryptic language of the poem appears to be an awareness of Cabrera's appropriation of racial minority identity (the negrita, the gitano) to satisfy the textual expression and sexual urgings of her queer desire.

Given the destruction of Cabrera's letters by the de la Parra family, we are forced to look at other textual information to read Cabrera's desire. The Lorca poem provides us with fossilized and oneiric, fragmentary elements that we may recompose as a way to elucidate her hidden and censured queer desire. We might also be able to look at Lydia Cabrera's landmark work, *El Monte*, to understand the ways in which her same-sex desire is articulated through African religion. For example, the brief mention of de la Parra at the beginning can be seen to function as a coded dedication of the work to her lover, as an endorsement of her novelistic production, and as an avowal of her same-sex desire:

> [la fotografía] de Calixto Morales, Oddeddei, retratado por la inolvidable escritora y distinguida venezolana Teresa de la Parra, que la vió con frecuencia y se complacía en platicar con ella durante su estancia en la Habana. Teresa guardaba el recuerdo de algunas frases lapidarias de la vieja iyálocha y de su cortesía de gran estilo. Y nunca olvidó a Calazán, actor inimitable, y a un pordiosero fabuloso, especie de Diógenes negro, que solía llevarle de regalo naranjas de china. Personajes novelables que la escritora emparentaba con el Vicente Pochocho en carne y hueso de las fragantes Memorias de Mamá Blanca y con otros tipos parecidos igualmente interesantes y simpáticos, conocidos en su infancia, en la hacienda Tazón, en una Caracas todavía de aleros y ventanas arrodilladas, que hubiesen revivido en el libro que soñaba escribir sobre la colonia. (Cabrera 1995, 11)

> [the photograph] of Calixto Morales, Oddeddei, taken by the unforgettable and distinguished Venezuelan writer Teresa de la Parra, who saw her often and rejoiced in talking with her during her stay in Havana. Teresa kept the memory of some succinct phrases of the old *iyalocha* and of her stylish courtesy. And she never forgot Calazán, an actor who cannot be imitated, and a fabulous beggar, a sort of black Diogenes, who used to grace her with oranges as gifts. Novelistic characters that the writer associated with the flesh-and-blood Vicente Pochocho of the fragrant Memories of Mama Blanca and with other equally interesting and likeable characters of her childhood, on the Tazón farm, in a Caracas still with tiled water spouts and kneeling windows that she would have liked to have revived in the book she dreamed of writing about the colony.

Cabrera here presents de la Parra as being surrounded by a community of Cuban black Lucumí practitioners. This is a supportive community of informants and friends who accept the two white women lovers without reservations. Lucumí is here presented as accepting of non-heteronormative sexual and romantic arrangements. Accordingly, in the narrative of the couple, Lucumí provides a queer-affirming Caribbean context that reflects and refracts the permissiveness of Europe and North America in the 1920s. While among these informants acceptance is both allowed and limited by the social class and race of the two privileged women, it is important to observe how de la Parra and Cabrera assume the role of students of black culture, therefore presenting Lucumí as a counterdiscursive, even if a bit escapist, cultural arena. This important passage prefaces at least eight other queer passages in *El Monte*, which we can use to redress the violence and absences in the epistolary record of the relationship. More importantly for our current study, we can see these passages as ways in which same-sex desire is articulated via Lucumí for Lydia Cabrera and that this discourse by proxy is enabled by a shared marginality, functioning as a transcorporeal code. Lydia Cabrera is interested in Lucumí because the symbolic representation of the body in the religion provides validation for non-heteronormative performances and identifications that are often abjected in Western Cartesian corporeality.

Lydia Cabrera does more than document the existence and acceptance of lesbianism within Lucumí; she also notes the requirement that female devotees of certain deities refrain from sex with men, fostering a queer social space in the religion:

> Abundan también las lesbias en Ocha (alacuattá) que antaño tenían por patrón a Inle, el médico Kukufago, San Rafael, "Santo muy fuerte misterioso" . . . Yewá, "nuestra Señora de los Desamparados," virgen, prohíbe a sus hijas todo comercio sexual; de ahí que sus servidoras sean siempre viejas, vírgenes, o ya estériles, e Inle, "tan severo," tan poderoso y delicado como Yewá, acaso exigía lo mismo de sus santeras, las cuales se abstenían de mantener relaciones sexuales con los hombres. (1995, 58–59)

> Lesbias [*sic*] abound in Ocha (allacuattá) who, in the past, had as their patron Inle, the Kukufango doctor, Saint Raphael, "a very strong and mysterious saint . . . Yewá, "our Lady of the Forgotten," virgin, who forbids her daughters all sexual intercourse; hence her servants are

always old, virgins, or already sterile, and Inle, "so severe," as powerful and delicate as Yewá, perhaps demanded the same of his santeras, who abstained from sexual relations with men.

While it might be tempting to interpret same-sex desire among women as a subsidiary and secondary consolation for forbidden heterosexual coupling, one may also see in this seemingly compliant reasoning a syncretic and subversive strategy that provides a protective explanation to safeguard a same-sex-loving female community from suspicious minds. In the same way Roman Catholic saints function as the outward, acceptable image of the orishas, this apparent interdiction provides a way to satiate the curiosity of strangers who might seek to harm the members of this alternative space. The presentation of lesbians as virgins plays on the same discursive strategy as pairing African gods with Roman Catholic saints, aligning lesbians and blacks as an essence that is thinly coated with a veneer of Western imagery to ensure its survival in a hostile and unknown environment. We see in this the coarticulation of same-sex desire and blackness through their shared marginal status in the writings of Cabrera.

There is a strong concern for linguistic designations of same-sex desire in Lucumí in the writings of Cabrera. The misspelling and deformation of "lesbianas" into "lesbias" exhibits a dissatisfaction with Western modes of identificatory desires and their imposition onto colonized populations around the world. The parenthetical Yorùbá term is one of several opportunities that Cabrera takes to present alternatives to non-heteronormative Western categories of *being* that still defy local and global patriarchial-reproductive models. The same-sex-loving female category of alacuattá is paralleled to a Yorùbá term for same-sex-loving men:

> "En esto de los Addodis hay misterio", dice Sandoval, "porque Yemayá tuvo que ver con uno. . . . Se enamoró y vivió con uno de ellos. Fue en un país, Laddó, donde todos los habitantes eran así, maricas, mitad hombres, que dicen nafroditos (*sic*) y Yemayá los protegía." "Oddo es tierra de Yemayá. ¡Cuántos hijos de Yemayá son maricas"! (Cabrera 1995, 56)

> "There is mystery in all this about the Addodis," says Sandoval, "because Yemayá had something with one. . . . She fell in love and lived with one of them. It was in a country, Laddó, where all the inhabitants were like that, faggots, half men, who they call *nafroditos* [*sic*] and Yemayá protected them." "Oddó is the land of Yemayá. How many sons of Yemayá are faggots!"

"Addodis" is the Yorùbá-retention lexicon for same-sex-loving men, which stands in a counterpointed relationship to the pejorative term "maricas." There are other categories of non-heteronormative desire that do not have to conform to Western models of alterity, Cabrera seems to say. And then there is another deformation of Western categories of being. Using the spelling "nafroditos" instead of "hermafroditas" functions in the same counterdiscursive manner as spelling "lesbianas" as "lesbias." Cabrera and the compiler of her field notes were meticulous in their Spanish spelling and in their phonetic spelling of Yorùbá words. Can *nafroditos* and *lesbias* be a mere oversight? Could we read an element of shame here? A love that dares not speak its name, in Spanish, but is brave in Yorùbá? Both words are clipped. There are syllables missing, which speaks to Cabrera's attempt to bite and detract from oppressive categories of alterity coming from the First World and a preference for the non-heteronormativity of subaltern spaces. And Cabrera reminds us that these spaces are real and material but also mythical, as there is a queerland that is also divinely governed and protected, "Laddó."

Through the portrait of Papá Colás, Cabrera presents a queer Lucumí practitioner who was respected, honored, and remembered by the religious community: "Este Papá Colás que ha dejado tantos recuerdos entre los viejos, era famoso invertido y sorprendiendo la candidez de un cura, casó disfrazado de mujer, con otro invertido, motivando el escándalo que puede presumirse" (1995, 56; This Papa Colás who has left so many memories among the old, was a famous invert and, surprising the naïveté of a priest, was married disguised as a woman, to another invert, generating the scandal that could reasonably be expected). The respect and honor with which Papa Colás's memory is held is underpinned by his courage. He dupes the Roman Catholic Church by cross-dressing, successfully deceiving a priest, and having that priest marry them according to the rites of a church that tried to stamp out the African spirituality of his community. In this sense, Papá Colás, whose very name is yet another shortened version of Nicolás, channels the orisha Eleguá, the trickster. Papá Colás is the embodiment of the counterdiscourse of resistance, overcoming, subversion, and ingenuity that characterizes the survival of Africans in the diaspora.

The term "invertido" recalls some of the late nineteenth-century sexology of Kraft-Ebbing and Havelock Ellis, which is part of a troubling set of medicalizing terms that we find in Cabrera's *El Monte*:

Desde muy atrás se registra el pecado nefando como algo muy frecuente en la Regla lucumí. Sin embargo, muchos babalochas, omó-Changó, murieron castigados por un orisha tan varonil y mujeriego como Changó, que repudia este vicio. Actualmente la proporción de pederastas en Ocha (no así en las sectas que se reclaman de congos, en las que se les desprecia profundamente y de las que se les expulsa) parece ser tan numerosa que es motivo continuo de indignación para los viejos santeros y devotos. "¡A cada paso se tropieza uno con un partido con su merengueteo!" (1995, 56)

From long ago, there is record of the abominable sin as something very frequent in the Regla Lucumí. Nevertheless, many babalochas, omó-Changó, died, punished by an orisha as manly and womanizing as Changó, who repudiates this vice. Currently, the proportion of pederasts in Ocha (not so in the Congo sects, in which they are treated with great disdain and from which they are expelled) appears to be so numerous that this causes great indignation toward the old santeros and devotees. "One runs into a group of them sashaying it up all the time!"

The passage reiterates the historical and numerically significant presence of queers in the religion. As troubling as it might be to hear outdated and loaded terminology for queerness such as "pecado nefando" and "pederasta," it is important to contextualize these as part of a passage that seeks to present how the world of African diasporic religions is not free from homophobia. Congo religions and extremely masculine Yorùbá orishas such as Changó can, according to some stories, reject homosexuals. Other male orishas can also be extremely unfriendly to queerness: "Sin embargo, los Santos hombres, Changó, Oggún, Elegguá, Ochosi, Orula, y no digamos Obatalá, no ven con buenos ojos a los pederastas" (Cabrera 1995, 56; However, the male orishas—Changó, Oggún, Eleguá, Ochosi, Orula, without leaving out Obatalá—do not look well upon queers). The virile Changó can be particularly hostile to same-sex-loving men:

No hace muchos años, Tiyo asistió a la escena que costó la vida a un afeminado que llamaban por mofa María Luisa y que era hijo de Changó Terddún. . . . Ah! Pero Changó no quería amujerado, y ya había declarado en público que su hijo lo tenía muy avergonzado. . . . Fué en una fiesta de la Virgen de Regla, María Luisa estaba allí y todos nosotros bromeando con él, ridiculizándolo. En eso, cuando a María Luisa le estaba subiendo el Santo, llegó otro negrito, un cojo, Biyikén, y le dio un pellizco en salva sea la parte. Ahí Changó mismo se viró como un toro

furioso y gritó: ¡Ya está bueno! Mandó a traer una palangana grande
con un poco de agua y nos ordenó que todos escupiésemos dentro y
que el que no escupiese recibirá el mismo castigo que le iba a dar a su
hijo. María Luisa estaba sano. Era bonito el negrito, y simpático. . . .
¡Una lástima! Cuando se llenó de escupitajos la palangana, se la vació
en la cabeza. Al otro día María Luisa amaneció con fiebre. A los diez y
seis días, lo llevamos al cementerio. Changó Terddún lo dejó como un
higuito. (Cabrera 1995, 57)

Not many years ago, Tiyo attended a scene that cost the life of an effeminate man whom they mockingly called María Luisa and who was a
child of Changó Terddún. . . . Ah! But Changó did not want an effeminate man and had already declared in public that his son had shamed
him. . . . It was during the feast of the Virgin of Regla. María Luisa
was there and all of us joked with him, ridiculing him. Then, when
María Luisa was going into trance, another black man who was lame,
Biyikén, came and pinched him in his holy poker so that Changó right
there became an angry bull and screamed, That is enough! He asked to
be brought a large bucket with some water and ordered all of us to spit
inside it and he who did not would receive the same punishment that
he was giving to his son. María Luisa was healthy. He was a beautiful
black and a nice fellow. . . . What a shame! When the bucket was full
of spit it was turned over his head. The next day María Luisa woke up
with fever. In sixteen days, we took him to the cemetery. Changó Terddún left him like a little fig!

Here, Changó is presented as intolerant of alternative masculinities. This
contrasts sharply with the acceptance that the queer man appears to enjoy
within the community. The grammatical cross-gender identification of a
female name described by masculine-suffixed adjectives presents to us the
naturalness with which they are received in the speech community and
mitigates some of the euphemism and circumlocution regarding sexual
organs and queer desire. Changó is the one who is criticized here for being
intolerant, presented as a bull and a bully, having no mercy on his queer
children and obligating his friends to punish them and bringing grief to
the community. Why must we see a deity as representing the aspired values of its worship community? Could it also not incarnate undesirable
traits worthy of condemnation? Can we not read this passage as a critique
of homophobia? The punishment can also be read as stemming from the

failure of the community to pay reverence to the subtleties of trance possession and to differentiate between the queer initiate and the hypermasculine orisha.

Moreover, it would appear that the problem with María Luisa is not so much his queerness but his misidentification with Changó. His is the tragic fate of being mismatched with a tutelary divinity. Let us note how, while both initiate and orisha are of the same sex, they are differently gendered in their roles. This tragic event happens during the feast of Changó's archetypal opposite, Yemayá, the Virgin of Regla, provoking the anger of Changó, who becomes jealous when his son apparently chooses to channel this other deity's persona.

Female orishas can also be severe with their queer initiates. Similarly to the way in which Changó punishes María Luisa, Oshún, in the passage quoted below, kills her queer initiates not because of their desire but for faking a trance and for their bellicose nature:

A las doce, cae Ch. Con Oshún. R. Que está en la puerta borracho, dice: A mí también ahora mismo me va a dar Santo y lo fingió. Entra al cuarto, vá a la canasta de los bollos, y se pone a comer bollos con miel. Viene Ch. Con Oshún a saludarlo y éste le manda un galletazo. Lo agarran, y le pega una patada. Le gritamos: ¡R. tírate al suelo! ¡Pídele perdón a Mamá!

—¡Bah! ese es un maricón. . . .

—No es Ch. ¡Es nuestra Mamá!

Oshún no se movió. Abrió el mantón, un mantón muy bueno que le habían regalado a Ch. los ahijados, y se rió. Levantó la mano derecha y apuntando para R. tocándose el pecho dijo:

—Cinco irolé para mi hijo, y cinco irolé para mi otro hijo

Y ahí mismo se fue

Ch. amaneció con cuarenta grados de fiebre y el vientre inflamado. R. amaneció con cuarenta grados de fiebre y el vientre inflamado. . . . Cinco días después murieron a la misma hora, el mismo día. (Cabrera 1995, 57–58)

At twelve, Ch. falls into trance for Oshún. R. who is by the door, drunk, says, "I am also going to go into a trance." He faked it. He comes into the room, goes to the basket with corn bread and starts eating it with honey. In comes Oshún to greet him and slaps him. They grab and kick him. We scream, "R., throw yourself on the ground! Ask mother for forgiveness!"

"Bah! He's a faggot!"

"It isn't Ch. It is our Mother!"

Oshún did not move. She opened the nice shawl that the godchildren gave to Ch. and laughed. She raised her right hand and pointing it toward R., touching her breast, said,

"Five irolé for my son and five irolé for my other son."

And just like that she left.

Ch. woke up with a forty-degree [Celsius] fever and the abdomen inflamed. R. woke up with a forty-degree fever and an inflamed abdomen. Five days later they died at the same time, the same day.

Here the orisha punishes her queer devotees for faking a trance and for fighting. Ch. is in a trance and R. fails to recognize that a transition of personalities has taken place. On top of this lack of reverence, R. fakes a trance. The genuine trance of Ch. clashes with R.'s dramatic one. The role of queers in the religion is problematically presented as driven by spectacle rather than sincerity, by unbridled passion and rage instead of true devotion. In this as well as the earlier María Luisa story, an important issue is that of the personality of the orisha blending with that of the devotee and the great risks inherent in misrecognition of the deity when the devotee is in a state of trance. Cabrera continues her thematic coding of queerness by giving us only the initials of their names. Is she also not eliding their personalities in order to highlight the transcorporeality that their narratives display as vessels of the divinity, as vectors of her persona and public display of power?

However, these anecdotes about the severity of punishment by the orishas are balanced by a story in which Changó, the most virile of the orishas, cross-dresses:

Una de las veces en que tuvo que esconderse de sus contrarios, porque si caía en sus manos le cortaban la cabeza, querían matarlo de todos modos, se metió en casa de Oyá. . . . Entonces Oyá se cortó sus trenzas y se las puso; lo vistió con su ropa, lo adornó con sus prendas, sus collares, argollas y manillas, e hizo correr la voz que se iba a dar un paseo. Changó y Oyá tenían el mismo cuerpo. Tiposo como ella, Changó salió vestido de mujer caminando igual que Oyá. . . . Los enemigos de Changó, muy respetuosos, creyeron que era la Santa, le abrieron paso y Changó pudo escapar. (Cabrera 1995, 233)

One of the times when he had to hide from his enemies, because if he fell into their hands they would cut his head off—they wanted to kill him anyway—he went into Oyá's house. . . . Then Oyá cut off her braids and put them on him; she dressed him with her clothes, adorned him with her jewelry, her necklaces, rings, and earrings and spread the rumor that she was going for a stroll. Changó and Oyá had the same body. As beautiful as she, Changó came out dressed as a woman, walking just like Oyá. . . . The enemies of Changó, very respectfully, thought he was the female saint, let him pass, and he was able to escape.

Some anecdotes on queerness enforce heteronormativity while others undermine it. There is an ambivalence that allows for a certain measure of openness. What is most important for us to see here is Cabrera's documented record of a long-standing tradition of queers in Lucumí, how the religion of Afro-Cubans helps her as a white Cuban to articulate her own sexuality, and how both of these issues can be explained through the peculiar representation of the body in this religion. Cabrera displays an incipient and unconscious knowledge of Cartesian and Afro-diasporic representation of the body:

> Pero antes de continuar, un paréntesis para que sepa el lector que desconozca a Cuba, que "subirle el santo" a uno o "bajarle el santo" o "estar montado" por el santo, "caer con santo," venir el santo a cabeza, se llama aquí a este fenómeno viejo como la humanidad, conocido en todos los tiempos y todos los pueblos que ocurre incesantemente en el nuestro, que consiste en que un espíritu o una divinidad tome posesión del cuerpo de un sujeto y actúe y se comporte como si fuese su dueño verdadero, el tiempo que dura su permanencia en él. De ahí que a la persona que es objeto de la intromisión habitual de un Santo, en cualquier Regla, se le llame "caballo" o "cabeza de santo." . . . El santo, (y el fumbi de los mayomberos) desaloja, valga la expresión reemplaza al Yo del "caballo." . . . El ego, pues del un individuo a quien "le dá santo"—es sacado. Arrojado por éste fuera de su cuerpo, o de su cabeza, "ori que es la que manda el cuerpo," queda anulado y lo sustituye el orisha, el npungu o el fúmbi . . . "baja" or "corona" espontáneamente, sorprende al "caballo" . . . entra en él, es decir "lo monta." (1995, 28)

But before continuing further, a parenthesis so that the reader who does not know Cuba will know that "climbing the saint," or "lowering the saint," or "being ridden" by the saint, or "coming down with saint," the saint coming onto the head, here, we call that phenomenon, old as humanity, known in all times and peoples, like that which always occurs in ours, which consists of a spirit or divinity that takes possession of a subject's body and acts and behaves as if it were its true master for the time in which it is with(in) him. From there, the person who is the object of the habitual invasion of a saint in any Regla is called "horse" or "head of the Saint." . . . The saint (and the *fumbi* of the *mayomberos*) expels, replaces even, the I of the "horse." . . . The ego of an individual who is with the saint is removed. Sent forth from his body or his head, "*ori* that is which governs the body," is annulled and is substituted by the orisha, the *npungu* or the *fúmbi* . . . "comes down" or "crowns" spontaneously, surprises the "horse" . . . comes into him, in other words "mounts him."

It is noteworthy that Cabrera uses an in/out metaphor in reference to the relationship between the spirit and body, but informants use a ridership terminology. While the differences between Western and African concepts of the body are evident through interpretation, this is a difference that remains unarticulated for Cabrera, but one which is seen to emerge closer to the surface, almost as the next logical step of her work: "Cualquier estado anormal psíquico supone para el negro la ingerencia de algún espíritu extraño, o de un orisha que penetra en una persona y toma el lugar de su yo, se entremete, en ocasiones sin desplazarlo enteramente" (1995, 30; For the black man, any abnormal psychological state supposses the ingestion of some strange spirit or an orisha that enters into a person and takes the place of its I, breaks in, on occasion without displacing him completely). The existence of partial states of possession shows that the in/out model is insufficient to account for the experience. In the Western sense, the anima or spirit is either in or out, so how can there be partial possession? The ridership metaphor, however, allows for levels of influence and passing, fleeting moments of contact between the divine rider and its human horse.

Wifredo Lam

When I peruse a museum exhibit catalog with Fran, he is captivated by the paintings of Lam. I wonder why Fran has never heard of him. Some of his paintings are in Cuban museums and certainly in New York. Fran tells me he

FIG. 4.3. The supra-cephalic horned face associated with Eleguá crowns the top of the head of the feminine entranced figure. Wifredo Lam, *Un coq pour Chango* (A rooster for Shango), formerly *L'Oracle et l'oiseau vert* (The oracle and the green bird), 1947. Oil on burlap, 42 × 35 in. (106.68 × 88.9 cm). © Artists Rights Society (ARS), New York / ADAGP, Paris. San Francisco Museum of Modern Art, fractional gift from Jan Shrem and Maria Manetti Shrem. Photograph by Ben Blackwell.

is not the museum type. He likes to be outdoors, communing with nature. "Es por eso por lo que me hice Santero, para estar más cerca de la naturaleza, trabajar con las plantas y los animales, y con todo lo que *Es*" (That is why I became a santero, to be closer to nature, to work with the plants and the animals and with everything that *Is*).

Wifredo Lam was born and raised in Sagua La Grande, a small town in the sugar-producing province of Villa Clara, Cuba. His father, Yam Lam, was a Chinese immigrant, and his mother, Ana Serafina Lam, was born to a Kongolese former slave mother and a Cuban mulatto father. His family, like many others, practiced Catholicism alongside their African traditions. Matonica Wilson, Lam's godmother, was a Lucumí priestess who exposed Lam to rites of the African orishas. His contact with African celebrations and spiritual practices proved to be his largest artistic influence.

In 1916, bowing to parental pressure, Lam moved to Havana to study law. During this period, he also began studying tropical plants at the botanical gardens. Disillusioned with academic teaching and painting, he left for Madrid in the autumn of 1923 to further his art studies. As a result of the

Nazi occupation of Paris, Lam left for Marseille in 1940, where he joined many intellectuals and surrealist artists and critics with whom he had been associated since he met André Breton in 1939. In Marseille, Lam and Breton collaborated on the publication of Breton's poem *Fata Morgana*, which was illustrated by Lam. In 1941, Breton, Lam, and Claude Lévi-Strauss, accompanied by many other European intellectuals, left for Martinique, only to be imprisoned there by German-sympathizing local officials. After forty days, Lam was released and allowed to leave for Cuba, which he reached in midsummer 1941.

Lam rediscovered Afro-Cuban traditions upon his return to Havana. There he sought a revalorization of Cuba's African heritage, which he felt was being undermined by discrimination and by tourism. His return to the Caribbean marked the climax of Lam's artistic development, as it is characterized by a rapid evolution and maturation of his style. Drawing from his study of tropical plants like the externally seeded marañon and his knowledge of Afro-Cuban culture, his paintings became characterized by the presence of the chimera, a hybrid figure composed of human, animal, and plant elements as well as the orishas. In 1946, he and Breton spent four months in Haiti, enriching his already extensive understanding and knowledge of African divinity and magic rituals through observations of Vodou ceremonies. Lam's syncretization of surrealist and cubist approaches with imagery and symbols from Lucumí, Palo Monte, and Abakuá during this period makes him a uniquely cosmopolitan artist. In 1943, he began his most famous work, *The Jungle*. Reflecting his artistic pinnacle and modernism's controversial relationship to African art, *The Jungle* depicts four figures with mask-like heads, half-emerging from dense tropical vegetation. Later that year, it was shown in an exhibition at the Pierre Matisse Gallery in New York and was ultimately purchased by the Museum of Modern Art and was exhibited beside Picasso's *Guernica*, to which it has been problematically compared. In 1952, Lam settled in Paris after having divided his time between Cuba, New York, and other cities in France.

Lam continued his strong engagement with the Caribbean from Europe in the decade following his departure. In solidarity with Cuban popular struggles, Lam exhibited a series of paintings at Havana University in 1955, to demonstrate his support for the students' protests against Batista's dictatorship. Similarly, in 1965, six years after the revolution, Lam showed his loyalty to Castro and his goals of social and economic equality by painting *The Third World* for the presidential palace. This engagement was recognized

FIG. 4.4. The scissors, the moon, and the verdant scenery reveal the context for Lam's masterpiece *The Jungle* as a ceremony for the orisha of herbalism, Osaín. In obsolescent Cuban Spanish Creole, La Manigua denotes the sacred natural world—the forest in particular. The dialogic nature between Lam and Cabrera's work is evident in the analogous titles of their best-known works: Lam's *The Jungle* and Cabrera's *El Monte* can both be translated as "the bush" or "the brushwood"—the "igbo" of igbodu. In this painting we appreciate the full gnosis and experience of Being achieved during the transcorporeal moment of ritual possession as the chimeric personae transcend and encompass all binarisms: human/god, plant/animal, male/female. In *The Jungle*, we discover that "We are One." Wifredo Lam, *The Jungle*, 1943. Gouache on paper mounted on canvas, 94¼ × 90½ in. (239.4 × 229.9 cm). © Artists Rights Society (ARS), New York / ADAGP, Paris. Inter-American Fund. Digital Image © The Museum of Modern Art. Licensed by SCALA / Art Resource, NY.

by the artistic establishment of the time. In 1964, he was awarded the Guggenheim International Award, and between 1966 and 1967 there were many retrospectives of his work throughout Europe. After a long life as the premier Caribbean surrealist artist, Wifredo Lam died on September 11, 1982, in Paris.

Cultural critics have had difficulty understanding Lam's work in its relationship to Lucumí. In general, we can distinguish several schools of thought that exhibit some regional specificities. There is a body of work in which critics, mostly from Cuba, gloss over or display anxiety regarding Lucumí. And there is a set of critics, mostly from the United States or France, who acknowledge the role of Lucumí in the work of Lam, but do so only in passing and stop short of any deeper theoretical discussions on the subject of corporeality.

None other than Fernando Ortiz, the premier Cuban ethnographer of the twentieth century, begins the tradition of attempting to erase blackness and Lucumí in Lam and his work:

> En Lam se habrían hallado influjos del expresionismo africano aún cuando aquél nada tuviera de negroide en su linaje ni en su aculturación cubana; le bastaría haber asimilado en Francia las tendencias del modernismo pictórico, en el cual ha sido honda la huella del arte afrooccidental, así en Picasso como en muchos otros artistas plásticos de su tiempo. (1950, iv)

> In Lam there are many influences of African expressionism even when he had nothing Negroid in his lineage or in his Cuban acculturation; it would have sufficed for him to have assimilated in France the tendencies of pictorial modernism, in which the mark of the art of West Africa has been great, evident in Picasso and in many other artists of his time.

What is at stake in the presentation of Lam as nonblack by the most respected figure in black culture in Cuba? Why present Lam as devoid of race? Is there not an element of tokenism here that presents Lam as the exceptional *negro avanzado* or as an honorary white?[1] Ortiz credits the presence of African cultural motifs to surrealism and not to Lam's background, effectively whitewashing him for the purpose of maintaining the fiction of an exclusively European artistic elite in Cuba. The erasure of Lam's blackness functions in a manner similar to the silencing of the black santero in the film

FIG. 4.5. The supra-cephalic Eleguá rests atop the head of the female figure in this mother-and-child composition. The idealized body of Santería/Lucumí is the physically and spiritually open and receptacular female body. Wifredo Lam, *Ibaye*, 1950. Oil on canvas, 104.5 × 87.6 cm. © Artists Rights Society (ARS), New York / ADAGP, Paris. Tate Gallery © Tate, London / Art Resource, NY.

Fresa y Chocolate, discussed in chapter 3. There is a co-optation of black spirituality for the production of a national culture that relies on the evacuation of the very populations producing this discourse.

Influenced no doubt by this colorless view of Lam, Max-Pol Fouchet, Lam's canonical biographer, continues this tradition of the elision of Lam's blackness, this time by invoking a universality in Lam that erases the very black ethnic specificities that inspire his work:

> Certes, il nous paraît pourtant nécessaire d'ajouter que ces *Figures*, aussi "africaines" soient-elles, ne ressortissent pas à ce seul fonds ou plutôt qu'elles rejoignent, à travers lui, un fonds plus général, universel. Dressés souvent "en majesté," elles s'apparentent aux plus anciennes images mythiques ou religieuses, dont elles sont, en notre temps, la résurgence, comme après un long cheminement au sein de l'être collectif. Profanes, crées par un incroyant, elles semblent néanmoins s'accompagner d'un Sacré primordial: les *Maternités* de Lam ressuscitent celles d'Akkad, de Sumer, d'Ur, de l'Europe romane, et dans ses *Nus* passe un reflet de Cyclades, de l'Égypte antique, de la Polynésie,

de l'Hellade des *kouroï*. Ainsi a-t-il réuni les formes archétypales d'une permanence de l'homme. (Fouchet 1984, 24)

Admittedly, it appears necessary for us to add that these so-called African figures do not come from that source, but rather that, through him, they rejoin a more general and more universal source. Often raised "in majesty," they resemble the most ancient mythical and religious images, of which they are in our times in resurgence, as after a long journey into the bosom of our collective self. Profane, created by a nonbeliever, they seem nevertheless to accompany a sacred primordial trope: Lam's *Maternities* resurrect those of Akkad, of Sumer, of Ur, of European Rome, and in his nudes passes a reflection of the Cyclades, of ancient Egypt, of Polynesia, of the Greece of Kouroï. In such fashion, he has reunited the archetypal forms of a human permanence.

Fouchet here dismisses blackness, Africanness, and Lucumí through an invocation of the universal. Why should the transgeographical and historical links in Lam's work function as a way to dismiss its African originary point of reference? What is the motivation behind this tendency in art criticism? Here it becomes evident how there is a certain social pressure to create a vision of Cuban high culture as Iberian. According to this dictate, while Cuban blacks might be the performers of folklore and cultural expressions deemed popular, they are not welcome in the world of high art and certainly not if this is to become the vision with which Cuba will be represented in erudite international social circles. The existence of a black Cuban artist who paints African-inspired images and is well respected abroad goes against the grain of Cuban racial hierarchies and artistic divisions of labor. To preserve these divisions, some have dismissed what appear to be very evident African religious motifs in Lam's work: "Lam's perception of orishas was clearly more evocative than literal" (Fletcher 1992, 185) because "Lam . . . no pinta ni . . . orichas ni babujales" (Ortiz 1950, ix; Lam paints neither orishas nor sorcerers).

When the complete erasure of Lam's blackness becomes untenable, many critics continue to display a great deal of ambivalence that forestalls any worthwhile discussion of race in Lam. For these ambivalent critics, Lam's mixed-race status and his membership in European artistic circles serve to diffuse African spirituality in a more global manner:

Lam's work immediately following his return to Cuba is profoundly anthropological. Paintings such as *The Jungle* are at once caught in this

FIG. 4.6. Supracephalic figurines, androgyny, and the camouflaging of the human within the plant world mark the transcorporeal body of the initiate in this painting. The displaced phallus, which here begins to evoke strongly the image of a pharaonic chin, begs to be read as Lam's bow to a mythological and ancestral Africa. Wifredo Lam, *Le Bruit*, 1943. Oil on paper mounted on canvas, 105 × 84 cm. © Artists Rights Society (ARS), New York / ADAGP, Paris. AM1985–97. On loan from the Centre Pompidou. © CNAC / MNAM / Dist. RMN-Grand Palais / Art Resource, NY.

modernist exploration of recognition and disavowal and a brilliant effort that distinguishes Afro-Cuban culture by using a "curtained" boundary or notion of a liminal space to mark the point of the exchange between the secular and sacred. (Merewether 1992, 22)

Whether it presents a definite rejection of Lam's African ancestry or foregrounds cultural eclecticism at the expense of the local, the effect is the same: the elision of blackness in the work of Lam. What is clear in the work of these critics is an antiblack racism in their refusal to acknowledge and discuss the African religious aspects of Lam's work.

Progressing beyond this sense of denial, other critics—also mostly from Cuba—exhibit a deep sense of anxiety, ambivalence, and disavowal regarding Lucumí in the work of Lam. Michel Leiris, one of Lam's biographers, vacillates between this denial and full acknowledgment through a highly ambivalent discourse: "A rationalist and a Marxist as well after his travels in Spain, Lam was not adept in santería or other Afro-Cuban cults. But we cannot doubt that he remained imbued with that sense of the supernatural to which he had access during his childhood (1970, vii). There are no records of initiate status for anyone into Lucumí because this is a religion that has relied on secrecy for its survival. How can the biographer claim to know that he had never been initiated? While there exist clear rituals that make public the induction and membership of a particular individual into the religious community, in inner circles of Lucumí, initiation is often discussed as a lifelong process of growth and evolution. In this sense, it is a mistake to call Lam a noninitiate. While it is known that his godmother was a Lucumí practitioner and her influence shaped him, there is a clear attempt here to make Lam conform to the white art world by toning down black spirituality and invoking a color-blind supernatural element.

Leiris's ambivalence has its origins in the writings of Fernando Ortiz, who is responsible for originating and perpetuating among cultural critics the erroneous idea that Lam's work is not about Lucumí. The following passage presents how Ortiz's denial engenders ambivalence as it is reconciled against hard evidence affirming Lucumí in Lam's canvases:

> Asimismo, algunos cuadros remiten a referencias de los sistemas mágico-religiosos afrocubanos, sobre todo la diminuta esferilla humanoide de ojos saltones coronada por dos cuernos, identificada con el ícono del orisha Eleguá, el santo Yoruba encargado de abrir y cerrar los caminos, el de las encrucijadas. La amistad con Lydia Cabrera fue decisiva en esta aproximación. La etnóloga conocía bien los mitos y la simbología de esos cultos, y lo acompaño a los recintos ceremoniales. Sin embargo, sus pinturas no traducen a cabalidad los atributos de deidad alguna, como tampoco recurren a una simbología precisa ni a una mitología carcelaria. "Lam no pinta orishas ni babujales", su imaginario anicónico, en las palabras de Ortiz era la resultante de una síntesis simbólica abierta. (Noceda 2002, 28)

> In a similar fashion, some paintings refer to the magical and religious system of Afro-Cubans, above all the small round humanoid figure with big eyes, crowned by horns, identified with the icon of the orisha Eleguá, the Yorùbá saint in charge of opening and closing roads, of intersections. The friendship with Lydia Cabrera was decisive in this approximation. The ethnologist knew very well the myths and symbology of these cults and accompanied him to ceremonial sites. Nevertheless, his paintings do not translate fully the attributes of a deity, as neither do they recur to a precise symbology nor to an imprisoned mythology. "Lam paints neither orishas nor sorcerers"; his

FIG. 4.7. Transcorporeal hermaphroditism as the orisha resignifies the personality and gender of the initiate during the moment of trance possession. Wifredo Lam, *Goddess with Foliage*, 1942. Gouache on paper, 41½ × 33½ in. (105.4 × 85.1 cm) (framed). © Artists Rights Society (ARS), New York / ADAGP, Paris. The Pierre and Maria-Gaetana Matisse Collection, 2002 (2002.456.32). The Metropolitan Museum of Art. Image copyright © The Metropolitan Museum of Art. Image source: Art Resource, NY.

anti-iconic imaginary, in the words of Ortiz, was the result of an open symbolic synthesis.

Noceda agrees with Ortiz yet overcomes his strict denial regarding Lucumí in Lam. It is important to note that while Noceda cites Ortiz as saying that there are no orishas in Lam's work, Noceda himself acknowledges the representation of at least one orisha—Elegúa—in Lam's work. In order to explain away the recurrence of this particular orisha, León Argeliers resorts to diminution and trivialization:

> Es cierto que Lam recurrió a algunas figurillas de la santería cubana, para situarlas entre sus hirsutos plantíos. Prevalecen unas figuras de la deidad Elebwa, en su advocación o "camino" que los oficiantes de la *regla de Ocha* llaman *masancío*. Pero el interés de Lam por estas figurillas era más *anecdótico* que plástico. (2002, ix)

> It is true that Lam utilized some of the figurines of Cuban Santería and placed them in his hirsute orchards. The images of the deity Ele-

guá prevail in the avatar that the initiates of the Regla de Ocha call *masancío*. But Lam's interest in this figurine was more anecdotal than artistic.

Among Cuban art critics of this ambivalent perspective, there is a general deferral of responsibility to Lydia Cabrera for any Lucumí content or interpretation in Lam's work. While the role that Lydia Cabrera played in Lam's transcorporeal *prise-de-conscience* and conversion to Lucumí exhibited in the paintings of his 1940s *retour au pays natal* is uncontroversial, the diversion of all discussions of Lucumí in Lam to Cabrera is a noteworthy rhetorical shift displaying a high degree of diffused cultural anxiety. Rojas-Jara epitomizes this discursive strategy when he argues, "Interestingly, friend and Ethnographer Lydia Cabrera titled many of Lam's paintings that contained what *she* identified as Santería references. Lam evoked these images, not literally as a devotee, but as a surrealist who associated them with the primitive" (1995, 61). While Noceda and others credit Cabrera with reintroducing Lam to Lucumí, Rojas-Jara argues that it was Cabrera who promoted a personal interpretation of Lam's symbology as Lucumí. According to this rhetoric, Lam is not painting orishas, but Cabrera is seeing them in his work and promotes such an interpretation by giving certain paintings Lucumí names. But in reality Cabrera was a specialist in Lucumí, and she recognized the religious images in Lam's work to such an extent that she might have named them according to some deities.

There is clearly a great deal of anxiety on the part of these Cuban critics about fully acknowledging the role of Lucumí in Lam. But these critics move beyond the mere erasure of Africanness in Lam exhibited by Ortiz. They admit the possibility of some content or possible interpretation of Lam's work as Lucumí but with caveats and disclaimers that display a nervous desire to whiten Lam and his work. Let us take note of the usage of the word "regress" in the following explication of Lam's *Femme sur Fond Vert* to see how Africanness fits into the overall work of aesthetic progress: "Aunque el rostro revela un nuevo acercamiento a las máscaras africanas, el fondo sigue siendo plano. Es evidente que Lam retrocede y que él lo sabe, razón por la cual abandona esta obra a medio hacer" (Medina 2002, 317; Even though the face reflects a new approach to the African masks, the background continues to be flat. It is evident that Lam regresses and that he knows it, and that this is the reason why he leaves this work incomplete). The erasure of blackness of the earlier generation yields to a reserved acknowledgment of an Africanness that is nevertheless akin to backwardness. This, troublingly,

FIG. 4.8. The depersonalization and psychological doubling reported by initiates during trance possession is illustrated in this femme cheval painting. Observe the continuation of the thematics of hermaphroditism in the location of the phallus on the chin of the distinctly female horse. The extrapelvic location of male genitalia allows for the preservation of somato-spiritual concavity in the initiate as androgyne. Wifredo Lam, *Satan*, 1942. Gouache on paper, 41⅞ × 34 in. (106.4 × 86.4 cm). © Artists Rights Society (ARS), New York / ADAGP, Paris. Inter-American Fund (710.1942). The Museum of Modern Art. Digital Image © The Museum of Modern Art / Licensed by SCALA / Art Resource, NY.

rearticulates a discourse of progressive development in which Africa represents the anterior and primal original from which all worthy endeavors should strive to distance themselves and outgrow in order to achieve completion and maturation.

All the while, there is a third school of thought that is characterized by an incipient acknowledgment of Lucumí in the work of Lam. While this represents a clear advancement in the revalorization of African religions, these acknowledgments stop short of a full understanding of the implications of the body in African diasporic religious cultures. The equine figure motif in Lam's paintings allows for an unequivocal presentation of African religious imagery in Lam: "La combinación peculiar de ser humano y caballo que transforman la figura en cuestión ofrece un símbolo visual de un estado de trance, que en los cultos afrocubanos se conoce como 'bajarle el santo'" (Martínez 2002, 22; The peculiar combination of human being and horse that transforms the figure in question offers a visual symbol of a state of trance, which in the Afro-Cuban cults is known as "coming down with the saint"). Cuban critic Juan Martínez remains a rare example of this interpretation of the horselike figure as an individual in trance. All the other critics who acknowledge the role of Lucumí in Lam are from the United States or France, locations from which a perspective of African continuities in Cuba might be more perceptible than in Cuba itself, given the particular racial formation of the island. Stokes Sims adds a gendered component to the equine figure when he writes:

> The inscriptions of the signs of the Abakuá society are a key part of the elaborate ceremonies that culminate in the possession of a devotee— who is symbolized by the femme cheval, since the devotee is "ridden" like a horse by the various orishas who manifest themselves during the rituals. (2002, 68)

While Stokes Sims's acknowledgment of the femme cheval as a Lucumí motif is signficant, he does not elaborate on the most important element he contributes to the development of the conversation: the gender of the horse. Why is the horse figure a woman? How might the woman's gender be modulated by the symbolic masculinity of the horse? In fact, most of these critics who do acknowledge the role of Lucumí do so only in passing, barely touching on the theme of possession without asking how this half-human, half-animal figure might serve as an illustration of the uniqueness of the Afro-diasporic conceptualization of the body. For example, Julia Herzberg, who is, in my opinion, the critic who pushes the conversation of Lucumí in Lam to its furthest point, does not advance much beyond a comparison of Lam's femme cheval to other Western artistic and mytho-logical motifs:

> Picasso's many preparatory drawings of the horses for *Guernica* along with his representations of minotaurs have features that influenced Lam's imaginative creations of this period. . . . A phenomenon of major religious significance and long-established tradition in Afro-Cuban religion is one in which the deity (orisha/santo) takes posses-sion of the practicant, who is referred to as the horse (caballo). . . . Viewed this way, Lam's mask face is often a metaphor for the horse in the phenomenon of possession. (1987, 28–29)

What is at stake in presenting Lam as derivative of Picasso and his hybrid figures as iterations of Greek mythological chimeras? Why insist on the Europeanness—the Spanishness, the Greekness—of an African religious phe-nomenon? Is there not an erasure of blackness that paradoxically co-occurs with an acknowledgment of this very concealed blackness? Continuing along

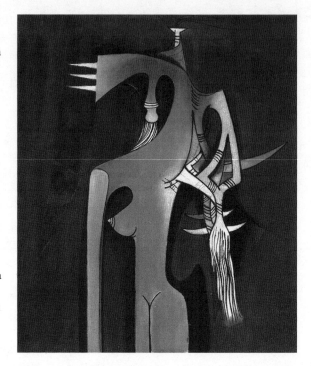

FIG. 4.9. The motif of the female horse becomes more evident in this painting, which also shows the androgynous ideals of Lam, who places the phallus and scrotum on the chin of the woman so as to preserve the openness required for sexual-spiritual possession. Wifredo Lam, *Zambezia, Zambezia*, 1950. Oil on canvas, 49⅜ × 43⅝ in. (125.4 × 110.8 cm). © Artists Rights Society (ARS), New York / ADAGP, Paris. Gift, Mr. Joseph Cantor, 1974. The Solomon R. Guggenheim Museum. Photo credit: The Solomon R. Guggenheim Foundation / Art Resource, NY.

these lines, Taillandier sees in the figure of the femme cheval yet another Lucumí idea. Beyond the idea of possession, this hybrid figure is the representation of syncretism: "Mais surtout le caractère androgyne de la figure en point d'interrogation serait un rappel de l'androgynie que résulte du mélange des personnalités de la sainte catholique et du dieu noir" (Taillandier 1970, 11; But above all, the androgynous character of the figure in the shape of a question mark would be a reminder of the androgyny that results from the mixture of personalities of the female Catholic saint and the black god).

The femme cheval is then the point of articulation for the phenomenon of trance possession and also for the system of correspondences between Catholic saints and orishas in the imagery of Lucumí. But couldn't we also go beyond this analysis and say that the chimera in Lam represents the unity of all in the cosmos as it represents the fusion of orisha and initiate—in its masculine and feminine genders—as well as the animal and plant world? Lam's femme cheval, in particular those in which the equine figure bears an Eleguá on her head, mirrors the idea of the body with an externally located spirit essence, emblematized by the cashew pear and its outer seed. This chimera operates as a meeting point of the secular and the sacred, modernism and Africanness, a liminal figure revealing the greater unity of Being. Taillandier elaborates further on the androgynous quality of the femme cheval figure when he says:

> Que signifie cette silhouette en forme de point d'interrogation? Au sujet de cette forme interrogative, je me suis beaucoup interrogé. Le point d'interrogation est tantôt à l'endroit, tantôt a l'envers. Peu importe. En bas se dessinent une épaule de femme et une glande mammaire. Le cou est un cou de girafe ou ce cou soudainement très long des danseurs cubains. Au bout de ce cou pend une tête qui est parfois triangulaire. Dans ce cas, elle porte une ou plusieurs cornes de licorne. Plus souvent, même très souvent, la tête est une tête de vieillard un peu démoniaque parce qu'elle est surmontée de deux cornes sataniques, chevaline par sa longueur et survirilisée: l'espace intermédiaire entre la bouche et le menton affecte l'apparence d'un pénis en érection; quant au menton, ses deux hémisphères séparés par une fossette ressemblent au double globe des testicules. En outre une barbe. (1970, 9–10)

> What is the meaning of this silhouette in the form of a question mark? I have pondered this interrogative form a lot. The question mark is backward and right-side up. This is a small matter. At the bottom there is a woman's shoulder and a mammary gland. The neck is a giraffe's neck or that long neck of Cuban dancers. At the end of this neck, there is a head that is sometimes triangular. In this instance, she bears one or several unicorn horns. More often, even very often, the head is the head of an old man, a little devilish, because it is mounted by two satanic horns, horselike in their length and supervirilized: the intermediary space between the mouth and the chin appears to be an erect penis; the two curves of the chin, separated by a dimple, resemble the double globes of the testicles in some, a beard in others.

Taillandier sees in the femme cheval a question that he tries to answer. His animalization of Cubans in his presentation of them as giraffe-like is troubling, as is his erroneous equation of Eleguá with the Christian devil. His Eurocentrism is evident in his reading of the horns of Eleguá as those of the unicorn. Nevertheless he recognizes the horse and sees the phallus on the chin but fails to develop its implications. Is the fragmented and recomposed penis-in-chin figure a homunculus-type mental representation of the body? Is it an Egyptian stylized beard? Is the chimera a type of sphinx? Is the fusion of female breasts and penises in a single body a commentary on Lam's own racial hybridity? Could we see the femaleness in the horse as a way to

FIG. 4.10. This painting reveals more clearly the facial features of the orisha Eleguá and those of the equine mother and child. The initiate is the horse of the spirit during ritual trance possession. Wifredo Lam, *Mother and Child*, 1957. Charcoal and pastel on ivory wove paper, 73.3 × 58.3 cm. © Artists Rights Society (ARS), New York / ADAGP, Paris. Lindy and Edwin Bergman Collection, 140.1991. The Art Institute of Chicago. Photograph: The Art Institute of Chicago / Art Resource, NY.

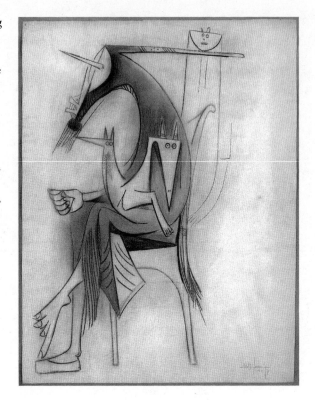

represent the openness of the idealized body-as-vessel in African religious representation?

The acknowledgment of Eleguá and the femme cheval as Lucumí images in the work of Lam provides an aperture for a consideration of the African conceptualization of the body through the figure of the bird in Lam:

> Si les oiseaux sont représentés de manière assez vague, on peut tout de même présumer que ce sont des vautours, messagers divin d'Olofi, la divinité suprême dont chaque oricha est une émanation. Pour les adeptes de la santería, Olofi, ou Olodumare, se loge dans la tête de chaque être humain. (Herzberg 2001, 116)

> If the birds are represented in a rather vague manner, we can nevertheless assume that they are vultures, divine messengers of Olofi, the supreme deity from which each orisha springs. For the initiates of Santería, Olofi, or Olodumare, resides in the head of each human being.

In *Flash of the Spirit: African and African American Art and Philosophy*, Robert Thompson explains the religious image of the sacred bird that Herzberg finds in Lam:

> According to traditional authority, shrines of the head also conceal, in the covering of the shining white shells, an allusion to a certain perching bird, whose white feathers are suggested by the overlapping cowries. This is the "bird of the head" (eiye ororo), enshrined in whiteness, the color of iwa, and in purity. It is the bird which, according to the Yoruba, God places in the head of man or woman at birth as the emblem of the mind. The image of the descent of the bird of mind fuses with the image of the coming down of God's *ashé* in feathered form. (Thompson 1983, 11)

The image of the bird and its relationship to the human and equine figures in Lam's paintings presents the unique relationship of the spirit to material bodies in Afro-diasporic religions. The use of the preposition "in" by Herzberg and Farris Thompson is not altogether accurate, as during trance possession the spirit-bird rests on top of the head of the initiate without truly residing within her. The body in Afro-diasporic religions is not the hermetic enclosure it is in European philosophy. Instead, the relationship between the body and its anima finds floral representation in the *Anacardium occidentale*, whose heart or seed—its cardium—queerly rests outside the pulpy corpus of the fruit. Thompson's usage of the ideas of perching and descent are more in tune with the idea that we see in Lam of multiple beings coexisting without entering, violating, or usurping identities. In this sense, Thompson moves us closer to an understanding of the transcorporeality that exists in Lam: the presentation of the body as vessel of the divine, hosting and transporting a multitude of subjectivities simultaneously.

I not only acknowledge the presence of Lucumí in Lam, but I see it as occupying a central role in his work without reservations of any kind. In contrast to the denials and ambivalences of these critics, I insist on the need to highlight the presence of Lucumí in Lam for the illustration of the transcorporeal self in the Afro-diasporic conceptualization of the body.

The differences between Cuban and First World (US and French) scholarship reflect variances in the representation of Cuban national identity both on the island and abroad. The various Cuban projects of independence and revolution have emphasized a whitened version of Cuban national identity that has difficulty finding a place for the religions of Afro-Cubans. To First World social scientists, Cuba is still imbued with some of the same discourses of exoticism that wealthy tourists expect from their island visit. The French love affair with the exotic erotic and the North American one-drop racial rule enforce a view of Cuba as an oversexualized black island paradise. Paradoxically, the exoticism coming from First World vacationers and ethnographers allows for the opportunity to reevaluate the most marginal of racial and religious groups on the island. While local Cuban racism effectively elides blackness from social science discourse, the racism of First World researchers actually pushes the lived realities of the most oppressed in Cuba to the forefront of academic discourse. Foreign ethnographers, like other First World visitors, tourists, and conquistadors, overturn the Caribbean social hierarchy to their advantage by aligning themselves with the most oppressed group, effectively reiterating alliances that have turned the existing social schema on its head and yielded, historically, the creation of the colony, the ferment of revolution, and the creation of the nation.

Lam's arrival in Cuba marks the beginning of a paradigmatic *retour au pays natal*, but also that of a mythical exodus, an *expulsion du pays étranger*. The return to African religious motifs is certainly not due solely to Picasso or psychoanalytic deployment of Africa as sociocultural and geographical reference for the subconscious. Lam's Lucumí imagery reflects Lam's racial *prise de conscience* after experiencing the threat of annihilation at the hands of the Nazis and his internment in a German-controlled concentration camp in Martinique. I propose that the paintings of this period are largely dominated by representations of humans in communion with the orishas. The small facial motifs atop the heads of many subjects with hermaphroditic traits as well as the strong theme of the female horse serve as vivid illustrations of my concept of transcorporeality in black Atlantic cultural production. In this sense, transcorporeality works with my original proposition that the cultural logic of the African diasporic body is that of a receptacular body that transports the essences of multiple and removable selves. Lam's work also allows us the opportunity to push forth a methodological understanding of transcorporeality, one in which the innovative synthesis of previously published information can be recorporealized, re-membered, and rearticulated like the bony joints of a composite corpus in order to advance an understanding of embodiment. Even as much as this transcorporeal understanding is underpinned in some previously published materials, this yields a never-before-synthesized understanding of Lam. This new under-

FIG. 4.11. In this painting, which functions as a study for *The Jungle*, we begin to observe how the transcorporeal body of the entranced poly-subjectified initiate begins to blend with the plant world, as the legs reveal themselves as indistinguishable from the stalks of sugarcane. Wifredo Lam, study for *The Jungle*, 1942. Tempera, with touches of pastel, on tan wove paper laid down on canvas, 177.4 × 121.9 cm. © Artists Rights Society (ARS), New York / ADAGP, Paris. Lindy and Edwin Bergman Collection, 138.1991. The Art Institute of Chicago. Photograph: The Art Institute of Chicago / Art Resource, NY.

standing of Lam sees his most significant contribution as the representation of the idealized sacramental body in the African diaspora as the entranced chimera, the liminal being representing the unity of all the cosmos, in its animal, human, plant, and divine forms. In a contestatory relationship to the hermetic enclosure of the Cartesian body, Lam's artwork presents the spiritual essence riding atop the material body, using it as a vessel for transportation and manifestation in the physical world. In Lam, the observer rarely sees small facial figures inside others. They are always stacked on top of one another. Heads over heads represent the supracephalic nature of the Afro-diasporic trance possession experience in which the deity rides, without entering per se, its human hosts.

In Lam, the open palms, concave heads often topped with baskets or plates, present the body as an open receptacle whose essence of being, its psyche, is

FIG. 4.12. The union of the female and male principles is emblematized in this allegorical marriage between Oshún, goddess of love, and Ogún, god of war and metallurgy. The supracephalic figures of the dove and the horseshoe indicate entranced bodies being ridden by these deities, respectively. Eleguá, the divinity who opens all gates and removes obstacles, is present as officiant and witness. Wifredo Lam, *Les Noces* (The wedding), 1947. Oil on canvas, 215 × 197 cm. © Artists Rights Society (ARS), New York / ADAGP, Paris. Inv. NG 33/66. Nationalgalerie, Staatliches Museum, Berlin. Art Resource, NY. Photograph: Jörg P. Anders.

multiple, external, and removable (figure 4.13). This allows for the transgendering of the body, as evidenced in the hybrid image of the female horse, whose breasted and phallic corpus embodies the androgynous ideal of Afro-diasporic religious discourse. The horse as woman articulates both the ridership metaphor for possession, in which the horse is the devotee, a devotee who must be ritually female—a category that would include passive homosexual men—in order to account for its open and receptacular function. Indeed, Lam's paintings provide a visual referent for the transcorporeal view of the body that makes Lucumí fertile ground for non-heteronormative subjectivities.

This transcorporeality is also evident in the trickster and border-crossing deity Eleguá, as it occupies an important place in Lam's semiotics. As the first and last orisha invoked in all ceremonies, Eleguá frames all the deities and in this way becomes a symbol for the entire pantheon in Lam. These Eleguás are mostly stacked atop the head of human or equine figures in Lam's paintings, presenting the transcorporeality of the Afro-diasporic body, which is modulated from multiple and removable divine external sources. Like Eleguá, birds become symbols of the divine who nest atop the head of initiates. The bird as symbol of the orisha emphasizes the transitory and temporary state of trance possession, in its fleeting nature. Lam's femme cheval evinces how this stacking or superimposition of beings has effects on gender. The paradigmatic figure of possession is androgynous. Transcorporeality allows for a transgendering of the body exhibited by the breasted and phallic femme cheval. Male and female, human and animal, divine and material, the female horse is a chimera representing the unity of Being. The liminal and chimerical being in Lam emblematizes Cuba's hybridity and at the same time also evokes a universality that is also reminiscent of another enclosed sea, the Mediterranean, in its Greek and Egyptian mythological references. In spite of those who would only want to favor these European referents, Lam's paintings are clearly both, and in this they reveal the same syncretic and integrationist approach as associating saints and orishas.

My friend Fran does not readily see the Lucumí symbols in Lam. Only after I decode them for him does he become conversant in Lam's Lucumí language. Our learning is a two-way street. After all I have learned from Fran, I am happy to help him understand the representation of Lucumí in high surrealist art. I have found myself processing my participation in the Yemayá beachside ceremony as an assistant to Fran. The relationship between the practitioner and the scholar mirrors that between the body and the spirit. Fran is the female horse, and I am like the winged creature that flies from afar into his hand or rests on his head for a while. Fran is the human who lives in one punctual space and time. I begin to see myself more like the Eleguá of the crossroads, the liminal being who brings knowledge from one realm to the other, as mediator between the popular and the academy. My cultural conversion involves a growing awareness of my role as disseminator

FIG. 4.13. Eleguá—metamorphosing into a sensuously hermaphroditic flower displaying both male and female parts, stamen and pistil—marries Oshún and Ogún. The yellow tones and the sexually suggestive flowers are an indicator of the seductive tone and mood of the event. The marriages presented in this painting and in *Les Noces* underscore the thematics of androgyny found in the figure of the femme cheval. Lam appears to say that the sacramental body is ultimately beyond this realm of binary oppositions. I argue that this body of the beyond/*au delà*/*del más allá* is the transcorporeal body, regendered, retaxonomized, deified in the moment of trance possession. Wifredo Lam, *The Eternal Presence (An Homage to Alejandro García Caturla)*, 1944. Oil and pastel over papier-mâché and chalk ground on bast fiber fabric, 85¼ × 77⅛ in. (216.5 × 195.9 cm). © Artists Rights Society (ARS), New York / ADAGP, Paris. Nancy Sayles Day Collection of Modern Latin American Art. 66.154. Museum of Art, Rhode Island School of Design, Providence. Photograph by Erik Gould, courtesy of the Museum of Art, Rhode Island School of Design, Providence.

of knowledge, spokesperson and theorist in the service of practitioners like Fran. In this sense, transcorporeality begins to reveal itself to me as an ethnographic methodology framing individuals and collectivities as bodies, which the scholar may ride and possess. Indeed, the work of transcorporeality can be conducted only by the composite chimeric body depicted by Lam, half scholar, half practitioner, entranced.

PART III

CANDOMBLÉ

QUEER CANDOMBLÉ SCHOLARSHIP
AND DONA FLOR'S S/EXUA/LITY

In *The Signifying Monkey*, Henry Louis Gates Jr. (1989) argues that the African trickster deity Eshu-Elegbara functions as a unifying trope between African and US African American discourses. In this chapter, I explore the survival of this African deity in another location in the Western Hemisphere—the city of Salvador da Bahia in Brazil—to make the claim that the figure of Eshu-Elegbara, far from remaining monolithic across the diaspora, shifts shapes in different New World contexts. While Eshu acquires a dismissive and combative stance toward the dominant Anglo-Saxon culture of North America, in Brazil, Exu contests dominant Lusitanian, and therefore Western, culture through a jocular and decidedly queer exhortation to cultural creolization. The character of Vadinho in Jorge Amado's (1966) *Dona Flor e seus dois maridos* affords us an opportunity to observe this phenomenon. After his death, Vadinho—a devotee of Exu—continues to appear to his wife and, as a spirit, is able to continue a sexual relationship with her. Realizing that the power of Candomblé has enabled Vadinho's return from the grave, Dona Flor decides to use the powers of this Afro-Brazilian religion to drive him out, so she can remarry. However, in the end she decides to keep both her ghostly stud and her homely, but living, husband. This ménage à trois embodies an embrace of cultural and ethnic hybridity that is quite distinct from the Eshu of Zora Neale Hurston or Ralph Ellison. Therefore, my study revises Gates's analysis by insisting that Eshu-Elegbara is a unifying feature of Afro-diasporic discourses not because of fixed spiritual attributes, but through its ability to survive through adaptive changes that often render it unrecognizable at first glance. One of the ways in which Eshu-Elegbara shape-shifts in Brazil is as an exemplary transgressive deity with respect to gender. The new orthography and shortened quality of his name in Brazil speaks to this New World evolution for the African deity, who in his new context becomes the master of gendered thresholds and crosses the boundaries of traditional forms of masculinity and femininity. The exposure of an existing tradition of queer Candomblé scholarship allows for an understanding of the religion as a vector for the proliferation of dissident sexual performances, behaviors, and categories. The trickster quality of the orisha Exu in Brazilian Candomblé enables a prominent non-heteronormative thematic element of Brazil's premier Afro-religious literary text, Jorge Amado's *Dona Flor and Her Two Husbands*, a queer reading that has until now remained unexplored in criticism and has been addressed by its author only in passing. This non-heteronormativity illustrates how the gender system operating in Candomblé is distinct from the Western binary of the body/soul and displays the transcorporeality of the self as removable, external, and multiple, contained within an open receptacular body.

History of Queer Candomblé Scholarship

In this chapter, I argue for the existence of a heretofore uncharted tradition of queer Candomblé scholarship that moves from a pathologizing period (1940–69) to one dominated by factualization (1970s) and culminates in a phase of elucidation (1980s–early 2000s), which moves close to the transcorporeal understanding that lies at the heart of my project.

The three main scholars of the pathologizing school are Landes, Bastide, and Ribeiro. Ruth Landes, in her landmark 1940 article "A Cult Matriarchate," equates homosexuality with vice. In a manner reminiscent of Ortiz's work on Lucumí, Landes writes, "Most of these caboclo 'fathers' and 'sons' are passive homosexuals of note, and were vagrants and casuals of the streets. . . . The ten or so 'fathers' whom I knew had come from the ranks of the street prostitutes and boy delinquents, and from the town's ruffians" (1940, 393, 396). In addition to her presentation of queers as social degenerates, Landes proposes that same-sex-loving men in Candomblé are usurping female gender roles. This elides any transgressive potential against binary gender roles and forestalls any discussion of solidarity between women and sexually dissident men: "They want one thing, for which the candomble provides widest opportunities: they want to be women. . . . Passive homosexual fantasies are realizable under the protection of the cult, as men dance with women in the roles of women, wearing skirts and acting as mediums" (Landes 1940, 394). Landes's "A Cult Matriarchate" paves the way for her most significant work, *The City of Women* (1947), in which she continues her pioneering work on gender in Candomblé. When she questions her informant about "a big man possessed by Iansá, the bisexual goddess," this is the response she gets: "Why, he's a man, Dona Ruth, in a world dominated by women! A true priest of the cult should be a woman, and I think Bernardino is honest enough about his cult practice to wish he were truly a woman, instead of just a man acting like a woman" (Landes 1947, 205). Here Landes introduces a spiritual logic through the notion of cross-gender possession, but retains the troublingly binary, and therefore simplistic, representation of male *pai-de-santos* as usurping femaleness.

In *Le candomblé de Bahia*, Roger Bastide continues the pathologizing of queer subjectivities, this time with a spiritual explanation for same-sex desire:

L'enfant, en naissant, vient au monde avec une âme; comme nous l'avons dit, la divinité n'entre au contraire dans le corps que quelques jours après l'accouchement, et elle reste dans un état de latence, tant que l'Orixá ne s'est pas manifesté par une crise de "possession." L'éini est du même sexe que le corps, les garçons ont une âme masculine et les filles une âme féminine; certes, cette règle peut souffrir des exceptions, et c'est ainsi sans doute que l'on explique les cas de pédérastie passive, assez nombreux dans certains terreiros bantous; ce ne sont cependant que des cas pathologiques. (1958, 267)

The newborn child comes into the world with a soul. As we have said, the divinity does not enter into the body until several days after the birth, and it remains in a state of latency since the orixá has not manifested itself through trance possession. The spirit is of the same sex as the body: the boys have a masculine soul and the girls a feminine soul. Of course, this rule has its exceptions, and this is how one explains passive homosexuality, so abundant in certain Bantu *terreiros* [communal and

physical space of Candomblé rituals]; these are no more than pathological cases.

This is a continuation of the pathological language in Landes, which also appears in Ortiz. Nevertheless, it is significant that the issue of the large numbers of queer men in the religion is addressed, and that it is addressed as a
complex relationship between the body and the gendered spiritual self. While
the influence of early sexology à la Karl Heinrich Ulrichs is palpable, particularly in the *anima muliebris virili corpore inclusa* (a female psyche confined in
a male body) concept, the important role of the body prefigures some of the
more advanced work that will only come to the fore some thirty years later.

It is important to remember that Bastide is writing in the late 1950s and
that the very mention of same-sex desire in the following paragraph, even in
its association with vice, is quite avant-gardist for the period:

> Il n'est pas bon de se marier quand on a également, fiancé et fiancée,
> un Orixá masculin, ou un Orixá féminin. Un babalorixá de Recife
> m'expliqua que ces mariages développaient chez les conjoints des
> goûts d'homosexualité et, d'une façon plus générale, des tendances
> vicieuses, tout au moins chez l'un des deux conjoints. (1958, 255)

> It is not good to marry when one has promised oneself to either a male
> or female orixá. A babalorixá in Recife explained that these marriages
> develop among spouses of homosexual tastes and, more generally, of
> vicious tendencies in at least one of the two spouses.

Bastide's *Le candomblé de Bahia* opens the path for the more ambitious work
he publishes only two years later, *The African Religions of Brazil* (1960). In
this work, Bastide continues the pathologization of same-sex desire through
its association with tragedy and compensation for heteronormative romantic failures. In general, same-sex desire is presented as a form of Freudian
stunted development:

> Elemental drives such as eroticism, whether homosexual or hetero-
> sexual (one makes love with the spirits to compensate for disillusion-
> ment in love in real life). Deep torment such as the guilt complex I
> have often observed in analyzing what the spirits say through their
> "media," which is just as likely to stem from an unresolved Oedipus
> complex. (Bastide 1978, 380)

The very title of Rene Ribeiro's 1969 article alerts us to the pathologizing
of same-sex desire in Candomblé. "Personality and the Psychosexual Adjust-

ment of Afro-Brazilian Cult Members" utilizes a developmental model to render same-sex-loving initiates as psychologically maladjusted people:

> Os homossexuais ou as pessoas sexualmente desajustadas podem aderir aos grupos de culto afro-brasileiros por muitas razões, entre elas a companhia feminina, a necessidade de exibirem seus manerismos ou de se identificarem com deuses femininos em grupos dirigidos por homosexuais, ou por homem e mulher austeros, igualmente dedicados ao controle do sobrenatural. (Ribeiro 1969, 217)

> Homosexual or sexually maladjusted people adhere to Afro-Brazilian cult groups for many reasons, including female companionship, the need to display their mannerisms or to identify with female gods in groups directed by homosexuals, or by ascetic men and women, equally dedicated to the control of the supernatural.

Ribeiro's homophobia is presented clearly here. In no uncertain terms, he portrays queer men as maladjusted and as exhibitionists who want to be with women because they want to identify as women. The association of queers with the supernatural resonates with troubling connotations of the occult, dangerous, and hidden. His acknowledgment of the largely queer male leadership is helpful in that it documents the numerical importance of queers in the tradition. In spite of the pejorative comments, Ribeiro's statement regarding queer male initiates' identification with female orixás functions as a building block for the full transcorporeal understanding of the regendered human body in trance communion with the divine. Complementing the queer cross-gender possession of a male initiate by Iansá that Landes presents, Ribeiro presents the important role that the orisha of femininity, vanity, and romantic love has for queer men:

> Oshum [sic], a divindade com uma reputacão mítica de volutuosa, entretanto, foi apontada como santa patrona de apenas um dos homossexuais e de três indivíduos com dificuldade de identificaçao sexual. Era, porém, a divindade secundária de todos os outros homossexuais (como seria de esperar conforme à tradição), mas somente nove dentre 25 indivíduos com dificuldade de identidade sexual ou inadequação sexual e tendências homossexuais tinham-na como deusa "de acompanhamento." (1969, 217)

> However, Oxum, a divinity with a voluptuous mythical reputation, was identified as patron saint of only one of three homosexuals and

individuals with sexual identification difficulties. It was, nevertheless, a secondary divinity of all other homosexuals (as expected according to tradition), but only nine out of twenty-five individuals with difficult sexual identity or sexual inadequacy and homosexual tendencies had her as an accompanying goddess.

As troubling as Ribeiro's presentation of queer men as riddled with psychological inadequacies and difficulties of identification is, his comments on queer men's assumption of Oxum, the female deity of sensuality and beauty, afford us a view of the nonprejudicial climate regarding same-sex desire in Candomblé. Oxum is presented as the tutelary deity of queer men—this in the 1960s. While there were few national laws anywhere in the world protecting queers, there is an Afro-religious community that welcomes and protects its queer members. Black diasporic cultures have paved the way for full inclusion of queer peoples in discourses of the nation, instead of the heavily mediatized representation of homophobic black peoples and enlightened, progressive white, upper-middle-class peoples.

In general, for Ribeiro, same-sex desire is presented as vice, mental illness, and aberrant behavior: "Exibiram graus variados de desequilíbrio emocional e conducta desviada, desde o homossexualismo aberto ou disfarçado a problemas de adequação sexual ai incluído o alcoolismo" (1969, 211; They exhibited varying degrees of emotional imbalance and deviant conduct, from open or disguised homosexuality to sexual inadequacy problems and alcoholism). In a manner reminiscent of Freud and early sexology from the late nineteenth century, he sees same-sex desire in men as stemming from problems with their mothers: "Homosexuais masculinos de classe baixa, criados naquelas famílias por mães solteiras e independentes" (210; lower-class male homosexuals raised in those families by single and independent mothers). In order to compensate for this single and independent mother, queer men seek to "procurar assumir os papéis femininos quando da possessão por divindades femininas" (210; ensure taking on feminine roles through possession by feminine deities). Not only is his pathologizing reminiscent of European philosophies of overbearing mothers and negligent fathers, it also bears a striking similarity to the Moynihan Report, which in the United States attributed black people's subaltern status to an alleged large incidence of single mothers and absent fathers in black families. Here, we see the formula for the normal as being predicated on a discourse of the nuclear family. According to Ribeiro, the inability to transcend the dominance of the single mother prevents them from achieving a normative ideal of manhood, engendering a masculinity suffused with infantile traits: "Mostraram dependência maternal, introversão, imaturidade, egocentrismo; alguns são exibicionistas, narcisistas, com sentimento de culpa, suspeita e timidez. Todos têm grande dificuldade no relacionamento com a imagem feminine" (211; They showed maternal dependency, introversion, immaturity, self-centeredness; some are exhibitionistic, narcissistic, with guilt, suspicion and timidity. All have great difficulty in relating to the female image).

In his discourse, there are strong contradictory desires toward the female image; queer men are attracted to women yet find difficulty with them. According to this narrative, male same-sex desire is presented as an inability to transcend the self, as stunted emotional growth, as arrested psychological development. Moreover, black people and queers are presented as social inferiors through their ascribed inability to pair up, reproduce, and rear offspring according to prescribed dictates.

The pathological description of same-sex desire and its preponderance within Candomblé circles has the effect of pathologizing Candomblé itself by marking it as the religion of the maladjusted, of the psychologically incompetent, and of social outcasts. The problematic implication of such an association is that these religious blacks—presented as racially dis-selected, uncivilized, and culturally infantile—should also foster the natural space for the abject and psychologically immature homosexuals.

The work of Landes, Bastide, and Ribeiro leads to a decade in which the preponderance of queers in Candomblé is presented as a fact, without judgment or analysis. While there is an absence of homophobia on the part of the researchers, there also isn't much to account for the reasons that queers are so present in these religions. This factualization phase is most readily depicted in the work of Leacock and Leacock, who in their 1972 book *Spirits of the Deep: A Study of an Afro-Brazilian Cult* present how there is "a widespread belief, both within and without the Batuque religion, that men who wear ritual costumes and dance in public ceremonies are either effeminate or, in most cases, active homosexuals. In fact, this belief is based on fact—some of the men are indeed homosexuals" (1972, 104). The Leacocks assert that the rumor is in fact true. And, while they attempt to maintain a detached stance toward the topic of same-sex desire, they do present the homophobic view of the larger Brazilian society and the fear of persecution that stems from such homophobia: "There is always concern that the terreiro will become a recognized gathering place for homosexuals and thus liable to public opprobrium and persecution by the police" (Leacock and Leacock 1972, 105).

Erika Bourguignon also acknowledges the great gender fluidity in Candomblé, but shows how Candomblé is not completely immune to this homophobia in greater Brazilian society:

> El ideal brasilero de "macho" está en conflicto con la imagen de una persona que padece la posesión de un espíritu durante el ritual cúltico. En un grupo por lo menos de cultistas, estudiado por estos autores, no se les permitió a los hombres experimentar el trance de posesión. Sin embargo, hay que notar que tanto hombres como mujeres pueden ser poseídos por espíritus masculinos o femeninos. Y parece que no hay objeciones contra el comportamiento masculino por parte de las mujeres que se creen poseídas por espíritus masculinos. (1975, 13)

> The Brazilian ideal of "the macho" conflicts with the image of a person possessed by a spirit during the cultic ritual. In a group of cultists studied by these authors, there were no men allowed to experience trance possession. However, it should be noted that both men and women can be possessed by male or female spirits. And it seems that there are no objections against the masculine behavior of women who believe themselves to be possessed by masculine spirits.

Bourguignon stresses cross-gender possession as a fact and acknowledges the common and unimpeded trance possession of female initiates by masculine deities. But neither Bourguignon nor Landes can tell us what enables these cross-gender possessions. Neither the factualists nor the pathologizers are interested in what accounts for the large numbers of queers in Candomblé. And it is the absence of these questions that sets these two groups apart from the new school of thought on queer sexualities in Candomblé from the 1980s to the present.

Peter Fry inaugurates this new queer scholarship on Candomblé in 1986 with his seminal essay "Male Homosexuality and Spirit Possession in Brazil." Here he condenses many of the passing comments regarding the reasons for the large number of queers in Candomblé, enlightening and elucidating this social phenomenon. The first reason he gives has to do with the singular ability that queers have to invest in relationships outside the constraints of the heteronormative family. This has an effect similar to that of the vows of celibacy in some monastic orders in various religious traditions:

> Pais or mães de santo who are married and maintain ties with their kinship networks, are therefore obliged to divert resources in order to meet their social obligations outside of the cult. Clearly, those cult

FIG. 5.1. Male pai de santo in trance for Obba, female orixá of marriage. Film still from *Dona Flor and Her Two Husbands*, Ancine (Agência Nacional do Cinema).

leaders who are not so encumbered can invest all their energies in social relations which are important in the cult context. Bichas find themselves in this situation. They rarely have children, and almost always maintain only the most tenuous links with their kinship networks. (Fry 1986, 141)

This position as outsiders allows queers an objective perspective on devotees' crises and problems, enabling them to therefore "provide impartial advice and counsel to clients" (Fry 1986, 149). In addition to this noncelibate, yet neomonastic religious space outside the traditional family, queer men have the advantage of being able to transcend gender roles and take over the roles of men and women: "[Queer men] can perform the roles of men and women: [the bicha] is in a category apart, and can use the privilege associated with both the male and the female role" (149).

Fry redeploys some of the essentialistic comments from the "pathologizing" scholarship and presents how "the majority opinion was that the bicha entered the cults either to be with men or else to show off before other bichas" (1986, 145). This can be seen as an exposure of homophobia and as a strategic way in which queers use Candomblé as a sexual marketplace and as a place to advance in status among their peers. The last interpretation that Fry provides for the large number of queers in Candomblé has to do with the performative. Candomblé allows queers to use an intrinsic talent for aesthetic embellishment and performative prowess: "Another interpretation offered for the presence of bichas in the cults was that bichas are more artistic than men and women and therefore better equipped to organize and participate in ritual" (144).

These interpretations provide a certain measure of satisfaction until 1995, when Patricia Birman forces a more nuanced response by asking more precise questions about the relationship between masculinity and homosexuality.

> A questão que não me parecia sufficientemente bem respondida ara a seguinte: haveria alguma razão para vinclar de modo tão freqüente e tão intenso possessão masculina e "homossexualidade"? Quais seriam esses elos e que formas assumiam? E que relação coma possessão? Seria preciso discutir o que se entende por "homossexualidade," por um lado, e por outro, o elo suposto com esse campo religioso específico. (1995, 6)

> The question that did not seem adequately answered was: would there be any reason for the frequent and intense association between masculine possession and homosexuality? What are these links and what forms do they assume? And what is the relationship to possession? One would have to discuss what is meant by "homosexuality," on the one hand, and on the other, the alleged link with that particular religious field.

Birman's question forces us to pay attention to the body and preface the transcorporeal understanding of the body that this present study proposes. Writing about Candomblé within the larger geographical context of the Lusophone Atlantic, James Sweet appears to provide a counterpoint and answer to Birman's question when he writes that

> the African transvestites reveal that the ideal spirit medium is the woman. Indeed, despite the presence of transvestite men as spirit mediums in Zulu society, divination is supposed to be the exclusive preserve of women. And gender exclusivity of spiritual leadership is not at all uncommon across the continent. Thus, the cultural feminization, if not the sexual feminization, of Africa's transvested homosexuals enables them to enter into positions of religious power. (Sweet 1996, 192)

The notion of cultural feminization moves us closer to an understanding of the large number and important role of queer men in Candomblé. There is a ritualized regendering of the body that queerness affords these men, which allows them access to the exclusively female domain of trance possession.

FIG. 5.2. An initiate consults the orixá. Film still from *Dona Flor and Her Two Husbands*, Ancine (Agência Nacional do Cinema).

However, I would like to take Birman's question and Sweet's response to the next level. Is there something about women's bodies in particular that physically or metaphorically makes them better mediums? Is there a commonality in the physicality and the uses of queer men and women's bodies that renders them superior incarnational vessels of the orixás? Answers to these more profound questions have been blocked by the channeling of the matter into transvestism, focusing on clothing, accessorizing, and bodily performance, rather than the philosophical conceptualizations of these bodies in religious rituals and everyday life.

Lindsey Hale in 2001 returns to Oxum's patronage of queer men to further the idea that the opportunity for cross-dressing is the folk explanation for the preponderance of gay men in the religion:

> Informants opined that men in Candomblé are most often gays enjoying the opportunity to dress and act as females and attract new lovers. Not surprisingly, given her image as the epitome of feminine sensuality, it was most often Oxum who was mentioned as the deity these men would portray. (2001, 224)

In contrast to Ribeiro, Hale discusses the role of Oxum but without negative connotations. The idea of Candomblé as sexual marketplace for queers is presented not as troubling but as part of the natural functions that a community offers its members.

But Hale would appear to have taken a step backward when elaborating on the topic, given the fact that, in 1997, the same author had made a more thought-provoking observation regarding the nature of cross-gender possessions:

> Father Gerônimo, a youngish-to-middle-aged man, works through the body of an elderly woman; Grandmother Catherine, who is very old indeed, is received by a man in his late thirties. In both cases, the juxtaposition of spirit and medium gender identities has strategic implications for the practical work of consulting: Gerônimo's masculinity mediates between women and their troublesome husbands; femininity, on the other hand, constitutes a bridge between Catherine's male medium and the women who seek her counsel, effacing what would otherwise be constraining impediments of shame and embarrassment in discussing intimate matters with a man. (1997, 405)

The multiply gendered body of the medium enables distancing, objectivity, and perspective that facilitates empathizing with and advising clients seeking guidance. The significance of Hale's observation goes beyond this, for here he hints at the fact that it is the identitarian difference between the medium and the spirit which legitimates the authenticity of the trance possession event. The differences in age, gender, and race between medium and spirit emphasize the other-bodied nature of the symbiosis and lend credibility to the trance. One may also see how the multiply identitarian trance would emblematize an idealized unity, effect a type of gendered/classed/aged/raced reconciliation that can speak from a putatively objective and therefore neutral guiding perspective. Hale is to be commended for the thought-provoking anecdote of this early article, even if his work loses steam later.

But if Hale appears to be losing sophistication as a more interesting observation is presented in his earlier work, Kulick in 1998 publishes what amounts to a non sequitur on the matter of transvestism in Candomblé. Against all the scholarship here elaborated, he rejects the notion that the transvestites of Salvador, known as travestis, play a strong role in Candomblé:

> In any case, because the assertion that the majority of Salvador's travestis are devotees of candomblé risks being repeated and disseminated as fact, I wish to clearly state here that the overwhelming majority of travestis in Salvador maintain *no* active involvement in candomblé *terreiros* and they cannot be considered "devotees" of candomblé in anything but the very weakest sense of the word.

Like a great percentage of the population in Salvador, the majority of travestis do believe in the power of the candomblé saints . . . [and] use Candomblé instrumentally. . . . But few travestis know *why* they do these things (they only know that they should do them to effect desired changes). And no travesti . . . regularly participates in candomblé *terreiros*. (Kulick 1998, 247)

This work does not fit in the overall trajectory of scholarship. This is an example of work that, while excelling in its data gathering and exegesis, is not informed and contextualized within a scholarly tradition on the topic. The lack of knowledge regarding the existence of a tradition of queer Candomblé scholarship, even among scholars of gender and religion, makes this study highly dubious. One wonders how it is possible to write a book about Salvador, the center of African culture in Brazil, and relegate the only discussion on Candomblé to a defensively toned footnote.

Matory, in 2005, elaborates his discussion on transvestism to a high point when he invokes the body through the language of sexuality and pushes the conversation to a more sophisticated level:

I have never heard any West African òrìsá priest speak of himself or his fellow priests as anything like a "homosexual" or as engaging in same-sex intercourse. I argue simply that the Afro-Brazilians have reinterpreted West African metaphors of spirit possession in the light of Brazilian gender categories. For many Brazilians in the 1930s and now, submission of a god's agency has seemed analogous to sexual "passivity," or the experience of being penetrated during intercourse. In other words, to Brazilians, a physically mountable man seems highly qualified, in a symbolic sense, to be mounted spiritually. (2005a, 212)

It is important to note here how Matory acknowledges the culturally constructed idea of same-sex desire and does not fall into the trap of homogenizing and globalizing from a First World perspective. It is noteworthy that he does not see the sartorial and performative disengagement between sex and gender as necessarily implying a non-heteronormative sexuality. His idea of New World reinterpretation is consistent with the discourse of creolization and the forestalling of a full discussion of same-sex desire in the African continent creates a discursive opening that allows this present study its raison d'être.[1] His is a sophisticated argument because in his insistence on the body, his argument hints at transcorporeality. So does Johnson, in passing, when he states that the ideal leader of a Candomblé terreiro is, at least in the important Ketu lineage, a subnation of Nagô (Yoruba-based) Candomblé, a post-menopausal woman, hence doubly cool. If the leader is male, he is often, though not always, openly gay. Regardless of actual gender, he or she occupies a structurally female position. (2002, 44)

I take Johnson's statement on the body one step further by postulating that, in fact, it is not the bodies of women which represent the ideal medium and that neither do queer men seek to emulate feminine bodies in ritual. The sacred body is the receptacular body, which both the female and masculine receptive bodies represent in sexual copulation and, by extension, in trance possession by a spirit.

The present study advances Johnson's work by positing that the body of the initiate is not so much penetrable as receptacular, for only the hermetic can be penetrated, and the Afro-diasporic body is concave in the way a saddle or a basket is concave and invites mountings and replenishings. In the chronology of queer Candomblé scholarship, the pathologizing period (1940–69) gives way to one dominated by factualization (1970s), which leads to a phase of elucidation (1980s–early 2000s). I propose that the next phase is transcorporeal, because it views the Afro-diasporic body as an open vessel transporting hosts, which are multiple, external, and removable.

Dona Flor e seus dois maridos

The literary and filmic presentations of Candomblé bear a complex relationship to this social science research chronology. Jorge Amado addressed Candomblé themes in many of his works, but often with a great deal of ambivalence, given his own participation in Candomblé ceremonies and his attempt to maintain what he perceived to be a professional distance to the religious themes he elaborated in his Bahian novels:

When Jorge Amado returns to Salvador as the locale for his next books, he exhibits a new but natural familiarity with Afro-Brazilian culture. Since at least 1944 he had been an *Oga* (a semi-administrative position) in the *candomblé* of Joãozinho da Goméia, and in 1959 he received the honorary post of *Oba* in the Candomblé Apo Afônjá. (Hamilton 1967, 248)

Je suis lié au candomblé pour des raisons de lutte contre le racisme et non pour des raisons religieuses. Je ne suis pas un spécialiste, simplement je te donne mon opinion. Je ne veux pas parler d'une chose que je ne connais pas, de toute ma vie je n'ai pas été à plus de dix ceremonies d'umbanda. (Raillard 1990, 79)

I am linked to Candomblé through the struggle against racism and not for religious reasons. I'm not a specialist; I'm just giving you my opinion. I do not want to talk about things that I do not know. In all my life I have not been to more than ten Umbanda ceremonies.

Jorge Amado's novel *Dona Flor e seus dois maridos* fits thematically in the second factualizing phase, even though it was published in 1966 during the pathologizing period. Moreover, it hints at the third, particularly in the ensuing film rendition by Bruno Barreto (1976). Taking this into account allows us to see how, in the case of Candomblé, cultural production in literature and film influences and foreshadows social science research.

Both the textual and cinematographic narratives of *Dona Flor* contain a strong Candomblé theme that is intricately bound to a non-heteronormative ethos. Each of the main characters stands for a Candomblé divinity. Teodoro is Oxalá, syncretized with Nosso Senhor de Bomfim. His name, "God lover," is symbolic of his piety, and the whiteness of his pharmacist garb reflects the colors of both Oxalá and Bomfim. The foods offered to Oxalá should not contain any spices, an important fact given the semantic associations between eating and sex in Brazilian Portuguese through the verb *comer*:

It is in the bill of fare of the *orixás* (*Dona Flor*, 395–96) that the eating-sex metaphor is the most explicitly used to polarize the personal and class features of the two spouses. Oxalá's aversion to all condiments and seasonings is clearly intended to be read as denoting the monotony and insipidness of Teodoro's sexual performance. Exu's lack of food biases is likewise meant to be a statement of Vadinho's sexual promiscuity. The social implications are obvious. Dietary and sexual contrasts may be regarded as paradigmatic of the intolerance/tolerance or regimentation/freedom oppositions that the novelist identifies with the middle-class-lower-class dichotomy. (Chamberlain 1990, 69)

The bland foods imply that Teodoro is sexually awkward and boring in bed: his amorous inadequacies contrast sharply with Dona Flor's oversexed first husband, Vadinho:

Dona Flor is married to that breed of charming scoundrel who, apart from being a constant source of problems for her, is able to provide the most exciting—and tender—love making she has ever experienced. . . . Dr. Teodoro Madureira is everything that Vadinho was not: responsible, mature and—unfortunately—essentially boring. (Ferrera-Pena 1987, 1382)

In fact, Vadinho is an incarnation of Exu. While this may appear to be something that was disclosed by the author, in reality, Amado only tells us that Exu was Vadinho's tutelary deity. Seeing how the personalities of the orixá and the person merge helps to make the argument for transcorporeality, for it is not just that the orixá represents or guides the character: the spirit communes with the living through a type of trance possession that is more than just a ceremonial and punctual event but is a pervasive condition that permeates all aspects of the daily life of those around Vadinho-as-Exu. Chamberlain eloquently captures the distinction between Vadinho and Teodoro:

Menos hermética—e talvez por isso mesmo mais efetiva—é a presença do sobrenatural afro-brasileiro em Dona Flor. Aquí os dois maridos relacionam-se, um e outro, com santos padroeiros iourbanos. O apolíneo Teodoro, segundo cônjuge de Flor, é protegido por Oxalá, que na Bahia se sincretiza com Nosso Senhor do Bonfim, Jesus Cristo. O dionisíaco Vadinho, por outro lado, é defendido pro Exu, o travesso orixá de orientaçao/desorientaçao, que muitos crentes identificam con Satanás. (1985, 720)

Less hermetic—and perhaps therefore more effective—is the presence of the Afro-Brazilian supernatural in Dona Flor. Here the two husbands relate to one another through Yorùbá patron saints. The Apollonian Teodoro, Flor's second spouse, is protected by Oxalá, who in Bahia is syncretized with Our Lord of Bonfim, Jesus Christ. The Dionysian Vadinho, on the other hand, is protected by Exu, the mischievous deity of orientation/disorientation, whom many believers identify with Satan.

Exu's colors are red and black, the latter color emblematizing a particular type of racialized blackness. Exu is omnivorous in his gastronomic and sexual appetites, preferring spicy food and sex. He is a trickster, inhabiting liminal zones, such as that between life and death, with great ease. Let us take note of how the following passage conveys how Vadinho embodies this liminality, which is the hallmark of Exu:

> Rodopiava em meio ao bloco, sapateava em frente à mulata, avançava para ela em floreios e umbigadas, quando de súbito, soltou uma espécie de ronco surdo, vacilou nas pernas, adernou de um lado, rolou no chão, botando uma baba amarela pela bôca onde o esgar da morte não conseguia apagar de todo o satisfeito sorriso do folião definitivo que êle fôra. (Amado 1966, 21)

> He whirled in the middle of the group, stomped in front of the mulatta, approached her in flourishes and belly-bumps, then suddenly gave a kind of hoarse moan, wobbled from side to side, and fell to the ground, a yellow slobber drooling from his mouth of which the grimace of death could not wholly extinguish the fatuous smile of the complete faker he had always been. (1969, 5–6)

A sexual dance, which could have led to the conception of life, leads, paradoxically, to the death of Vadinho. His moan was both one of climactic ecstasy and giving up the ghost. The smile on the corpse mocks the pain of death. Barreto's superb film rendition captures the spirit of the text and of the orixá when he presents Vadinho dancing with the mixed-race woman—whose racially hybrid status marks her as yet another border crosser—while he is dressed as a woman and wearing a large phallus under his skirt. Bastide presents the phallus as the symbol of Exu, which has led to his troubling reinterpretation in Christian mythology: "Le phallus d'Éxú, autant que ses cornes, nous paraît donc responsable de son identification brésilienne avec le démon" (1958, 190; Exu's phallus as well as his horns appear to be responsible for his Brazilian identification with the devil). This questionable demonic association pervades the representation of Exu:

> In the backyard of many residences or on the exterior of business establishments a cult priestess has "seated" Exu, the demigod messenger of the Yorubas. His presence, often marked by a black devil-like figure (sometimes two, one male and the other female) fashioned in cast iron, protects the residents or personnel from evil. . . . Believers frequently leave these offerings at intersections, Exu's favorite haunt, for purposes of revenge or to win the attentions of a recalcitrant lover. The messenger of the gods can be induced with the proper offering to carry out diabolical acts. (Hamilton 1970, 361–62)

This erroneous analogy to the Christian devil is one that Amado perpetu-
ates in his narrative when the Candomblé priest reads the oracle to determine how to appease the visiting specter of Vadinho:

> Dizem ter sido o Asobá Didi quem fêz o jogo para o finado e os búzios
> por três vêzes confirmaram: o santo de Vadinho era Exu e nenhum
> outro. Se Exu é o diabo, como consta por aí? Talvez Lúcifer, o anjo
> decaído, o rebelde que enfrentou a lei e se vestiu de fogo.
>
> Comida de Exu é tudo quanto a bôca prova e come, mas bebida é
> uma só, a cachaça pura. Nas encruzilhadas exu aguarda sentado sôbre
> a noite para tomar o caminho mais difícil, o mais estreito e complicado,
> o mau caminho no dizer gereal, pos Exu só quer saber de reinação.
>
> Exu mais reinador o de Vadinho. (1966, 421)

> They says [sic] it was Asobá Didi who cast the shells for the departed,
> and three times they came up with the same answer: Vadinho's pa-
> tron deity was Exu and no other. If Exu is the devil, how did he get in
> there? Perhaps Lucifer, the fallen angel, the rebel who defied the law
> and cloaked himself in fire.
>
> Exu eats anything in the way of food, but he drinks only one thing:
> straight rum. At the crossroads Exu waits sitting upon the night to take
> the most difficult road, the narrowest, the most winding, the bad road,
> it is generally held, for all Exu wants is to frolic, to make mischief.
>
> Exu the great mischief-maker, Vadinho's patron deity. (1969, 409–10)

Amado's rearticulation of the Exu-devil association speaks to his capitaliz-
ing on folk beliefs when he himself knew of the impossibility of fully analogizing both religious personae. Amado was well aware of Exu's attributes
since he had a personal and professional identification with Exu: "o logotipo dos livros de Jorge Amado é um Exu, muito serelepe, desenhado por Carybé, e *Exu* é também o nome da revista editada pela Casa de Cultura Jorge
Amado" (Seljan 1999, 315; the logo on Jorge Amado's books was an Exu, very
cute, designed by Carybé. *Exu* is also the name of the journal edited by Casa
de Cultura Jorge Amado). Also, "Exu era o logotipo de Jorge Amado, ape-
recendo na contracapa dos livros é no papel timbrado de sua correspondência"
(Seltzer Goldstein 2000, 55; Exu was Jorge Amado's logo, appearing on the
back cover of his books and on his stationery).

The association between Vadinho and Exu goes beyond that of a tutelary deity but encompasses a full identification between orixá and character. When Dona Flor feels compelled to seek assistance from a Candomblé

FIG. 5.3. Jorge Amado is transcorporeally identified with his namesake saint São Jorge, here syncretized with Santiago Matamouros since both saints are hunting knights on horseback. This slayer of dragons and Moors is in turn interpreted in Candomblé as the warrior orixá Ogum. Photographer Pierre Verger references trance possession in the purposeful mounting of the saint atop the head of the somnolent, entranced author of *Dona Flor*. The orixá, in its guise as Catholic saint, rides the initiate as horse, with whom it merges. Their union liquidates the monster of egoic conscious-ness, bringing the hybrid divine-human construct into a full awareness of Being. Photograph by Pierre Verger. Used by permission of Fundação Pierre Verger.

priest to perform a ritual to ward off the spirit of Vadinho, it is the spirit of Exu who is invoked, not to tell his godchild to stay away but to address Exu directly:

> Para lhe garantir tranquilidade, livrá-la de ôlho-mau, de qualquer doença, das ameaças do egun inconformado a atraí-la para sua morte, dona Flor devia cumprir obrigação de monta, não um despacho simples,

não ebó qualquer. Exu, cabeça do finado, se pusera em contra, em pé de guerra. Dionísia dissera ao ojé para não medir despesas. (Amado 1966, 510)

To assure her tranquility, protect her from the evil eye, from any illness, from the menace of the spirit of the dead, which was dissatisfied at not taking her to her death, Dona Flor had to fulfill a costly vow, not a simple charm, an insignificant hex. Exu the guiding spirit of the dead man, was opposed, and was on a war footing. Dionísia had told the witch-doctor not to take expense into account. (1969, 494)

While Vadinho and Teodoro can readily be associated with orixás, the same cannot be said for Dona Flor, who has traditionally been studied as a referent for human agency vis-à-vis the supernatural powers of divine beings. However, upon closer inspection, we see that Dona Flor, too, is strongly syncretized with a deity worshiped in Afro-Brazilian religions. Through her liminality Dona Flor is an Exua, a particular female version of Exu. She is between men and is of mixed race. She displays vacillation and indecision regarding her choice of husbands. In the end, her comfort in ambiguity clearly marks her as a mistress of the crossroads. Her refusal to make a choice between a marriage of love and a marriage of convenience presents her as being beyond moral binaries. Like Exu, she is fickle and capriciously changes her mind at the last minute, when she decides to undo a spell that would have sent Vadinho to the underworld and makes a space for him in the same bed she shares with her living husband:

Vadinho is saved from being annihilated by the rites of the Macumbistas only by Flor's anguished declaration of love. Amado has presented a case of true love in Flor and Vadinho's relationship. It is a love that can conquer even death. Vadinho's possession of Flor is complete. First as a virgin, and then again as a woman married to another man, Flor cannot deny her need for Vadinho. (Lowe 1969, 81)

Dona Flor's control over the various ritually gendered aspects of funerary rites speaks to her masculinization and sacramental androgyny. Mikelle Smith Omari-Tunkara reminds us that the rituals and art forms associated with death in candomblé Nagô are broadly divided into male and female categories: the Àxèxè as funerary, burial, female, occasional, and caring and the Egún as ancestor, lineage, stable, and male (2005, 109). Moreover, Dona Flor's control over them articulates a reinvigoration of tradition: "The funerary rites thus comprise the breaking of bonds and the liberation of the spiritual elements that constitute a human being (Prandi 2008, 441). There is a disturbing decline in the importance of funerary rites in Brazilian Candomblé that threatens to break the ritual circularity of life cycles (Prandi 2008, 445). Her control over both realms, the heaven of Bonfim-Teodoro and the underworld of Exu-devil-Vadinho displays her character as a gatekeeper between the terrestrial and the otherworldly, the key trait of Exu in its ancestral Yorùbá name: Eshu-Elegbara. According to Lowe, she embodies maleness and femininity, further hybridizing her character: "Flor's 'contrasexuality' (her male *animus*) emerges in the course of her development as a character and empowers her to take the dominant, decision-making role in defining her relationship with her two husbands" (2001, 126). The trickster quality of Exu is evident in her comic and erotic solution to have her cake and eat it too by accepting a duality outside the conventions of heteronormativity. When Dionísia asks Dona Flor if the ghost has stopped bothering her, "Dona Flor sorriu com embaraço e disse:—Ou eu deixei de me assombrar. Já não preciso de mais nada" (Amado 1966, 510). "Trying to hide her embarrassment, Dona Flor smiled and said: 'Or I got over my fright. I don't need anything more'" (1969, 495).

Moreover, in her role as an Exua, Dona Flor becomes an emblem of Brazilian creolization. Even though the text and certainly the movie appear to evacuate racialized blackness, symbolically, ethnicity is addressed through the color and syncretic associations of Exu (black, demon) and Oxalá (white, savior). Flor's choosing not to choose between the two husbands is as much a creolization of beliefs as it is a womanist integration of sexuality and wifeliness and an emblematizing of the Brazilian ideal of racial reconciliation. Contrast this with the US version of the movie, *Kiss Me Goodbye*, in which Sally Field does choose one lover over the other.

Dona Flor is a type of female Exu or Exua, widely worshiped in Kimbanda, a specialized religious tradition devoted to Exus. In *The Taste of Blood: Spirit Possession in Brazilian Candomblé*, James William Wafer narrates the myth of a particular Exua called Maria Padilha, whose associations with Dona Flor warrant our attention. A woman has two daughters who do not get along. Maria Padilha is the beautiful older sister of Pomba Gira. She is in charge of household tasks while Pomba Gira is spoiled by gifts and affection, the difference creating friction between the two. At age seven, their brother Manuel feels sexually attracted to Maria Padilha and at fourteen rapes her, and she vows to take revenge on her brother. Once grown, Maria Padilha marries a king and acquires wealth through marriage. She then leaves her husband to become a prostitute, seduces her brother, stabs him seven times, and drinks his blood. Maria Padilha is in turn killed by her brother's lover, rules over hell, and is governess of brothels. She returns from the dead to kill her sister, Pomba Gira. Both Maria Padilha and Pomba Gira are Exuas, and their brother Manuel has come to be known as an Exu called Sete Facadas. In this myth, Tranca Rua often appears as well, as one of the seven husbands of Maria Padilha (Wafer 1991, 11–13). According to Pressel:

> The exu and his feminine counterpart, the pombagira . . . have led es-
> pecially wicked lives. Since they failed to make it to heaven, they are
> usually said to be without "light." The spirits of persons who commit
> suicide automatically become *exus*. The *exus* spend much of their time
> in cemeteries, which are regarded as particularly dangerous places for
> mediums with undeveloped spiritual abilities. (1977, 337)

While the sweet and light Dona Flor may seem light years away from the twisted and wretched Maria Padilha, they are both torn by their attachment to two men, one a respectable man and the other an Exu. Before crafting the clever ending of his story, Amado had intended for the story to end with Dona Flor descending to the underworld with Vadinho:

> Amado is on record that he had planned a different ending for Dona
> Flor. In the first, contemplated ending, Amado had Flor despairing
> over giving herself back to Vadinho and then vanishing with him
> under the *candomblé* spell which she had initiated. . . . According to
> the author, however, Flor "rebelled" and took over, calling Vadinho
> back and thus creating a richly symbolic tale that has seduced readers
> all over the world. (Lowe 2001, 126–27)

In spite of its transformed, conciliatory ending, the story line of Dona Flor retains many aspects of the myth of Maria Padilha in Dona Flor's liminality. Most notably, the Exu and Exua qualities of the Maria Padilha myth survive strongly in the Dona Flor text, which can be most palpably felt in the concern that both narratives have for the privileging of the non-heteronormative.

The myth of Maria Padilha marks the worship of Exus in Candomblé, and particularly in Kimbanda, as the realm of the non-heteronormative. The following list of themes serves as ample evidence of the counterdiscursive element of the myth: single motherhood, illegitimacy, family discord, poly-andry, incest, rape, prostitution, nonreproductive sexuality, revenge, murder, and symbolic reverse rape by a woman of a man by stabbing. While the myth does not speak directly of same-sex desire, the strong non-heteronormative discourse allows for the receptivity of queers in these religious communities. And the association between queers and Kimbanda is evident in the history of this religious tradition. In Brazil, there are records of this association as early as the colonial period. *The Denunciations of Bahia* (1591–93) documents how Francisco Manicongo—a black slave or freedman and a cobbler's apprentice— was accused by the Inquisition in Brazil of refusing to wear proper masculine attire, wearing women's clothes and/or a type of loincloth allegedly associated with gender-variant males engaging in same-sex eroticism. He is called a *jimbandaa*, "passive sodomite" in the language of Angola and Congo. The word "jimbandaa" engenders kimbanda, a female or gender-variant male shaman, according to various sources: "Kimbandas are mostly women, but also gender-diverse, homoerotically inclined males or transgender transsexual women" (Conner and Sparks 2004, 43). Also, "the term kimbanda has survived in Brazil as Quimbanda, an African-Brazilian spiritual tradition associated with sorcery. Its association with sexual and/or gender complexity seems to have been forgotten or suppressed" (Conner and Sparks 2004, 45). Quimbandas were passive homosexuals, transvestites, berdaches, high priests of sacrifice in Angola, where they inhabited a category of sexually dissident male sorcerers who lived as women and were persecuted by the Portuguese Inquisition in Africa, Portugal, and Brazil (Mott 2007, 78). Therefore, we can boldly assert that the very name of the religion in the Americas whose main worship is that of the Exus is founded on queerness.

Dona Flor e seus dois maridos is a novel in which transvestism, homoeroticism, and androgyny play an important role, lending the narrative a strong non-heteronormative aspect. The novel begins with cross-dressing. The very first sentence of the text reads,

> Vadinho o primeiro marido de Dona Flor, moreu num domingo de carnaval, pela manhã, quando, fantasiado de baianas, sambava num bloco, na maior animação, no Largo Dois de Julho, não longe de sua casa. Não pertencia ao bloco, acabara de nêle misturar-se, em companhia de mais quatro amigos, todos com traje de baiana. (Amado 1966, 21)

> Vadinho, Dona Flor's first husband, died one Sunday of Carnival, in the morning, when, dressed up like a Bahian woman, he was dancing the samba, with the greatest enthusiasm, in the Dois de Julho Square, not far from his house. He did not belong to the group—he had just joined it, in the company of four of his friends, all masquerading as *bahianas*. (1969, 5)

FIG. 5.4. Transcorporeality in the carnivalesque. Film still from *Dona Flor and Her Two Husbands*, Ancine (Agência Nacional do Cinema).

This begins the novel with the strong theme of Exu as master of the crossroads, with Vadinho as his human avatar falling dead as he dances. The commingling of male and female attire and bodily performance emphasizes Exu-Vadinho's personality as a border crosser. Amado takes great pains, however, to explain that Vadinho and the other revelers' cross-dressing is pure carnivalesque play with no implications whatsoever in terms of sexual behavior:

> O fato de estarem fantasiados de baiana não deve levar a maliciar-se sôbre os cinco rapazes, todos êles de macheza comprovada. Vestiam-se de baiana para melhor brincar, por farsa e molecagem, e não por tendência ao efeminado, as suspeitas esquisitices. Não havia chibungo entre êles, benza Deus. (1966, 24)

> The fact that they were wearing the typical dress of the Bahian women should not give rise to any doubts about the five friends' masculinity. They had dressed up in that fashion the better to fool around, to enjoy themselves and have fun, not because of any deviant inclinations laying them open to suspicion. There was not a faggot in the whole lot, praise to God. (1969, 7)

The assertion of heterosexuality is what seems carnivalesque and comical here, not the cross-dressing. There is great anxiety in the passage regarding the presentation of transvestism, which would appear to be Amado's way of providing some sort of retraction or apologia that would allow the por-

FIG. 5.5. Cross-dressed Vadinho channels phallic Exu. Film still from *Dona Flor and Her Two Husbands*, Ancine (Agência Nacional do Cinema).

trayal of a gender-transcending performance. In this sense, *Dona Flor e seus dois maridos* manages to articulate the language of the pathologizing school, while at the same time promoting a more open and eventually less biased presentation of dissident gender identifications. The cross-dressing acquires an added layer of complexity with Vadinho's performative phallus:

> Vadinho, inclusive, amarrara, sob a anágua branca e engomada, enorme raiz de mandioca e, a cada passo, suspendia as saias e exibia o troféu descomunal e pornográfico, fazendo as mulheres esconderem nas mãos o rosto e o riso, com maliciosa vergonha. Agora a raiz pendia abandonada sôbre a coxa descoberta e não fazia ninguém rir. Um dos amigos veio e a desatou da cintura de Vadinho. Mas nem assim o defunto ficou decente e recatado. (Amado 1966, 24)

> Vadinho had even tied under his white starched petticoat a huge cassava tuber, and at every step he raised his skirts and displayed the outsized, pornographic trophy, causing the women to cover their faces with their hands and let out malicious giggles. Now the tuber hung over his bared hip and elicited no laughter. One of his friends noticed it and untied it from Vadinho's waist. But not even so did the dead man look decent and modest. (1969, 7–8)

In both Africa and the Americas, Exu is often associated with the phallus, and his devotees and mediums, male and female, can often be seen wearing wooden or tuberous appendages in the shape of a penis for the purposes of simulating a sexual play that both contrasts with and complements that other aspect of Exu: death. The performative sexual play of Exu functions as a form of comic relief for the anxiety elicited by his role as grim reaper. His transcending of binarisms—joy/sorrow, life/death, and terrestrial/underworld—acquires a more nuanced aspect in his performative gender. By exaggerating femininity through the folkloric bahiana dress and masculinity with an oversized phallus, and by commingling both of these extravagantly gendered depictions in one body, Exu in Vadinho helps to deconstruct heteronormativity and the long list of signifying binarisms that are underpinned by this construction.

The non-heteronormative element of Dona Flor is also evident in a strong subtextual and coded homoerotic desire between Vadinho and Teodoro. There are intimations of a psychosexual ménage à trois relationship that is homosocial in the way in which Eve Sedgwick redeploys René Girard's notion of triangulated relationships. Borrowing the title of Eve Sedgwick's groundbreaking work, in bed and in life, Dona Flor is "between men":

> Êle também é teu marido, tem tanto direito quanto eu. Um bom sujeito êsse teu segundo, cada vez gosto mais dêle. . . . Aliás, quando cheguei, te avisei que a gente ia se dar bem, os três. . . .
> —Vadinho!
> —O que é, meu bem?
> —Você não se importa que eu te ponha chifres com Teodoro?
> —Chifres?—passou a mão na testa lívida—Não, não dá para nascer chifres. Eu e êle estamos empatados, meu bem, os dois temos direito, ambos casamos no padre e no juiz, não foi? (Amado 1966, 520)

> "He is your husband, too, he has as much right as I. He's a good fellow, I like him better all the time. Besides, remember when I got here I told you that we were going to get along well, the three of us. . . ." "Vadinho! You don't mind my putting horns on you with Teodoro?"

> He ran his hand over his livid head. "Horns? No, there are no horns involved in this. He and I are tied, babe: we both have our rights; we were both married by priest and justice of the peace, weren't we?" (1969, 505)

The mockery of church and state heteronormative nuptial ceremonies operates through bigamy and same-sex desire. This non-heteronormative aspect of

FIG. 5.6. Cross-dressed phallic Vadinho moves away from the golden-attired female dancer channeling Oxum in order to perform a lascivious homoerotic dance with a short-statured harlequin. Film still from *Dona Flor and Her Two Husbands*, Ancine (Agência Nacional do Cinema).

the novel is underpinned through the gender fluidity of Candomblé, made possible through the imagining of the idealized human body as a fruit that is externally seeded, as in the case of the *castanha de caju*. This corporeal externality and receptacularity then enhance Exu's role as the paradigmatic boundary transgressor in the pantheon of Candomblé deities. Regarding Exu's gender transgressions, Henry Louis Gates writes,

> The various figures of Esu provide endless, fascinating references to the critic's role in interpretation and to the nature of interpretation itself. Esu, like interpretation, is ageless. Despite the fact that I have referred to him in the masculine, Esu is also genderless, or of dual gender, as recorded Yoruba and Fon myths suggest, despite his remarkable penis feats. (1988, 29)

In addition to Exu, Jorge Amado presents a few other Candomblé orixás as androgynous: "Yemajá tôda de azul vestida, longos cabelos de espuma e caranguejos. No rabo da prata três sexos lhe nasceram, um branco de algas, outro de verde limo, o terceiro de polvos negros" (1966, 531). "Yemanjá, dressed all in blue, with her long hair of foam and crabs. Her tail of silver held three different sexes, one white of seaweed, the other scum green, the third of black powders" (1969, 515).

FIG. 5.7. The transcorporeal threesome. Film still from *Dona Flor and Her Two Husbands*, Ancine (Agência Nacional do Cinema).

Cobra imensa, Oxumarê vinha nas côres do arco iris, macho e fêmea ao mesmo tempo. Coberto de serpentes, a cascavel e a jararaca, a coral e a víbora, e seguido por cinco batalhões de hermafroditas. Empurraram Vadinho por uma ponta do arco-íris, era um macho retado quando entrou, saiu sestrosa rapariga, donzela derretida. Com seu tridente Exu desfez o arco-íris. Oxumarê enfiou o rabo pela bôca, anel e enigma. (Amado 1966, 531)

In the form of [a] huge snake, Oxumaré displayed the colors of the rainbow, male and female at the same time. Covered with snakes, the rattlesnake and the pit viper, the coral snake and the adder, and followed by five battalions of hermaphrodites. They caught Vadinho up in one tip of the rainbow; he was a male in all his masculinity when he entered; he emerged a timorous female, a wilting maiden. With his trident, Exu dissolved the rainbow. Oxumaré put its tail in its mouth, ring and enigma. (1969, 515–16)

The following extended quote of the exchange between Dona Flor and Babalaô Didi is important given the treatment that film director Bruno Barreto gives it in the film version of *Dona Flor*:

Um negro alto e magro, perfil agudo, face enigmática, ainda relativamente jovem, ouvido com atenção e respeito por mecânicos e choferes do ponto de táxis,—ao saber a identidade de dona Flor e o motivo dessa compra de flôres, dela se aproximou a lhe solicitar algumas de empréstimo e por um momento apenas. Um pouco surprêsa, donha Flor o satisfez, estendendo-lhe o colorido ramalhete onde êle próprio escolheu, num ciuidado ritual, três cravos amarelos e quatro saudades roxas; quem seria êsse homem e por que tomava dessas poucas flôres?

Do bôlso do paletó extraiu um fio trançado de palha da costa, um mokan, com êle amarrando cravos e saudades num pequeno buquê e dando um nó.

—Desamarre quando arriar na cova Vadinho. É para o egun dêle se aquietar.—e disse em nagô, diminuindo a voz:—Aku abó!

Eis que o negro era o babalaô Didi, zelador da casa de Ossain, mago de Ifá; e só passando muito tempo dona Flor aprenderia seu nome e seus podêderes, sua fama de adivinho, seu pôsto de Korikoê Ulukó-tum no terreiro dos eguns, an Amoreira. (Amado 1966, 216–17)

A tall, lean Negro with a sharply etched profile, an enigmatic expression, still relatively young, who was listened to with attention and respect by the mechanics and chauffeurs of the taxi stand, on learning who Dona Flor was and the reason for the purchase of the flowers, came over to her and asked her to lend a few of them to him for a moment. Somewhat surprised, Dona Flor did as he asked, holding out the bright bunch from which he himself selected, with religious care, three yellow carnations and four red scabiosas. Who could this man be and what did he want with those few flowers?

From the pocket of his coat he pulled a braided thread of African straw, a mokan, tying the carnations and scabiosas into a small bouquet with it, and making a knot.

"Untie them when you put them on Vadinho's grave. It's to propitiate his patron saint," and he added in Yoruba, lowering his voice: "Aku abó!"

This Negro was the babalão Didi, caretaker of the shrine of Ossain, a sorcerer of Ifá; and it was only much later that Dona Flor learned his name and his powers, his reputation as a fortuneteller, his post of *Korikoê Olokótum* at the *candomblé* center in Armoreira. (1969, 205–6)

Baretto switched the babalaô from male to female to make the point of gender fluidity in Candomblé and, as shorthand, given the time constraints of the film, for the transcorporeal, spiritually receptacular nature of the Afro-diasporic body.[2] The only other black character in the film (Dona Flor is a

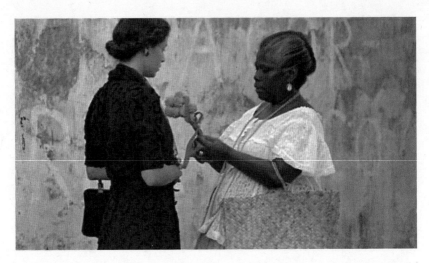

FIG. 5.8. Dona Flor receives an amulet from a Candomblé initiate who is regendered in her transmutation from novelistic to filmic character. Film still from *Dona Flor and Her Two Husbands*, Ancine (Agência Nacional do Cinema).

mulatta, Vadinho a blond, and Teodoro belongs to the Portuguese-descended elite of Brazil) is also strongly trans-identified with respect to gender and spirituality. The male babalaô who performs the ceremony is surrounded by female *filhas-de-santo* and is wearing the female garments of the orixá of marriage Obba. As a result, both the novel and the film deliver a strong non-heteronormative message in what would superficially appear to be a narrative of heterosexual lust.

The androgynous representations of Yemanjá and Oxumarê work with the cross-gendered aspect of Exu to lend Dona Flor's narrative a strong non-heteronormative discourse. In fact, Exu is the master transgressor of norms. This quality can be traced to one of the most important myths about him: "the Carnivalesque essence inherent in the myth of Exu is only complete when we examine the celebration of Odun-Elegba . . . [in which] the grotesque 'bodies forth' the cosmos" (Abodunrin 1996, 59). In this myth, Exu disagrees with Oludumaré, the supreme deity, for investing the power of creation in Obatalá, the deity of creation. Exu places a gourd of palm wine in front of Obatalá's hut—a drink that, after a hard day of creating, he consumes. While drunk, Obatalá creates the deformed, the crippled, the blind, the albino, in short, the Other. Therefore, the nonnormative owes its existence to Exu.

This transgression of sexual and identitarian normativity is open to same-sex desire. This non-heteronormativity is further underscored by the homosocial aspect of the triangular love relationship of the narrative and the transvestism of Exu-Vadinho. This places the novel thematically in the elucidating phase of research in spite of its chronological place within the pathologizing phase. In the way in which fiction predates and prefigures critical research, we can witness the avant-gardist symbiotic relationship between literature and cultural studies work in Afro-diasporic cultural production.

TRANSATLANTIC WATERS OF OXALÁ

Pierre Verger, Mário de Andrade, and Candomblé in Europe

The epilogue of *Macunaíma* (1928), Mário de Andrade's celebrated novel narrating the national odyssey of a mythical and magical Brazilian citizen and everyman, ends with the protagonist's parrot flying off from Brazil to Portugal upon the death of his master. Reading this parrot as a representation of Oxalá, the orixá who is the master of all heads and who is often represented as a bird upon a staff, I seek to re-create this flight by elaborating upon ethnographic interviews with informants in Salvador da Bahia and Lisbon in the first part of this chapter. After engaging these ethnographic interviews with new scholarship on Candomblé in Portugal, I continue with an extended exegesis of Mário de Andrade's novel as a transcorporeal text, working through the author's connection to another queer cultural producer of Candomblé, Pierre Verger. Emphasizing Oxalá's attribute of wisdom and his symbolic association with waters, I apply intellectual pressure to the necessity of studying Oxalá-as-knowledge traversing the Atlantic from Africa to the Americas in the centuries of the slave trade and thence to a surprising flourishing in Europe in recent years.

FIG. 6.1. Bird on the staff. Pierre Verger, *The Opaxorô of Oxalá*. Used by permission of Fundação Pierre Verger.

From Salvador to Lisbon: The Ethnographic Flight of *Macunaíma*'s Bird

The green door opens. Pai A can see me now.[1] After an hour's wait, I enter his office in the Pelhourinho, the historical center of Salvador. Pai A is a Candomblé pai-de-santo, an activist and community leader in Salvador da Bahia. He is a tall, lean man of olive complexion in his late forties. According to him, Afro-Brazilian religious groups need the organization he leads because they require recognition from the federal state governments for their protection from legal prosecution, and their social destigmatization. For a Candomblé pai- or mãe-de-santo to be recognized as a minister of religion, he or she needs to be certified by the state. It is necessary to have an activist nonprofit organization that can document the intellectual formation of the pai- or mãe-de-santo, most often in the way of Yorùbá language learning and knowledge of herbalism, and can persuasively argue that this training is equivalent to that of a seminary or the ecclesiastical training of other established religious groups.

Pai A is proud to assert that his work has produced a social context that is conducive to the thriving of Candomblé. "In Brazil, Candomblé is official," he says. "Article 5 of the Constitution guarantees it." The achievement of this new openness in Brazil has led his organization to now turn its sights toward Portugal, which is considered the future, a new frontier. It is more challenging to practice Candomblé in Portugal because they don't have the herbs and the animals required for rituals. However, "Portugal gives us hope," he tells me. Using an interesting vegetative metaphor, he says, "For us Candomblé practitioners in Brazil, Portugal is new territory. It represents growth and expansion." In general, he seems to revel in these floral and faunal conceits. He explains that the internet is good for information, but it is not equivalent to life in the *terreiro*: "We need connection to nature. The role of nature is very important so there will be differences and adaptations in Portugal."

When I ask Pai A about the elision of Africa from his organization, he says, "Africa already has lots of orixás, while Portugal doesn't have that much in that respect. In this lies the need to establish closer ties to Portugal than to Africa through the organization." He pauses and looks up for a few seconds. I can hear the wheels in his head turning. After a long five seconds, he continues, "Portugal Europeanized us; it is time to take African culture there." I feel he now invokes Africa merely because I brought up that important historical link—but even here I see an erasure of it as a geographical locale with people currently living in it who are serving the same spirits. I am troubled by Pai A's articulation of a rhetoric that problematically reorients the origin of orixá devotion from Africa to Brazil. Later I will travel to Lisbon to make a personal assessment of the transformation of Candomblé as it traverses the Atlantic to the former colonial center.

"Oh, you are a child of Oxalá. I can see that," Pai B tells me as he scrutinizes me at the threshold of his house the first time we meet. Pai B is a pai-de-santo in his early fifties with a very vibrant terreiro in the suburbs of Lisbon. He is Portuguese but was initiated in one of the historical and prestigious Candomblé houses in Salvador da Bahia, in Brazil. Prior to his initiation, he studied in Rome for the Roman Catholic priesthood. As a result of this experience, he is very fluent in Italian, and when I can't find a Portuguese word, we slip into

Italian very easily. His eyes glimmer when he remembers his seminary days, but the happy reverie ends abruptly when he recalls his need to part with the Roman Catholic Church. I know he is queer, even though we have never used that term or any other to label ourselves. It is a tacit understanding. Words would make the obvious redundant. Most pai-de-santo are queer, statistically. His male partner, Pai C, is also Portuguese, in his early forties, and also active in the Candomblé community. They both live together in the residence above the terreiro where the community meets. They have met my partner. When we go out to dinner, the easy camaraderie of two gay male couples is palpable and enjoyable. Pai B and Pai C have a dog, and we talk a lot about it, since my partner and I are also dog parents. The Candomblé community is full of straight couples in their thirties and forties with children. They are all white Portuguese, mostly upper-middle class. When I get some ash in my eye, a man from the congregation—a medical doctor—has a look at me. I make friends with a woman who is an expert seamstress and talk about the wonderfully designed robes she has made for everyone in the group. They are all skilled and educated professionals. The parents easily leave their children to Pai C, so he may guide them in a *xirê*, a round dance, while the drums beat during the ceremonies. "Gay men as auxiliaries of reproductive heterosexuals," I think. "We cut the bride's hair, dress the groom, plan their weddings, gentrify neighborhoods for them to move into, and we even babysit and educate their offspring. Candomblé does not seem to offer an alternative to gay male socialization in Western societies." Conscious of my own ability to descend into a form of critical negativity, I bring myself back to the consciousness of being in the ceremony. The drumming had lulled me into a light trance. I sit in front of the fellowship of practitioners, with Pai B to my left and Pai C to my right. I am the scholar of African diasporic religions who has come to their community to talk about his research. The children seem thrilled to have a guest speaker and have many questions for me: How did you become interested in Candomblé? Have you ever been ridden by a deity? I try to answer in such a way that my research in the Caribbean and Africa bears on the topic. I feel that making connections with other Afro-diasporic traditions in different locales is what I have to offer to the group, a geographical expansion of their range of knowledge. I am not so sure this strategy always worked. Twice removed from Africa, Candomblé in Portugal sees itself as exceptional.

The terreiro is the heart of a very well-organized community with events every day of the week. However, there are other important community spaces. There is the priests' apartment where dinners are held several times a week. Pai B is an excellent cook. He displays a caring maternal nourishing in the stirring of the chicken in the pot, in the serving of the pasta on the plate. As if wiping the sweat from his brow, he brags about the dozens of people he feeds at his house every week. Then there is the shop that sells Candomblé paraphernalia—fabrics, clothing, statues, herbs—to practitioners from all over Portugal. A copy of the community's glossy magazine is prominently displayed on the counter. Some of my short articles have been published in it. The magazine also serves as the organ of a national council of Candomblé practitioners that Pai B and Pai C founded. On the second floor of the shop, Pai C keeps an herbarium full of leaves in various stages of drying, grinding, and packaging. Pai C explains to me the names and functions of some fifty different plant species in pharmacy jars and some ten others in the process of dessication. The second floor includes a small tailor shop where an initiate makes the dresses that will be exhibited and sold below, and which the members of the house wear during ceremonies. I focus on an industrial-grade sewing machine and what appear to be at least three distinct unfinished initiation robes strewn about. The office is the only secluded space in the shop. This is where Pai C reads the *jogo de búzios* to his clients in private. The office has a desk full of recent books in English and Portuguese on Candomblé scholarship. Pierre Verger's book on herbalism, *Ewe*, sits atop a pile of other books. There is the Ifá tray upon the desk. There is an Exu effigy that Pai C tells me is alive.

Pai C tells me that Candomblé is changing in its diasporic expansion into Europe. "We have to adapt. Europe is a new environment." This can be more clearly seen in changes to the required initiation time. "In Portugal we accomplish in seven days what would take a month or a year in Brazil or Africa," he remarks, without any pride in the new expediency because there is a clear concern for preserving tradition. "We cannot deny the reality of time in First World societies," he adds. Another main area of cultural change has to do with the choice of natural materials. As a result of Portugal's more temperate climate, certain plants easily found in Brazil or Africa are simply not available. So the community in Portugal needs to be creative and use different plant species. "In the end all plants are related," Pai C says. Another important area of change involves the law. "There can be certain laws in Europe that make it more difficult for us to gain recognition and the indoctrination of children is often invoked to limit us," he says. Of course, I have to ask about changes in the ethnic makeup of the Candomblé houses in Europe. I ask Pai B if they have any black initiates in the house. He says, "Yes, I have one from

São Tomé. He is now in Berlin." I think it is odd that there would be only one, who is not Brazilian.

Then there is the matter of how Candomblé changes in highly technological societies. Aside from the magazine, the community uses the internet to disseminate much of its information. Their website is full of calendars, directions, and archives of photos and videos. This is certainly the most technologically inclined Candomblé house I have ever seen. However, they are critical of the degenerate way in which some diasporic communities have used the internet. They laugh at what they call Pai Google and ridicule initiations by internet, in which people put their heads on the screen. "Real community is still at the heart of a functioning community," Pai C tells me. Both Pai B and Pai C agree on the importance of keeping tradition in the diaspora. They are also very critical of the anything-goes attitude in the diaspora. Already, the devotion to orixás has become lax through Umbanda, in which Amerindian spirits and discarnate and archetypal spirits are also welcomed in the heads of initiates. "Now, the spirits taking over the initiates don't even have to be dead. One can even go into trance for Madonna!" exclaims Pai C in dismay.

There is the general sense among Portuguese Candomblé communities that they are the preservers of a religious tradition that in Brazil has been corrupted by commercialism. However, I find it hard to reconcile this statement with what takes place in their shop: they read the oracular jogo de búzios for a fee and sell paraphernalia for Candomblé practitioners. I look around and wonder what is the price for a large Yemayá boat, which sets the white and light-blue color palette for the entire lower floor. I also see the prices on the ritual clothes, African textiles, and statues of orixás, among which the Exus predominate.

I can see that my questions on diasporic Candomblé have sparked interest in Pai B, and, very passionately, he tells me that Brazilian Candomblé has been unfortunately weakened by poverty and that you can see this through the role played by food. I look around the room and see twenty-five people in the house, all enjoying Pai B's cooking. Pai B is proud to tell me that every day there are at least fourteen people for dinner at the house. Pai C joins in to add how horrified they have been on travels to Brazil to observe their hosts putting ice in the *vinho verde* that they brought over as a gift. He gives me names of contacts in Salvador so that when I go there, I can make my own assessments regarding the differences between Brazilian and Portuguese Candomblé eating practices.

He explains the relatively larger numbers of Candomblé practicioners in Brazil by presenting hunger as a motivator: "In Brazil people go to Candomblé ceremonies because they give them something to eat there, but in Portugal people come because of faith. People in Portugal are very devout." It is true that much of Candomblé involves eating together. But I am not sure that this commensalism is nobler in Portugal than in Brazil. In fact, many of the comparisons between Portuguese and Brazilian Candomblé seem to me to be very nationalistic and Eurocentric, the latter impression being all the more surprising as it is coming from the devotees of a religion that is African in origin. But Pai C insists that Candomblé in Portugal honors practices of commensalism much better than in Brazil. "Here we cultivate a more domestic feel than in Salvador. Here the kitchen is also an open space for noninitiates." It is true that the cooking in Lisbon is performed out in the open, and everyone in the congregation socializes while the pai-de-santo cooks for the entire congregation. I remember witnessing the way in which Pai B stirred the spaghetti and chicken with liturgical splendor. In Bahia, the space of the kitchen and the dining room are much more separate. I conclude that the Portuguese claim of a more egalitarian Candomblé has some validity. Pai B and C seem proud to have democratized Candomblé, at least in the kitchen, through Portuguese culinary customs.

While Pai B and C articulate a clear sense of being in the diaspora, I see an uncertainty vis-à-vis Portugal's relationship to the source. Africa is never mentioned; it remains obscured, elided. Their view of Brazil is one of rude and crude ritualistic decadence. Portugal, on the other hand, is the keeper of the flame and the repository of the real tradition. The imaginary relationship between origin and telos remains anxiously dyadic. On the one hand, the pais must be initiated in Brazil or at least spend considerable time there, yet there is an operating belief that the Axé, the divine life force, is no longer available at that place of initiation. So the site of arrival—Europe—is crowned, it seems, as the new displaced center. My conversations with Pai B and Pai C show me that the initial source must be rendered decadent in order for the subject to be propelled into the journey of diasporic migration. The symbolic destruction of one's place of memory, beginning, infancy, and initiation enact the discursive bridge-burning that guarantees linear travel and growth. The pain of the migrants, whether as individuals or as ideologies, is that teleologies have damned them to make their own return impossible, forcing them to sink roots in a new location.

Afro-Diasporic Religion in Portugal Scholarship

The flight of *Macunaíma*'s bird to Lisbon is prophetic in that it signals a rerouting of the trajectory of travel in the circulation of Afro-diasporic religious knowledge in the twenty-first century. Echoing Pai A, scholars seem to point to the role of Portugal as the new frontier of Afro-religious diaspora knowledge and practices in the Lusophone world. Aside from provincializing Europe, it largely recasts Brazil as a new center of the Afro-Lusophone world. When this redrawing of the discursive map occurs, it produces a narrative in which Candomblé is a religion whose origin is Brazil, a schema that enacts a problematic elision of Africa.

The historical trajectory of Candomblé to Portugal can be traced to the "massive migration from Northeast Portugal to Brazil in the 40s" (Pordeus 2000, 9). Even though many families did not return to Portugal, it is possible to surmise that those who did make their way back brought with them some experiences of involvement with Candomblé communities in Brazil. Highlighting Pai B's insistence on a democratic Portuguese Candomblé, after the many decades of *Obscurantismo salazarista*, the growth of Candomblé communities in Portugal can be read as breaking the shackles of political dictatorship:

> A instalação da Umbanda, en 1976, das igrejas pentecostais e outras, permite dizer que, em Portugal, existe uma relação direta entre o proceso de democratização e a liberação desse imaginário, que traduziria uma inquietação social recusando os limites do presente e as condições reais do futuro. O fenômeno da possessão na Umbanda Portuguesa marcaria o fim de um period social e se encarregaría de um duplo significado: o desequilibrio de uma cultura e a acceleração de sua transformação por intermédio do imaginário social. (Pordeus 2000, 8)

> The introduction of Umbanda, in 1976, of Pentecostal churches and others, allows us to say that, in Portugal, there is a direct relationship between the process of democratization and liberalization of this imaginary that would translate a social need refusing the limits of the present and the real conditions of the future. The phenomenon of possession in Portuguese Umbanda would mark the end of a social period that carries a double meaning: bringing about the imbalance of a culture and an acceleration of its transformation through a social imaginary.

Adding Portugal to the Brazil-Africa dialogue on Candomblé further complicates an area of scholarship that was already in limbo at the outset.

Whether Candomblé is an African or a Brazilian religion has been the subject of much debate. Even when ritualistic innovations are used to argue for the Brazilianness of Candomblé, there remains the matter of semantic shift in what are considered cultural retentions:

> In characterizing Candomblé *terreiros*—above all the purest ones—as havens of Africanness and resistance, authors who adopt this methodological stance implicitly accept that the presence in Brazil of cultural traits that originated in Africa necessarily indicates black resistance. The authentic transformation of Africanisms into proofs of resistance signals acceptance of the given that the meaning of cultural traits is determined through origin, without considering the fact that, whether real or supposedly of African origin, cultural traits may have different meanings in Brazilian society. (Dantas 2009, 1)

The reintroduction of Portugal in the elucidation of knowledge circulation in the Lusophone Atlantic world might actually allow us to understand, rather than confuse, the ways in which cultural knowledge is imagined to travel by populations in the diaspora: "Just as Africa appears as a symbolic paradise and a source of legitimation of the cults in the New World . . . so, too, Brazil emerges in Portugal as the source of these Afro-Brazilian cults" (Saraiva 2007, 189), proving the difficulty of a conceptualization of diaspora as a network and the persistence of an overly simplified origin-destination binary and linear conception of travel.

Departing from the position of most scholars, including my own, on the topic of Candomblé origins, Guillot presents an image of an idealized Africa and a forgotten Brazil in Portugal: "Le voyage initiatique au Brésil n'est pas obligatoire. . . . En fait pour le Portugais, le Brésil n'est pas nécessairement considéré comme la Terre-Mère du candomblé et de l'umbanda" (2009, 215; The initiatory voyage to Brazil is not obligatory. . . . Actually for the Portuguese, Brazil is not necessarily considered the mother country of Candomblé and Umbanda). Similarly, Guillot continues, "La réinterpretation de leurs parcours religieux amène donc certains chefs de culte et initiés portugais à affirmer l'héritage 'africaine' du Portugal" (2009, 210; The reinterpretation of their religious trajectory brings certain leaders of the religion and Portuguese initiates to affirm the "African" heritage of Portugal). Guillot's assessment regarding the religion's geographical source is very much at odds with my own work and that of other scholars such as Saraiva and Pordeus, who note that "Brazil always appears as the mother-land, the origin of the Umbanda cults. In order to assert his/her authority, a pai- or mãe-de-santo is either a Brazilian or has lived in Brazil in order to acquire the knowledge and expertise necessary to perform his/her role" (Saraiva 2007, 189).

Um dos aspectos da legitimidade do convertido às religiões luso-afro-brasileiras é, como referi anteriormente, o facto de a manifestação se ter iniciado no Brasil, onde pode realmente ser encontrada a "pureza religiosa." Quase todos os dirigentes das comunidades passaram por esse processo, mesmo que por pouco tempo. E, de volta às comunidades, enquadraram essas filiações, de modo bem visível, como certificado de adesão a uma das tants federações que congregam os terreiros existentes no Brasil. (Pordeus 2009, 151)

One of the legitimizing aspects of converts to Luso-Afro-Brazilian religions is, as I said previously, the fact of being initiated in Brazil, where one can truly find "religious purity." Almost all the leaders of these communities would pass through this process, even if for a brief period. And upon returning to these communities, they will draw upon those connections, in a very visible way, as a certificate of belonging to one of the many federations that unite the existing terreiros in Brazil.

The gross differences between Guillot's findings and those of most other scholars make one wonder just where and how she obtained this information. It would seem, however, that Guillot did obtain firsthand knowledge from participation in Candomblé communities, as she is able to confirm their surprising ethnic makeup in Portugal. Corroborating my own personal observations and those of at least three other scholars, Guillot's work confirms that the population of the Candomblé communities in Portugal consists overwhelmingly of white bourgeois Portuguese and very few Brazilians: "Cependant, le phénomène étudié ne peut être réduit à l'immigration brésilienne, vu que la majorité des fils-de-saint et de très nombreux chefs de culte sont des Portugais" (Guillot 2009, 209; However, the phenomenon studied here cannot be reduced to Brazilian immigration, since the majority of children of the saints and many leaders of the religion are Portuguese).

Most of those who take part in the performances in these *terreiros* are exclusively middle-class Portuguese. . . . In contrast to the African populations in Portugal, Brazilians in Portugal rarely select the religious options that are available in the context of the diaspora. . . . They state that the Portuguese would look down upon them if they were known to frequent Umbanda or Candomblé cults. (Saraiva 2007, 188)

We have already looked at how Candomblé becomes attractive for the Portuguese as a tool of liberation from the ideological repression of the Salazar dictatorship. Some of the Candomblé community's alliances, particularly through the shop, with Celtic and Druidic religions seem to express a desire on the part of the Portuguese to reconnect with their own pre-Christian past. That this is accomplished through Afro-diasporic religions is problematic, as it renders the religious practice purely utilitarian and de facto casts Candomblé as universally primeval. When the myth is articulated as "Africa and Brazil meet in Portugal," it actually recenters—and recapitalizes—Portugal by reinscribing it as a clearinghouse and foyer for the entire Lusophone Atlantic world. Appropriation and co-optation of African heritage enact a recentralization of Portugal under the guise of egalitarianism and diversity. As described by Guillot, the mythical unity of Africa, Brazil, and Portugal that is created through the rhetoric of lusotropicalism allows Portuguese initiates to appropriate and co-opt Candomblé rituals and present the religion as a positive result of colonization (2009, 217). In this sense, participation in Candomblé might serve as an expiation of colonial guilt for the Portuguese participants and explain the dearth of Brazilian migrants—who might be more interested in acquiring respectability through assimilation—in Portugal.

Macunaíma's Bird and Oxalá

Mário de Andrade's modernist novel *Macunaíma* can help us to bridge the Lusophone Atlantic in more enabling ways. The novel deserves a reappraisal as the foundational literary representation of Afro-Brazilian religions, as it is surprisingly suffused with orixá motifs for the period and presents us with the earliest instance of trance possession in any literary work. Fittingly, the novel ends in a transcorporeal moment as the third-person omniscient narrator of the story fictionally reveals himself as the very author of the manuscript we are reading. While the revelation of the narrator as author, the fusing of both personae, and the *mise-en-abîme* created by this technique are not innovative literary devices, de Andrade deploys them toward the representation of a distinct Afro-diasporic spirituality when we take into account the manner in which this hybrid literary construct accessed the knowledge of the story he is recounting:

> O papagaio veio pousar na cabeça do homem e os dois se acompanheiraram. . . . Só o papagaio conservava no silêncio as frases

e feitos do herói. Tudo êle contou pro homem e depois abriu asa rumo de Lisboa. E o homem sou eu, minha gente, e eu fiquei pra vos contar a história. (1965, 228)

The parrot came down and perched on the man's head, and the two went along together. . . . Only the parrot had preserved in that vast silence the words and the deeds of the hero. All this he related to the man, then spread his wings and set his course for Lisbon. And that man, dear reader, was myself, and I stayed on in order to tell you this story. (1984, 168)

The bird sutures Africa, the originary source of the Oxalá it represents, with Brazil, the habitat of parrots and the scene of the novel's plot, and Portugal, the eventual destination of the masterless bird. Instead of "Africa and Brazil meet in Portugal," the novel recenters Brazil by presenting it as the entrepôt between Africa and Europe.

Through the use of a literary frame that effectively creates a tale within a tale, we are presented with the novel as a type of foundling text. The revelation of this literary technique at the end of the text closes a narrative circle that began with the foundling child. The presentation of the narrator as the discoverer and author/transcriber of the story posits him as the collective spokesperson of a people, the African griot whose recitation blurs the boundaries between fact and fiction. More poignantly, however, here de Andrade cleverly evokes the feelings of disorientation and depersonalization that characterize the experience of trance possession by inducing a frustrated catharsis in the reader, who is propelled away from the illusory pleasure of the novel and forced to consider the assemblage of the text in his hand by the narrator-cum-author. The parrot that had been following Macunaíma during his entire life journey finds a new host in the figure of the narrator-author, achieving an intricately sedimented persona who also functions as the literary equivalent of the trance possession initiate at the heart of the Candomblé ritual experience. In this sense, the parrot is an Amazonic transfiguration of the dove, an element of supracephalic iconographical relevance in both Roman Catholicism and Yorùbá spirituality: as the symbol of the Holy Spirit atop Jesus's head during his baptism on the Jordan and the animal referent for Oxalá, most visibly seen atop the Opaxorô, the walking staff borne by the initiate when in trance for the old, wise, and arthritic avatar of this deity, Oxalufan. The zoological and white color symbolism shared by both Jesus and Oxalá also coincides with their common association with wisdom and compassion and their preeminent positions in their respective pantheons—

all elements that facilitated the syncretism between the two deities in colonial Brazil. Slaves who were able to preserve and transform their Yorùbá deities by disguising them as Catholic saints also capitalized on the role of the dove atop the head of the human vessel as a sign of anointing and rite of passage marking the beginning of a spiritual mission in both religious traditions. An additional common trait shared by the dove-instantiated missions of Jesus and Oxalá that was certainly used by Brazilian slaves to suture both narratives involves the association of both spiritual figures with water. The baptismal Jesus and dove on the Jordan parallel two important festivities that associate Oxalá and water: the Waters of Oxalá and the Lavagem do Bonfim.

The Waters of Oxalá

The Waters of Oxalá marks the beginning of the ritual year of Candomblé. On the decreed Thursday, the initiates must prepare themselves for the big event through the ritual of Bori (offering of the head) or Obi (ritual feeding of an orixa)—depending on the Candomblé house. Fully charged by divine power, or Axé, all dressed in white and keeping absolute silence, the initiates line themselves in descending order of years as initiates to the saint and follow the *iyalorixá* or *babalorixá* right before dawn in a procession toward a water source to refill the cisterns of ritual water that will wash and feed the various orixás for the next liturgical year. In the time of Mãe Senhora, one of the most celebrated Candomblé matrons, the water cisterns were filled outside Ilê Axé Opó Afonjá, her terreiro. This was the source of Riacho, next to the Lagoa da Vovó in San Gonçalo do Retiro. After her passing and with the encroachment of the city of Salvador upon the religious community, a water source inside the terreiro began to be used instead. Once at the well, the iyalorixá fills each initiate's vase. The group returns to the terreiro carrying the waters, and each one empties her vase into a basin in front of the shrine for Oxalá. This procession to and from the well is repeated three times, and on the last the vases are not emptied but are allowed to remain full in front of the altar. At this point, the iyalorixá takes a seat on the throne and, as she goes into trance for Oxalá, dips the bunched leaves into the water. The initiates present themselves one by one in front of the throne and refill the vase of their own orixá with new water for the coming liturgical year. This having been accomplished, one of the initiates brings Oxalá's Opaxorô, the orixá's staff that is decorated with a crown and a bird at its pinnacle, from seclusion and restores it to its customary position. This breaks the quiet solemnity of the ceremony and a joyous circle dance, the xirê, celebrates the return of Oxalá to its proper place.

The Waters of Oxalá has been studied by scholars in relationship to the orixá whose name it bears, as it performs Afro-diasporic oral traditions, and in terms of community building. Curiously, however, there is very little scholarship that addresses the role of water symbolism in this ritual. The Aguas de Oxalá are the foundational part of a "ritual cycle for the creator/father deity Oxalá that begins the annual series of private ceremonies and public festivals for the *orixás*" (Omari-Tunkara 2005, 47). Noting the preservation and performance of African orality in Brazilian Candomblé, Paul Christopher Johnson (2002, 143) stresses that most practitioners are unaware of the oral narrative that underwrites the ritual. Assuming that performers require an uninitiated scholar to explain to them the literary sources of their religious practice seems problematic. Nevertheless, his explanation of the ritual through the idea of containment and circulation is noteworthy, even when it misses the role of water in this movement. I would like to highlight the symbolism of the ritual of the Waters of Oxalá as the waters of the Atlantic, as a referent for exile and scattering, of home and migrancy. The best-known version of the oral tale of Oxalá goes something like this:

> The Ifá oracle advises Oxalá not to go see Xangô. But Oxalá insists, and Ifá recommends that he not complain or refuse service to anyone he should meet on the road. Oxalá meets Exu on the way and helps him three times to lift the palm oil gourd onto his head, but on the last attempt, Exu tricks him and spills the palm oil onto Oxalá. As advised by Ifá, Oxalá does not complain. Oxalá goes to the river and changes his clothes. Then, he finds Xangô's runaway horse but is accused of stealing it. This leads to seven years of wrongful imprisonment which coincide with seven years of infertility in the world: crops fail and women are barren. Ifá is consulted and this leads to Oxalá's release. Xangô is reunited with Oxalá and sends him home with many gifts.

The tale is performed allegorically through the ritual of Waters of Oxalá. Johnson discusses the main message of both the ritual and the story as being that of the containment of secrets. Departing from his interpretation, I see the ritual and its narrative as a moral tale regarding the dangers of capturing wisdom-knowledge. The very nature of Logos is shared flow and movement. Making knowledge static leads to unfruitfulness at best or danger at worst. The initial scene of the story reveals a foundational imbalance when the god of wisdom becomes the recipient of advice instead of its proclaimer. Ifá declares that a visit of Oxalá-as-cool-wisdom is unfit for its antipodal Xangô-as-explosive-virility. Ifá's impeding Oxalá's necessary movement and forcing him to heed his advice is dangerous. However, there is still something more dangerous than supreme wisdom stopping its flow to hear the advice of subordinates. When wisdom actually heeds this advice, terrible consequences ensue. The silence that Ifá recommends to Oxalá only enables his abuse at the hands of the trickster Exu. The flow of Oxalá's wise words must not be impeded. When Oxalá relinquishes the autonomy of his fluids and fluidity to others, there is a soiling of the divine natural order, as exemplified by Oxalá's tarnished robe. The cleansing stream allegorizes the self-regenerative ability of wisdom when it is allowed to resume its course. Oxalá's unsuccessful attempt to return the runaway horse speaks to the risk of abuse that prophets face when those they seek to help fail to see the helpfulness of their message. Wisdom loses its divine power when it remains static. The fruits of sexual reproduction, the domain of Exu and Xangô, wither when these orixás dare take a higher seat than Oxalá. Wisdom must flow in order for the natural order to resume, a dictum that is performed by the initiates refilling the vases with new water every year with an iyalorixá representing—and in trance for—Oxalá. Oxalá's wisdom must circulate like water in and around the terreiro and also throughout the world. Through and in spite of the horrors of the transatlantic slave trade, the movement of orixá devotion to the Americas is seen as an inevitable and unstoppable circulation of spiritual knowledge as powerful as the very wind and ocean currents that brought it from Africa. As the iyalorixá restores the Opaxorô that had been ritually concealed and thereby enacts the reestablishment of the natural order after Oxalá is liberated from his wrongful imprisonment, I focus on the bird atop the ceremonial staff. In my mind's eye, this bird merges with de Andrade's bird flying to Lisbon. This leads me to ask myself how the circulation of wisdom globally might involve more than just the proverbial return to an ancestral Africa and encompass a necessary transformative passage through the former European colonial center.

The Lavagem do Bonfim

The Lavagem do Bonfim is another feast reinforcing the association of Oxalá with water and its metaphysical flows. It is ritualistically performed through the movement of pilgrims, the waving of streamers, and reiterating the earlier Waters of Oxalá, the spilling of water—this time as a sacramental cleansing of the steps of a historically significant Bahian church. After Carnival, this festivity—taking place on the second Thursday in January since 1754—is certainly the most well-attended mass event of Salvador da Bahia.

The feast begins at 10 A.M. when thousands of participants congregate in front of the Igreja da Conceição da Praia for an eight-kilometer pilgrimage to the Igreja de Nosso Senhor do Bonfim. The procession is led by baianas in folkloric dresses—turbans, large skirts, bracelets, and necklaces—carrying *água de cheiro*, water perfumed with flowers. Behind them are large groups of the faithful, often the same ones that make up the Carnival samba groups, such as the Filhos de Gandhi. Everyone wears white, the color of Oxalá, the orixá syncretized with Our Lord of Bonfim. After a little over an hour, those in the procession arrive at the Igreja of Bonfim, where crowds of onlookers and participants greet them and cheer them on as they wash the steps leading up to the church. Many have eaten the *acarajé* fritters. Most are wearing *fitinhas do Bonfim*, cloth strips tied in three knots around the wrists, each knot representing a secret personal request to Oxalá that will be granted when the strip falls off naturally. As everyone chants hymns to Bonfim, the Bahianas spill the water and place flowers on the steps, in a ritualistic act of cleansing. Aesthetically turning the steps into a waterfall, the church turns into a symbolic water source of the type so central in the earlier Waters of Oxalá ritual of African origins. But there are Christian sources as well, such as the passage of Jesus and the woman at the well and the story of the woman who cleans Jesus's feet with expensive perfume. In addition to Yorùbá and Christian sources, Bastide in *Estudos afro-brasileiros* and Câmara Cascudo in *Dicionário do Folclore Brasileiro* present European sources for the practice. The practice of washing churches was customary in Portugal (Bastide 1946a, 22). Interestingly, there is the possibility of Mediterranean sources dating to antiquity for this ceremony when one takes into account the practice of washing the steps of the Parthenon—Panatenéia—and how it might have syncretized with the African washing of ritual objects in Salvador (Cascudo 1972, 489).

In 1890, the archbishop banned the Lavagem do Bonfim, a restriction the police enforced. Ultimately unable to suppress the powerful popular force and flow of the pilgrims, the archbishop—like Xangô in the oral tale—recognized the need to liberate Oxalá and allow him to circulate freely. However, as state power acknowledges its inability to contain wisdom, it finds a way to co-opt it to further its control, something it does, curiously, through music. Composed in 1923 by João Antonio Wanderlei and Peiton de Vilar, the hymn to Bonfim ostensibly celebrates the recuperation of the statue of our Lord of Bonfim from the Portuguese one hundred years earlier,

an emblematization of the successful struggle for Brazilian independence
enabled by the power of Oxalá:

Glória a ti neste dia de glória
Glória a ti redentor que há cem anos
Nossos pais conduziste à vitória
Pelos mares e campos baianos.

Chorus:

Dessa sagrada colina
Mansão da misericórdia
Dai-nos a graça divina.
Da Justiça e da Concórdia

Glória a ti nessa altura sagrada
És o eterno farol, és o guia
És, Senhor, sentinela avançada
És a guarda imortal da Bahia

Aos teus pés que nos deste o direito
Aos teus pés que nos deste a verdade
Trata e exulta num férvido preito
A alma em festa da nossa cidade.

Glory to you on this day of Glory
Glory to you redeemer that a hundred years ago
guided our parents to victory
through Bahian seas and fields

Chorus:

From this sacred hill
mansion of mercy
give us Divine Grace
Give us Justice and Harmony

Glory to you in these sacred heights
You are the everlasting light, you are the guide
You are, Lord, the watchman
You are the Immortal guardian of Bahia

At your feet you gave us the law
At your feet you gave us the truth
and it rejoices in fervent homage
The festive soul of our city.

The hymn, popularized by Caetano Veloso in his 1968 album *Tropicália ou Panis et Circensis*, is devoid of direct references to Yorùbá or Candomblé motifs and only references the Christian side of the syncretic figure. In its capturing of a spiritual narrative for nationalistic discourse, Oxalá, the deity of wisdom and peace, is presented as a god of war, evoking the misjudgment of Oxalá in the mythological story in which the political power of Xangô misinterprets Oxalá's return of a lost animal as theft. Consequently, the history and yearly performance of the hymn points to the difficult truce between political and spiritual power in Brazilian society. Moreover, the capturing of the statue of Bonfim by Portuguese troops is a political iteration of the concealing of Oxalá's Opaxorô, and both articulate the detrimental consequences of state sanctions on the free movement of wisdom. The return of the statue of Bonfim to its church ritually marks Brazilian independence, wedding both discourses to another layer of syncretic associations. The fact that the statue had been crafted in Portugal did not, in the eyes of Brazilians, imply its necessary return there during the war for independence. Just as the water well moves inside the terreiro as a result of urban encroachment upon the lagoon, the source-origin-totem moves from the outside to the inside during the political phases of boundary demarcation and territorialization. In this way, the Lavagem do Bonfim functions as the Christianized and nationalistic version of the Candomblé ritual of Waters of Oxalá. And the hymn of Bonfim functions as the Brazilianized and textualized version of the vernacular myth of the theft of the statue of Bonfim, which in turn has roots in the African story of Oxalá. Even as the very political power that is reprimanded in the tale for its confiscation of wisdom attempts to co-opt its message, the core teaching remains strong: the state must curtail its tendency to suppress knowledge since its very power depends on the free circulation of this knowledge.

Even as Bonfim is liberated from the shackles taking him back to Portugal, it is significant to note that Mário de Andrade presents this deity as traveling there freely in the image of the bird of Macunaíma. Writing his novel during the centenary of the Brazilian struggle for independence, at the same time as the hymn, de Andrade presents the movement of Bonfim to the former colonial power with a greater degree of fluidity than that presented during the actual war. Macunaíma's parrot, an avatar of the bird atop the staff of

Oxalá, signals the movement of Afro-Brazilian spirituality back to the colonizing center, contributing to the postcolonial project that has the provincialization of Europe at heart. Here, the Waters of Oxalá are resignified to mark the beginning of a new era of knowledge circulation across the Atlantic in which the fountainhead is Brazil, and Portugal becomes just one more step in its epistemological cascade—a decolonial flow that contrasts sharply with the vision of the Lusophone world espoused by Lisbon Candomblecistas in the twenty-first century. When the parrot lands on the head of a character that we soon come to identify as the narrator and writer of *Macunaíma*, we have a clear example of a transcorporeal moment paralleling Wifredo Lam's paintings with supracephalic orishas and Hector Hyppolite's use of birds as symbolic representations of Vodou lwa. The fact that the bird will go to Portugal, presumably to find a new host there, speaks to de Andrade's belief in Brazil's overtaking of Portugal and the need for the former colonial center to be reshaped by its once largest colony. Nearing the bicentennial of Brazilian independence, we come to see the prophetic nature of de Andrade's novel, as Brazil's economy has greatly surpassed that of Portugal, and the flow of goods, peoples, capital, and its gods has reversed. If the statue of Bonfim had been crafted as a replica of one in Portugal for the purpose of religious conversion in the colony, what does it mean for this derivative statue's fame to have eclipsed its Portuguese original and for the syncretized Bonfim-as-Oxalá to acquire a growing following in Europe? Herein lies the subversive, postcolonial message of the Waters of Oxalá processions and pilgrimages as they produce a redirection of the circulations along the waters of the Atlantic, which leads to an engulfing and capturing of the former colonial seat of power. As such, de Andrade's novel functions as an important literary event that anticipates the arrival of Candomblé in Europe that I discussed at the beginning of the chapter and to which I return in the final section. For now, however, I would like to discuss de Andrade's work in relation to the work of Pierre Verger, the most famous photographer of Candomblé and unquestionably the greatest visual disseminator of knowledge of the religion worldwide.

Queer Candomblé Convergences: Verger and de Andrade

Verger and de Andrade deserve to be studied together as they both circulate across waters. They both display aspects of Oxalá as intellectuals who produced the most foundational works legitimating and valorizing Candomblé.

In terms of nationality, they are both liminal and cosmopolitan yet epitomize a distinct Brazilian intellectual perspective and affect. Even if Verger flees Europe, and de Andrade—in his novel—metaphorically flies toward it, both are mesmerized by the specter of the Old World, which can be kept at bay only by documenting and creating an authentic, even folkloric, Brazilian culture capable of standing on equal footing with modernist European highbrow aesthetics. Like other privileged queer researchers on African-derived religion in the first half of the twentieth century—see chapters 2 and 4—blackness provides a discourse with which to articulate the love that dares not utter its name. The strong network between these various queer scholars is evidenced in Verger's dedication of his 1982 book *Orisha* to Lydia Cabrera, where he hints at a possible initiation of Lydia through a stylistically and queerly coded, unspoken understanding: "A Lydia Cabrera hija predilecta de Yemayá con el cariño y amor de Fatumbi" (To Lydia Cabrera, favorite child of Yemayá, with the care and love of Fatumbi).

Like Cabrera and Fichte, Verger and de Andrade's queer corporeal experience enabled them to appreciate the cultural and therefore relativistic representation of the human body. This knowledge of the body is evident in their transcorporeal representation of the self in photographs and literature. Both artists' sexual alterity drew them to investigate possible alliances with other disenfranchised groups in Brazil, their work with Candomblé communities being the most notable example of this solidarity. Both experienced a relief from their sexual marginality by immersing themselves in the cosmological view of African diasporic religions, whose corpus of rituals, oral narratives, and performance is suffused with a knowledge of the body in relationship to Spirit. Verger and de Andrade discovered in Candomblé a cultural assemblage whose highest state displays a fluidity between gender and sex distinct from Western options of embodiment. And yet the Oxalá in them was often balanced by and was at odds with their sexualized orixás—Verger was initiated into Candomblé as a child of Xangô, and de Andrade has strong identifications with Exu—allowing us to read their lives as partnered and sequential, according to the oral tale of Aguas de Oxalá.

While the queer gaze is something they share, Verger's sometimes takes the form of a detached festishization while for de Andrade the perspective is much more introspective and invested in a psychological and national self-crafting. In this chapter, my purpose is not so much to expose the fetishism of the gaze of either artist or to present how this gaze might be overcome or transcended; rather, I seek to make visible how the aesthetic production of Verger and de Andrade complicate ideas of outsider/insider, observer/ initiate, foreigner/native, and how the framing of this instability leads to a lucid understanding of the cosmopolitanization of Candomblé, particularly in Europe.

Pierre Verger

Spanning the breadth of the twentieth century and both sides of the Atlantic, Pierre Verger was born on November 4, 1902, in Paris and died in Salvador on February 11, 1996. He was a writer, ethnographer, and war correspondent, even though he always insisted that above all he was a photographer (Le Bouler 2002, 28). Verger starts to assume his role as an ethnographer through his interaction in person and in writing with his friend Bastide (Lühning 2002, 7). Regardless of the stamp we want to put on this professional output, Verger's life will be remembered as that of a modern-day saint, comparable in some ways to an Atlantic Buddha—better yet, like Oxalá, since Verger's wisdom also circulates across the waters.

He leaves his upper-class life in Paris in 1932 for the warmer climes of Brazil, Africa, Haiti, and Cuba, finally settling in Brazil in 1946. There, he is initiated into Candomblé as a son of Xangô and becomes an Ogã in the terreiro Opô Afonjá of Mãe Senhora and in the Opô Aganju in Salvador. In Bahia, he creates the Museo Afro-Brasileiro. In 1953, he travels to Africa, where he becomes a babalaô, studies Ifá divination, acquires the honorific title of Fatumbi (reborn in Ifá), and becomes visiting professor at the University of Ife in Nigeria. His foundational photographic and textual documentation of African-derived religions on both sides of the Atlantic reveals him as veritable diplomat and messenger between two worlds:

> O autor de *Orisha* trouxe da África para a sua "mãe spiritual" Maria Bibiana do Espíritu Santo, mais conhecida pelo nome de Senhora, uma missive do Alafin de Oyo conferindo-lhe o título de *Ianassô*, assim com objetos sagrados: um instrumento de música chamado *xerê* [*sic*] e um "machado de raio." (Le Bouler 2002, 21–22)

The author of *Orisha* brought from Africa to his "spiritual mother" Maria Bibiana do Espíritu Santo, better known by the name of Senhora, a missive from Alafin Oyo giving him the title of *Ianassô* and sacred objects: a musical instrument *xirê* and a radius ax.

FIG. 6.2. Verger captures the moment in which the black male subject looks back at him, overturning momentarily the Hegelian dialectic of the master and the slave. Photograph by Pierre Verger. Used by permission of Fundação Pierre Verger.

Pierre Verger's queerness is something of an open secret in Candomblé circles. In the photos from Verger's *Dieux d'Afrique*, some of which are reprinted in this chapter, young men are the ones who figure most prominently in single portraits: no other gender or age group receives such focused and affective treatment in Verger's work. Writing on these photographs, Serra says, "Nas fotografias de Verger, vêem-se os trasvestidos em bloco.... São extravagantes e sonhadoras 'mulheres' de brinquedo que os homens incorporam" (2006, 34; In the photographs of Verger, we see the transvestites.... They are extravagant and dreamy playful "women" that men personify). Here, Serra captures the complexity of queer representation in the work of

Verger for, curiously, this queerness seems to work toward a reification of normativity:

> Mas é bom lembrar que esse travestimento também tem ainda, para muitos, um sentido de afirmação masculina. Exemplo disso está na figura de um personagem inesquecível de Jorge Amado, o grande macho sedutor Vadinho, malandro e galã que more fantasiado desta maneira em pleno carnival

> But remember that this transvestism also still has, for many, a sense of masculine affirmation. One example is the figure of Jorge Amado's unforgettable character, the great male seducer Vadinho, a trickster and heartthrob who lives this way fully during Carnival.

These photos and many more are kept at the Pierre Verger Foundation in a poor neighborhood in Salvador. Through major Brazilian and European funding, it preserves the house in which Verger lived, transforming it into a museum and cultural center. Visitors can walk into his bedroom and study and take notice of the African design he used in the layout of the house: sixteen stair steps, one entrance, and one exit to the house. During a research visit to the Pierre Verger Foundation in Salvador in September 2012, the response of an archivist who knew Pierre Verger personally, through an acknowledgment and quick dismissal, best exemplified to me the ambivalence with which the topic is addressed:

> What goes on between four walls has nothing to do with his professional life. Everyone knows he was homosexual. But if you say that people will try to dismiss his work. Verger is above and beyond homosexuality. Homosexuality is private. Who is able to say he could not be a babalorixá if the orixá says he is one!

Similarly, Luiz Mott was shot down during a question-and-answer session at a photo exhibit of Verger in Salvador for bringing up Verger's queerness (Conner and Sparks 2004, 239). It becomes, therefore, important for me to redress this lacuna here by presenting Verger's important early contribution to the understanding of gender making in Candomblé. Even as he displays an obliqueness with regard to queerness, he lays the foundations for my theorization on transcorporeality.

Pierre Verger's work is criticized for not being harsh enough regarding slavery. For example, he writes that the contemporary reader ought not to judge slave owners and traders because one cannot use the morals of one era to understand another (Verger 1992b, 6, 8). Yet overall Verger was a solid historian of Candomblé. He is unique among scholars of the early colonial period by analyzing the lack of unity among different groups of Africans:

> Les Africains à Bahia étaient souvent séparés les uns des autres par des questions religieuses, par des rancunes anciennes de nation à nation et par le souvenir des guerres qui les opposaient en Afrique. Le Malheur commun ne réussissait pas toujours à les leur faire oublier. (Verger 1968, 521)

> Africans in Bahia were often separated from each other by religious issues, old grudges between nations and by the memory of wars that opposed them in Africa. Common woes were not always able to make them forget.

Original for the time, he is also keenly aware of the cross-fertilization and communication that continued occurring during and after the slave trade, challenging those who saw the migration of African populations and ideas unidirectionally: "Além disto, um vai-e-vem se organiza entre as duas costas do oceano Atlântico, para assegurar o abastecimento dos produtos da África indipensáveis à celebração dos cultos dos deuses africanos" (Verger 1981, 229; In addition, a back-and-forth is organized between the two shores of the Atlantic Ocean, to ensure the supply of necessary African products for the celebration of the cults of African gods).

More specifically, Pierre Verger displayed keen awareness of the role of gender in Candomblé. He was one of the first to theorize that women are leaders in Candomblé because the market jobs they have traditionally held are better remunerated than those held by men. This allows women to buy their freedom and to gain the financial and social status that would enable them to establish Candomblé houses (Verger 1992a, 109). However, he considers Ruth Landes's *The City of Women* a bizarre text, perhaps threatened by her comments on gender. He critiques Landes's comments on male homosexuality by saying that homosexuality in Candomblé is not restricted to males. Let us not miss how his challenge to Landes's observations allows him to skirt the issue of his own desire. He says that queer men cannot be drawn to terreiros to be with women since in Africa most of the priests were men (110). He adds that it is not true that there are more female priests than men but that the more respected houses are led by women because they tend to be more traditionalist, and this enabled them to preserve ritual (111).

FIG. 6.3. Fetishism, desire, and reverence in the photographic portraiture of Pierre Verger. Photograph by Pierre Verger. Used by permission of Fundação Pierre Verger.

It is also important to point out that Verger remains a pioneer in our understanding of trance possession:

> Ha uma coisa muito interessante no candomblé: em princípio, um orixá é um antepasado da família, que às vezes se apodera da pessoa, e então ela cai no santo, como se diz, sem fingimento, numa possessão verdadeira. Quem não tem sangue africano, como eu, infelizmente não é possuído pelo orixá. . . . Há pessoas sem sangue africano que também caem no santo, entram en transe. Mas é um transe de expressão, e não de possessão. O orixá é uma espécie de arquétipo do comportamento da gente. Quando se apossa de uma pessoa, ela revela o que está escon-

dido em seu inconsciente, passa a exprimir sua personalidade verda-
deira. (Le Bouler 2002, 29)

There is a very interesting thing in Candomblé: in principle a deity is a
family ancestor, which sometimes takes possession of the person, and
then he falls into trance, as they say, without pretense, a real possession.
He who does not have African blood, like me, unfortunately, is not possessed by the deity. . . . People without African blood also enter into
trance, but it is a trance of expression, not possession. The deity is a
kind of archetype of the behavior of people. When it comes upon a
person, it reveals what is hidden in the unconscious, expressing his true
personality.

Here, he makes a distinction between two different types of trances:

Transe de expressão . . . transe no qual nos tornamos nós mesmos.
Transe de manifestação da personalidade profunda das pessoas.
Quando entra em transe, o adepto do candomblé comporta-se incon-
scientemente como o orixá que é o seu arquétipo e libera a parte de si
mesmo que ficou recalcada. (Le Bouler 2002, 30)

Trance of expression . . . trance in which we become ourselves.
Trance of manifestation of the deep personality of people.
When adepts of Candomblé enter into a trance, they behave unconsciously like the orixá that is their archetype and free the part of
themselves that was repressed.

Verger uses his insight on trance possession toward an early understanding of queerness in Candomblé. There is a keen interest in the way in which
gender and sex avoid normative convergences. Yet Verger's obliqueness, deferral, and defensiveness, through the use of syntactical negation here and
in earlier quotes, reveal a possible anxiety regarding disclosure of his own
desire. With respect to cross-gender trance possession, he writes,

L'*Orisa* étant immatériel, ne peut se manifester aux êtres humains
qu'à travers l'un d'entre eux qu'il choisit pour lui server de monture,
de médium, généralement appelé *iyaworisa*, femme de l'*Orisa*; le sexe
n'est pas impliqué dans ce nom, c'est l'idée de possession par l'Orisa qui
est exprimée. (Verger 1957, 71)

The *orixá* being immaterial, cannot be manifested to humans but
through a person that he chooses for himself to serve him as a saddle,

as a medium commonly called *iyaworisa*, wife of the *orisha*; the gender is not involved in this name; it is the idea of possession by the orisha that is expressed.

Similarly, he displays the same type of negative grammatical construction when he discusses the initiation process:

> Les elégùn sont souvent appelés iyawóòrisà, ou simplement iyawó, femme de l'orisha. Ce terme s'applique aussi bien aux hommes qu'aux femmes et n'évoque pas une idée de conjonction charnelle, mais celle de sujétion et de dépendence, comme les femmes l'étaient autrefois aux hommes. (Verger 1982, 19)

> The elégùn are often called iyawóòrisà or simply iyawó, wife of the orixá. This term applies to both men and women and does not evoke a sense of carnal conjunction, but that of subjection and dependence, as women were once to men.

If men can be brides of the orixás, it is because gender and the institution of marriage are resignified—queered—in Candomblé, Verger seems to say, through negation and anxiety.

Liminality in Mário de Andrade and Macunaíma

Mário de Andrade must be read as a liminal writer whose ethnic identity, sexual orientation, and literary output transcended definitions based on binary Manichean ideals. The canon of Brazilian literature has "tragically whitened" Mário de Andrade (Haberly 1983, 154) as it has sought to downplay and erase de Andrade's mixed-race ancestry. The fact that de Andrade came from an upper-middle-class family in São Paulo, that his maternal grandfather had been a provincial governor and his father had been a successful accountant, are all factors that have been used to present him as a white elite Brazilian, a whitening that is clearly evident in the pink hue used to portray him on the 500,000 cruzeiro bill.[2] And it is important to note how this whitening coexisted at times with an exaggerated representation of his African heritage: "Newspaper caricatures of him and passing comments seem to highlight his negroid features: broad nose, dark complexion, his teeth and jaw as evidencing prognathism" (Ancona Lopez 1983, 44). In fact, "Mário's skin color was the legacy of Indian ancestors; the contours of his nose and lips, so evident in photographs,

FIG. 6.4. Money laundering, b(r)anque(amento): Brazilian currency note displaying the troubling Latin American practice of Europeanizing wealthy, prominent, or accomplished black and indigenous citizens in portraiture. This case literalizes the common adage that money whitens.

portraits, and caricatures, were clearly African. Mário occasionally referred to his triple ancestry" (Haberly 1983, 137).

It is necessary to take stock of the full measure of Mário de Andrade's mixed-race ancestry, without limiting him to being either black or white—or indigenous for that matter, even if this last category was seldom ascribed to him—because his hybridity informs his work. Haberly discusses the way in which de Andrade uses the figure of the harlequin to articulate the multiplicity of his ethnic background: The central image of the Hallucinated City / Paulicéia Desvairada is the harlequin, whose suit of many colors, madcaps, and masks speak to the contradictory diversity of São Paulo and the multiple, patchwork racial identities of the author (1983, 140). More pertinent to the present study, Haberly discusses the main character of *Macunaíma* as a continuation of this motley fool: "Macunaíma, like Mário's harlequin, is at once black and red and white: He is born a black-skinned Indian, but becomes white, blond and blue-eyed when he bathes in the water that fills a footprint left by Saint Thomas" (153). I would like to propose that in addition to the European figure of the multicolored court jester, accepting the fullness of his racial ancestry, in true hybrid fashion, de Andrade is also invoking in Macunaíma the African trickster Exu—whose symbolic colors are also black and red. Not unlike other liminal figures of world myths—Charon/Kharon, Phlegyas, Coyote—the òrìṣà Eshu-Elegbara of the Yorùbá pantheon can be read as a symbolic ferryman of cultural goods from subaltern to elite populations; he is a no/mad whose identity is constantly in flux and open to interpretation.

We know that de Andrade was particularly fond of Exu. He commissioned an Exu piece from Bahia for his collection, made especially for him by a pai-de-santo (Rossetti 2004, 42). Likely due to a desire to redress the ethnic and cultural whitening to which he was subjected by the literary establishment, in true trickster fashion, Mário de Andrade used his position in elite circles to valorize the role of African culture within the context of Brazilian nationalism:

> Em meados dos anos 20, Mário de Andrade já se documentava também sobre a música nos cultos afro-brasileiros. Por volta de 1925, cita, por ejemplo, informações que lhe deu Pixinguinha sobre a macumba carioca—que vai aparecer em Macunaíma. Em 1928/29, na viagem ao Nordeste, como dissemos, "fecha o corpo" no catimbó de dona Plastina, em Natal; publicou ainda, em O turista aprendiz, várias crônicas sobre "fetiçaria brasileira," procurando delimitar áreas, influências africanas e ameríndias, o sincretismo. Em 1933, comunica seus estudos sobre "Música de feitiçaria no Brasil" em conferêrencia no Rio de Janeiro, em outubro. Estuda a influência negra no folclore, divulgando as conclusões sobre "Os congos," no Rio de Janeiro, em julho de 1934. (Rossetti 2004, 40)

In the mid-twenties, Mário de Andrade was already documenting music in Afro-Brazilian cults. By 1925, for example, he cited information that Pixinguinha gave him about Macumba from Rio that would appear in *Macunaíma*. In 1928–29, during the trip to the Northeast, as we said, he "closed on the body" in Catimbó of Dona Plastina in Natal. He also published in *The Tourist Apprentice* several essays on "Brazilian witchcraft" seeking to delimit areas of African and Amerindian influence and syncretism. In October 1933, he announced his research on "Music of Witchcraft in Brazil" at a conference in Rio de Janeiro. He also investigated the black influence in folklore, disseminating the findings in "The Congos," in Rio de Janeiro in July 1934.

For his ethnographic research on music, photography, and inspiration for his novel, de Andrade leaves for the blackest area of Brazil: "Longe do cosmopolitismo de São Paulo, ele busca um outro Brasil—nos anos 20—pelas bandas do Norte e do Nordeste, lá mesmo onde fez nascer seu Macunaíma" (Carnicel 1994, 11; Away from the cosmopolitanism of São Paulo, he seeks another Brazil—in the twenties—in the north and the northeast, the very place where he birthed his Macunaíma). Macunaíma's travels from country to city to deserts in Brazil in quest for an identity mimic de Andrade's own ethnographic research throughout large parts of Brazil's territory. These parallel pilgrimages serve to reiterate the necessity of knowledge circulation proposed by the story of Oxalá.

In spite of his institutional whitening, de Andrade remained invested in black Brazilian studies. Throughout his career, Mário de Andrade corresponded with Arthur Ramos about research on black cultures. This is particularly noteworthy as this took place during a period of police persecution of Candomblé terreiros. In 1934, de Andrade sent an essay, "A Calunga dos Maracatus," to be published in the proceedings of the First Congreso Afro-Brasileiro, organized by Gilberto Freyre. He was also supportive of the 1937 II Congreso by sending representatives through his government department (Rossetti 2004, 40).

It becomes important to discuss blackness in de Andrade's life and work in order to redress a tendency to overlook this important aspect in scholarship. De Andrade's work is often seen as paradigmatic regarding Brazilian cultural production, yet blackness as a component of this production is often driven out of the conversation: "Harmonização das culturas formadoras do amálgama nacional . . . um componente expressivo do carácter nacional" (Russeff 2001, 114; Harmonization of national cultures forming an amalgam . . . an expressive component of the national character). Curiously, even Bastide, who wrote extensively on Candomblé, seemed wary of commenting on the Africanness of de Andrade's work, perhaps out of fear of insulting a national literary establishment not yet ready to accept the full breadth of its origins:

> Não se pode encontrar um livro mais especificamente brasileiro que Macunaíma. Toda literatura tem seus tesouros ocultos. Obras há que podem ser traduzidas, e saboreadas, tanto por estrangeiros como por nacionais; mas algumas têm um sabor secreto de tal maneira se acham ligadas ao mais profundo da sensibilidade étnica; são como feras que só obedecem ao domador que conhecem, amadas que só se dão ao homen eleito. São livros para uso interno. Macunaíma está entre eles. (Bastide 1946b, 45)

> You cannot find a more specifically Brazilian book than Macunaíma. All literature has its hidden treasures. There are works that can be translated, and enjoyed, both by foreigners and nationals, but some have a secret flavor that links them to deeper ethnic sensitivity; they are like beasts who only obey the tamer they know, mistresses who only give themselves to their chosen man. They are books for internal use. Macunaíma is among them.

The liminality of de Andrade's ethnicity parallels that of his sexual orientation. In 1929 Mário de Andrade severed contact with Oswald de Andrade—another important figure of the modernist movement who in spite of the shared last name is not related to Mário—after Oswald proclaimed Mário's effeminacy in the *Revista de Antropofagía* (Cannibalist review), a literary supplement of the *Diario de São Paolo*: "Our Miss São Paolo, translated into the masculine" signed with the pseudonym Cabo Machado, an allusion to a sensuous male character from a 1926 poem by Mário de Andrade. There is a literary basis for the assumption Oswaldo raised about Mário's sexuality. De Andrade articulates a rare, early queer voice in some of his literary works. For example, in his poem "Carnival in the Hallucinated City," the male cashier transforms himself into a sexy Bahian girl. Also, in his short story "Federico Paciência" in his collection *Contos Novos* there is the development of clear romantic friendship between two students. Lafetá in *Figuraçao da intimidade: Imagens na poesia de Mário de Andrade* addresses this homoeroticism obliquely in de Andrade's poetry by calling it "Um vulcão de complicações" (A volcano of complications) and "Canto do mal do amor" (A lovesickness lament) and the expression of "desejo sexual que tem sua realização impedida" (1986, 39; sexual desire that had its consummation forestalled). Continuing the circumlocution, Lafetá says that as a poet de Andrade nears the nucleus of some terrible truth. Something abominable, "*nefasto*," that cannot be told (Teixeira dos Santos 1994, 95–96; Werneck de Castro 1989, 91–92; Lafetá 1986, 158). Moacir Werneck de Castro in *Exílio in Rio* finally directly addresses what other critics only hinted at: "Ressalta a questão de um componente homossexual de sua personalidade, sugerido na pesquisa de Lafetá" (1989, 92; Highlights the matter of a homosexual component to his personality, implied in Lafetá's research). Critics see de Andrade as embodying an unaccomplished sexuality, sublimated due to the repressive mores of the period (Teixeira dos Santos 1994, 96; Werneck de Castro 1989, 93), one that nevertheless emerges in coded form in his literary works and in his pederastic correspondence with aspiring young poets (Alves 1973, 152).

The liminality of de Andrade continues with yet another scandal. Curiously, the most innovative and inventive Brazilian writer of his generation endured serious accusations of plagiarism. Mário de Andrade's "Anthropophagist Manifesto" owes a great deal to Oswald de Andrade, yet the latter is not given credit in the text. Moreover, large sections of *Macunaíma* appear to be found texts, sometimes copied almost word for word from various collectors of Indian folktales. In 1931, "Raimundo Morais declara ser *Macunaíma* cópia das lendas colhidas por Koch-Grünberg" (de Souza 1999, 212;

Raimundo Morais declares that *Macunaíma* is a copy from folktales gathered by Koch-Grünberg). Here he is referring to the second volume of *Vom Roroima zum Orinoco* by German ethnographer Koch-Grünberg, published in 1924. De Andrade, who appears to steal entire sections of this text for his novel, never gives Koch-Grünberg any credit, unless we count the last paragraph of the last chapter as a confession of his peccadillo: "Dizem que um professor naturalmente alemão andou falando que aí por causa da perna só da Ursa Maior que ela é o sací... Não é não! Sací inda pára neste mundo espalhando fogueira e trançando crina de bagual... A Ursa Maior é Macunaíma" (de Andrade 1965, 224); "It is said that a certain professor (German, of course!) goes around asserting that because it has only one leg, the Great Bear is really Saci, the little one-legged Negro boy. But no! It is not! Saci is still with us in this world, letting off fireworks and painting the manes of horses. The Great Bear is Macunaíma" (de Andrade 1984, 165). De Andrade not only steals the story from Koch-Grünberg's book but has the audacity to imply that the German ethnographer had the story wrong. This highlights the fact that the ethnographer himself was nothing more than an intermediary between de Andrade and the indigenous informant, who is the first traceable source of the narrative. The charge of plagiarism forces us to question the notion of origins in *Macunaíma*. De Andrade's satirical inclusion of the written source of the narrative points to the necessity to find even earlier sources that can expose literary theft by foreign ethnographers. De Andrade's comical statement about the German ethnographer deflects the charge of plagiarism away from himself and points an accusing finger at Koch-Grünberg instead.

The image of the bird in Macunaíma reiterates de Andrade's liminality, especially in its relationship to language.

> O comércio de signos, o mimetismo lingüístico do herói, metaforizado na imagem do papagaio—o que repete e reduplica linguagens—constituem a marca autoral desta obra-prima do Modernismo brasileiro, uma das mais agudas reflexões sobre e identidade nacional. (de Souza 1999, 13)

> The commerce of signs, the hero's linguistic mimesis, metaphorized in the image of the parrot—who repeats and reduplicates languages—constitutes the authorial mark of this masterpiece of Brazilian modernism, one of the most acute reflections over national identity.

De Souza gestures toward the role of the bird as linguistic trickster, whose parroting functions as a mimicking device through its camouflaging, its repetitions, its doublespeak. The verbosity of the bird contrasts with the late onset of speech for the protagonist, who acquires language proficiency later than his peers. Writing in and for a New World country whose lingua franca is that of the colonizer, de Andrade sought to represent the extremes of fluency and the linguistic genocide of African and Amerindian languages that characterizes modernity in the Americas. The parrot is the bard, and the griot is the transmitter of the oral narrative of the nation to the transcriber-cum-author: "Only one parrot remains to converse with Macunaíma, to witness his ascension into the sky, and to teach the hero's language and deeds to a stranger and, thereby, to us. The parrot then flies away . . . to find a new life in Portugal" (Haberly 1983, 151).

This transmission of the narrative from the parrot's beak to the transcriber's quill points to the liminality of *Macunaíma* in terms of genre. The claim to truth and authenticity involved in the "manuscript found in a bottle" motif would seem to work against the ingenious creativity of the text. Interestingly, de Andrade never referred to *Macunaíma* as a novel but as a *história* or *rapsódia*. The indeterminacy of the text's genre diminishes the charges of plagiarism, as the standards of innovation for novelistic production are not the same as those for history, for example. Also, those who devalue the text by criticizing its difficult language, popular syntax, native and foreign languages, and the inclusion of every dialect within Brazilian Portuguese see this as chaos because the text does not live up to literary expectations that it never sought to fulfill, given its status as a nether text. Like Lydia Cabrera's *El Monte* and Fichte's *Xango*, the narrative style is transcorporeal. The phenomenon of trance possession takes over the author and the book, yielding a mediumistic genre between orality and textuality, fact and fiction.

The transcorporeality of the text finds maximum expression in the chapter "Macumba," which is the first literary representation of trance possession in an Afro-Atlantic religion. While it contains elements of primitivism that were commonplace in the simultaneous black modernist trans-linguistic literary movements of Antropofagía, Negrismo, négritude, and the Harlem Renaissance, this exoticism works toward a validation of Candomblé as a religion. It is particularly commendable given that there was an intense police persecution of terreiros during this time. Haberly provides us with a clear synthesis of the events that take place during this complex chapter of *Macunaíma*:

> The link between sex and power is most explicit in the episode of the macumba ("voodoo") [*sic*] ritual in Rio, a tangle of inverted sexual identities and the most brutal and terrifying section of the text. The

ceremony calls up Exu, the male African deity of evil, who takes over the body of a fat Polish whore. As Macunaíma copulates with the whore possessed by Exu, it becomes clear that the hero is really Exu's son, and is therefore fornicating with his own father. As a reward for Macunaíma's sexual prowess, Exu works sympathetic magic: The hero beats and tortures the whore's body in a fit of almost incomprehensible sadism, but all her wounds are transferred to the body of Pietra in São Paulo—Macunaíma's first victory over his great adversary. (1983, 155)

Let us unpack the multiplicity of personhood in this passage. The first trans-corporeal moment occurs when Exu claims Macunaíma as his *filho-de-santo*, his spiritual child:

Todos estavam nus também e se esperava a escolha do Filho de Exú pelo grande Cão presente. Jongo temível. . . . Macunaíma fremia de esperança querendo o cariapemba pra pedir uma tunda em Venc-eslau Pietro Pietra. Não se sabe o que deu nêle de sopetão, entrou gin-gando no meio da sala derrumbou Exú e caiu por cima brincando com vitória. E a consagraçao do Filho de Exú novo era celebrada por licenças de todos e todos se urarizaram em honra do filho novo do icá. (de Andrade 1965, 75)

Everyone was also naked by now, and awaited the choice of the son of Exu by the great Devil now present. The dance was terrifying. . . . Macunaíma quivered with anticipation, longing to beg the devil to bring about Venceslau Pietro Pietra's downfall. Caught off guard by the unforeseen break of good luck about to open in front of him, he reeled into the middle of the room, knocking Exu over and falling on top for a triumphant fuck. The consecration of this new Son of Exu was acclaimed by all; they all howled hurrahs in honor of the new son of the devil. (1984, 55)

This association between Exu and Macunaíma is described by de Andrade and interpreted by Haberly as sexual, using the language of male same-sex eroticism. This becomes more clearly presented in the second transcorpo-real moment when an unnamed Polish whore—already embodying a very liminal national and sexual identity—goes into trance for Exu:

A polaca vermelha tremendo rija pingando espuminha da bôca em que todos molhavam o mata-piolho pra se benzerem de atravesado, gemia uns roncos regougados meio chôro meio gôzo e não era polaca mais, era

Exú o juruparí mais macanudo daquela religião. . . . Quando acabou, a fêmea abriu os olhos, principiou se movendo bem diferente de já-hoje e não era mais fêmea era o cavalo do santo, era Exú. Era Exú, o romãozinho que viera ali com todos pra macumbar. (de Andrade 1965, 75)

The red-haired whore, in jerking spasms, spewed froth from her mouth in which they all moistened their thumbs to bless themselves with the sign of the cross; she groaned with harsh croaking grunts, half sobbing, half gloating; she was no longer a whore but had become Exu himself, the most direful devil of the macumba cult. . . . When she stopped, the whore opened her eyes and began to move, but in a style quite different from before. She was Exu, the devil himself, who had come to make one of his rare visits to a macumba rite. (1984, 55–56)

In becoming the vessel for Exu, the Polish whore becomes the paradigmatic example of the concept of transcorporeality as the deity regenders the initiate. The body of the initiate is no longer referred to as female because male Exu is controlling it. This transcorporeal passage from de Andrade predates much of the current scholarship on cross-gender trance possession, like mine and Daniel's. Let us look at the change in gender pronouns:

Yansan had taken a young man in the front row of male participants. The *xirê* continued with welcoming songs to her, but s(he) was not taken out of the room. His shoes and white T-shirt were taken off, and then she was wrapped with a white headscarf and a long length of multicolored fabric from her armpits to her ankles. (Daniel 2005, 196).

Almost describing the possession of de Andrade's Polish whore by Exu, Daniel writes, "Yansan is a female *orixá* and, like most of the *orixás*, both men and women may receive her in their bodies. When she arrives, the person who receives her is understood socially as suprahuman female, despite his/her gender. Gender is flexible and shifts according to the divinity" (2005, 290). This multilayeredness of personhood acquires even more strata as a result of Exu's granting an audience to listen to the requests of his devotees. A butcher asks that his business do well. A woman asks for a job so she could marry. A doctor asks to be able to write Portuguese well. Everybody asks virtuous requests of Exu, except Macunaíma: "E o herói pediu que Exú fizesse sofrer Venceslau Pietro Pietra que era o gigante Piaimã comedor de gente" (de Andrade 1965, 76); "So the hero asked that Exu bring down hideous sufferings on Venceslau Pietro Pietra, the giant, Piaiman Eater of Men" (1984, 56). Macunaíma is the only one whose request is granted, yet it is the only one that is thoroughly negative. Exu remains unbaffled by the selfish and vindictive desires of mortals and grants Macunaíma's wish in a most surprising way:

> Então foi horroroso o que se passou. Exú pegou três pauzinhos de erva-cidreira benta por padre apóstata, jogou pro alto, fêz encruzilhada, mandando o eu de Venceslau Pietro Pietra vir dentro dêle Exú pra apanhar. Esperou um momento, o eu do gigante veio, entrou dentro da fêmea, e Exú mandou o filho da a sova no eu qu estava encarnado no corpo polaco. O héroi pegou uma trance e chegou-a em Exú com vontande. (de Andrade 1965, 76)

> The happenings that followed filled the onlookers with horror. Exu took three little sprigs of lemon verbena blessed by an unfrocked priest, threw them into the air, crossed himself and commanded Venceslau Pietro Pietra's duppy to enter his, Exu's, body, there to be given punishment. He waited a moment and the giant's duppy came and entered the body of the female medium; Exu told his son to give a hiding to the duppy now lodged in the whore's body. The hero seized a door bar and lashed Exu with a will. (1984, 56–57)

The Polish whore, who was already mounted by Exu, adds another layer of personhood by also incorporating the nemesis of Macunaíma, Venceslau Pietro Pietra, also known as Piamã. Reminiscent of the supracephalic figures in Wifredo Lam's paintings and the externality of the *castanha de caju* to its accessory fruit, this third transcorporeal moment in the chapter shows the multiplicity of personhood and the fluidity of gender afforded by trance possession. The characterization of this initiate by de Andrade as a whore implies her proficiency at being able to be ridden by many men, in this case, simultaneously. This allows Macunaíma to carry out his desire for revenge by giving his opponent a thorough thrashing. However, this beating is described as a sexual act, allowing him to fuck (up) his same-sex adversary through the voyeuristic tutelage of Exu via the body of the Polish whore. In fucking a body that is inhabited by his spiritual father, Macunaíma's sex fight is more than a homoerotic act. The fact that he is fucking Exu, Piamã, and the Polish whore simultaneously characterizes him as the ultimate sex taboo breaker: the main actor in a carnal and spiritual sadistic bisexual orgy in which prostitution and incest figure prominently. And let us not forget that his sexuality is nonprocreative. Earlier in the text, Macunaíma smashes his testicles with a rock and gets coconuts as substitute, but piranhas devour his coconuts. With respect to sexual mores, this 1928 novel is a pioneering work. By utilizing the transcorporeal modularity that the Afro-diasporic body preserves in the Candomblé-Umbanda continuum of practices, de Andrade is able to present a unique characterization of the human body as the abode of multiple and removable selves.[3] As a result of this feat, *Macunaíma* can be commended for pushing the boundaries of the body beyond any imaginable potential hitherto represented in literature. In a formidable manner, *Macunaíma* transgresses the boundaries of textuality, language, and corporeality.

The narrative of *Macunaíma* is an Odyssean journey that juxtaposes the world of the city and the countryside and attempts to reconcile both of these national profiles in the liminal body of its hero-citizen, Macunaíma. Perhaps better than any ethnographer, Bastide presents to us the difference between urban and rural trance experiences in Candomblé:

> So we can establish a kind of law that whenever group control is relaxed, mysticism ceases to be the expression of collective models and becomes an individual expression of the way people experience the transformations of the social structures. . . . The trance of the candomblé still represents the triumph of the superego, i.e. of the collective norms, while the trance of syncretistic or improvised sects is the triumph of the self. . . . The one we have briefly sketched for Afro-Brazilian trance has brought out the importance of closed societies and groups open to outside influences, thus leading us into the problem of acculturation. The susceptibility of this trance to infiltration by personal drives seems to me to be associated with the individualization of the black in the industrialized big cities as he has been proletarianized through contact with whites. (1978, 380–81)

Bastide here appears to be saying that the real Candomblé is rural and black, and its trance experience positions the initiate in a place in conformity with the array of social spaces in a manner that can best benefit the group. The urban terreiro, by contrast, has been contaminated by the individualization that characterizes Western societies. We see Bastide's idea illustrated in Macunaíma's egocentric and vindictive reasons for going to the big city: "Pois então tinha resolveu tomar um trem e ir no Rio de Janeiro se socorrer de Exú diabo em cuja honra se realizava uma macumba no outro día" (de Andrade 1965, 69); "So he decided to take the train to Rio and seek the help of Exu, the powerful devil from Africa, in whose honor a macumba rite was to be held the following day" (1984, 50–51). Perhaps the most visible effect of the corrupting influence of the city is Macunaíma's association of the orixá Exu with the Christian devil. The specific characteristics and personality of Exu are deformed and limited by this gross association. His incipient ego has been further corrupted by the big city as Haberly presents: "Macunaíma, weakened and contaminated by the modernity of São Paulo, is still obsessed with sex, but his generative potential is forever eliminated during his stay there" (1983, 156). The city is presented as sterilizing, a view that contrasts with the fertility of the jungle. That Macunaíma is able to navigate both worlds attests to his liminality.

Macunaíma's textual, linguistic, and corporeal transgressions reinscribe those of his equally liminal author. The ability of de Andrade and his literary protagonist to traverse these boundaries is most aptly presented in the flight of the bird to Lisbon, representing the intrinsic need that wisdom has for wide circulation.

Epilogue: Lavagem de la Madeleine

From Lisbon, *Macunaíma's* bird has taken flight to other European capitals. Most notable among these new destinations is Paris, which since 2002 has been the site of the largest outdoor Candomblé-themed gathering outside of Brazil. The highlight of the festivity is the resignification of the Église de la Madeleine in Paris as the Igreja de Nosso Senhor do Bonfim by the Brazilian community in Paris. Since La Madeleine is architecturally a re-construction of the Parthenon, the relocation of the washing of the steps at this Parisian church re-creates also the Panatenéia, the European source of the ceremony that syncretized with Yorùbá ritual in Brazil. It took Brazilian migrations to Paris to have Oxalá revive the worship of Athena and high-light the connection of this Greek deity with the Christian female apostle, Mary Magdalen, who is the patroness of the church. Through the arrival of former colonial subjects, the center rediscovers its own past traditions and returns to its own entangled roots. But for Brazilians in Paris, La Madeleine was chosen consciously because of its prominent steps, reminiscent of those leading to the Brazilian church of Bonfim, and through the associations that Mary Magdalen has with anointing Jesus's feet, interpreted as a kind of "washing," and in her textual assimilation with the "woman at the well." In fact, when attending the festival, I was surprised to hear how few times the name Bonfim was invoked. I see this as yet another moment of trans-corporeality by which Oxalá is regendered from its male avatar to a female prototype in the European diaspora. Despite the moving French-Brazilian ecumenical ceremony celebrated at La Madeleine as part of the festivities, in which a Catholic priest and a babalorixá prayed the Our Father in French, Portuguese, and Yorùbá, I sensed very little mixing between the belief systems. Whatever specific Christian figure is used to represent Oxalá remains inconsequential, for it functions as only a thin veneer for the continuation of orixá devotion wherever Oxalá may relocate. Little does it matter that the pilgrimage marching from Place de la République to La Madeleine is more carnival than spiritual, unlike its Brazilian original.

My eyes notice but purposely see beyond the Brazilian Tourism Office booth, the dance workshops, the capoeira performances, and the myriad caipirinhas. I shrug off the concerns that this pilgrimage is embedded in a five-day Brazilian national festival and that it is taking place in mid-September instead of in January, as in Bahia. One must make certain concessions in diaspora. That is the spirit of creolization: survival through adaptation. What really matters is that Oxalá continues flying across the waters, circulating his wisdom, unimpeded by pessimistic oracles and trickster gatekeepers. As I stand among hundreds of pilgrims dressed in white on the steps of La Madeleine, my eyes are finally opened, and in a whirlpool of water created by the circular dancing motion of the Baianas' brooms I see a mystical Gulf Stream being set in motion by a gigantic Oxalá composed of a dozen women whose white flowing skirts turn miraculously into flying parrot wings.

CONCLUSION

Transcripturality

When the initiates exit the igbodu, they are in a state of trance and are revered by their new communities as the personification of their tutelary orishas or lwas. Many new initiates report their initial trances as dramatic occurrences, in which their sense of awareness is thoroughly displaced and replaced by the divinity. At this early stage of the initiates' development, the orisha or lwa may direct messages meant for their new spiritual children to the congregation at large for the wider membership to relay to the neophytes once the ceremony is over. These messages are often prefaced by the formula "Go tell my horse . . ." which gives Zora Neale Hurston's celebrated early work on Vodou its title. As the initiates progress in the practice, however, they may be able to retain more and more of their awareness during trances. Many experienced priests of the religion confess to having developed the ability to retain such full consciousness while the divinity is on their heads that they are able to go about their quotidian life as they easily slip in and out of trance throughout their day. This self-reflexivity of the performative has great relevance to the texts examined in this study, as many of these cultural producers seem to have been operating under these highly advanced forms of trance as they worked creatively through various artistic media. As a suggestive call to further work on these cultural producers, on the phenomenon of trance possession, and as a coda to this book, I propose the theoretical neologism of transcripturality as the act of cultural creation—painting, photography, film, and particularly writing—in an altered or exalted state of consciousness that mirrors trance possession and prompts or suggests a similar experience in the receiver of such a work of art. Transcripturality then functions as the specific textual manifestation of the broader theoretical concept of transcorporeality as the external, multiple, and replaceable self of the Afro-diasporic body presented in this book and whose botanical referent finds ripened expression in the externally nutted cashew pear. The novels studied in this book—Jorge Amado's *Dona Flor e seus deus maridos* and Mário de Andrade's *Macunaíma*—not only provide narratives in which trance possession is evident; stylistically and rhetorically, they perform this very corporeal trascendentality. Similarly, the films I selected to analyze—Bruno Barreto's *Dona Flor e seus deus maridos* and Tomás Gutiérrez Alea and Juan Carlos Tabío's *Fresa y Chocolate*—replicate the creolized, otherworldly quality of the Afro-diasporic religions they discuss through the deployment of a syncretic magic-realistic narrative that vacilates between reason and the metaphysical. Likewise, the visual artists Wifredo Lam, Hector Hyppolite, and Pierre Verger communicate and almost induce the state of trance possession that their paintings and photographs depict to enraptured audiences, prompting them to wonder under what psychological conditions such works were created. Nowhere is the rescripting potential of transcorporeality more palpable than in the femme cheval paintings of Lam, which, when decoded through the figure of the cashew pear, reveal the capability of the orisha to rewrite the gendered program of the initiate in trance. The cashew nut hanging from the fruit analogizes the scrotum and penis dangling from Lam's horse's face to expose the generative and sexual qualities of the orisha's bond with his human vessel during the trance experience. Here, trance possession can be read as a form of testicular implantation, whose virilizing effect on the female subject transcripturalizes her gendered narrative beyond all dualities.

Most shockingly among all of these various fields, because of its claims to objectivity, detachment, and rationality, is the emergence of a discourse of transcripturality, a rhetoric that performs the very state of trance possession it analyzes, in ethnography. The work of anthropologists Hubert Fichte and Lydia Cabrera exhibits this transcripturality in their ethnopoesis, in the disorienting quality of their unredacted field notes, in the spiralist quality of their interviews, all of which replicate the dizzying turns of the dancing initiate as he exits the igbodu. Similarly, the tradition of female Vodou ethnography outlined in the work of Zora Neale Hurston, Maya Deren, Katherine Dunham, Karen McCarthy Brown, and Mimerose Beaubrun evidences and upholds transcripturality in their parallelism of the ethnographic text with the body of the initiate, the initiatory process, and the phenomenon of trance possession. The radiance of the trance possession moment progressively reaches an infectious quality, of which I have become conscious in the preparation of this book, particularly when I felt the narrative taking on a channeled, mediumistic quality.

The way I experience, interpret, and present transcripturality in the present work is in the form of the text as a possessed body, allowing for the very texture of the corpus of information to duplicate and mirror the modular corporeality of the human body as it meets the divine. This book displays transcorporeality through the conceit of the text as the initiatory chamber, the repository of secrets, and in the consequent interpellation of the reader who, having learned the mysteries, as an initiate. The way in which the chapters work as bodily limbs and rite-of-passage steps also has functioned as my way of illustrating the idea of transcripturality, as a way to use form to highlight, as it converges with, content. It is my conviction that the style in which a cultural or scholarly product is rendered ought to be shaped in dialogue with its message in much the same way as the initiate is subjectified in her union with the divine during trance. While transcorporeality sought to provide a mechanism to understand a distinct Afro-diasporic conceptualization of the self, transcripturality becomes the critical apparatus through which we can appreciate how cultural works also have their own very similar forms of embodiment, how—in their very canvases, films, and pages—works become entranced by the subject matter they depict. Transcripturality, creolizing queer studies, hears the echoes of Judith Butler's (1993, ix) famous question "What about the materiality of the body?" and boldly responds with queer/ies of its own: "What about the immateriality of the body? What about the materiality of spirit, *Judy*?" as it offers a discursive technology that encodes within itself the very subject of its study and presents it as an extreme example of Butler's reinterpretation of J. L. Austen's speech-act theory as performativity. Transcripturality calls for a new poetics of Afro-diasporic texts in which the article, the monograph, the edited volume, are allowed to be possessed by their subject matter in the same way as the initiates of Candomblé, Vodou, and Santería surrender their bodies to the orishas and lwas. Let us imagine what such a transcriptural praxis would look like using the very structure of

Yorùbá and Ewe/Fon ritual sacramentality. I invoke Eshu-Elegbara—also called Legba, Eleguá, and Exu—the master of the crossroads to clear all blockages and to open the gates for a new and self-reflexive scholarship of black Atlantic religions and cultural life. I call on the rulers of wisdom—Obatalá, Dambala, and Oxalá—to descend upon all scholars and artists of the black diaspora not only so that we may produce works whose style mirrors content but so that together form and message transcend Cartesian dialectics because these not only limit the bodies of humans, they also restrain texts from reaching their full queer potentiality. As Erzulie Freda and Oshún/Oxum come down, I see monographs on individual orishas and lwas that are organized, dressed, and danced according to those particular deities' colors, norms, and values. As food offerings are presented to the various orishas and lwas, I see edited volumes on commensalism that replicate in their structure the very act of eating together during and after a ceremony. The Marassa Twa and Ibeji crown the Ori of writers creating tripartite works on the transatlantic slave trade. Yemayá/Iemanjá and Lasirèn undulate as they foreshadow the incoming tide of a layered style for works on African diaspora religious altars, which are often multileveled—as if in rhythmically spaced waves. Ogún/Ogum/Ogou and Changó/Xangô lend their aegis to forthcoming works on the cultural geography of the West Indies that will deploy an archipelagic or volcanic style, in organicity with their content. Transcripturality means allowing our texts to be inhabited by the spirits in the same way devotees go into trance. If the bodies of initiates can be regendered in trance, then we must allow our texts to be re-genre-d by the transcriptural moment of composition, which, in times of deep inspiration, we feel more like transcription, even dictation. The ceremony of the book is coming to a close as the drumming slows its pace and the catharsis of reentering the world begins to dawn, now that the full force of the trance subsides. Dear reader, your new world is waiting outside; exit now the igbodu—dreamy, yet awake—looking back at yourself with, through, and in the luminous, multiple pairs of eyes of your new spiritual family.

NOTES

1. Igbodu, without the accent, is the Yorùbá spelling for the initiation chamber.

2. *Orisha* is the English spelling of Yorùbá *òrìṣà* and analogous to Spanish *oricha* and Portuguese *orixá*. Because many practitioners of Candomblé and Santería see Brazil and Cuba, respectively, as the sources of their religions, I have sought to retain the spellings in the language of use by the various communities in which I conducted field research. For example, some practitioners might not consider Nigerian Ọṣun, Cuban Ochún or Oshún, and Brazilian Oxúm as the same divinity and would even question whether the idea of the orisha is identical across the black Atlantic.

3. The liberatory potential that black Atlantic religions provide for the performance of queer subjectivities need not force us to conclude they are spaces devoid of troubling hierarchies and exclusions. Sobering reminders preventing us from a descent into a romantic primitivism on these religions are the traditional proscriptions against women in the Ifá priesthood, ceremonial prohibitions of premenopausal women slaughtering four-legged animals, and the antagonism that certain hypermasculine divinities can bear toward trans-identified devotees. Interestingly, it is precisely through the interstices of these gendered interdictions that queer men are able to carve a niche for themselves, as they are free of the interdictions against women and can also carry out the paradigmatic feminine sacramental role of being mounted by the gods. For a more extended study of the exclusions that persist in Lucumí communities for queer people and women, see Pérez 2016, particularly chapter 4, "Gendering the Kitchen" (111–40).

4. Transcorporeality is clearly within the literature on the embodied religious perception and behavior currently discussed within the field of religious studies. Over the last decade, there has been increasing attention to the human body not as a historical or biological artifact, but as a multisensory interface between spiritual and physical realms that is continually reconfigured through ritual practice. Some call this "body pedagogics" (Csordas 1990; Mellor and Schilling 2010) or "sensuous ethnography"

(Stoller 2004; van Ede 2009) and get insights from anthropology and neuroscience. There is also the introduction to a special issue on the body in *Religion and Theology* (2014), which reviews the literature in this emerging subfield within religious studies. Furthermore, the reader is directed to the special issue of the *Journal of Religion in Africa* (2007), volume 37, issue 3, which deals with the instability of categories or units of analysis and the problematics of definition when theorizing about black Atlantic religions.

5. All translations are my own unless otherwise noted. Special gratitude to Eric Anton Heuser for his help in decoding the most complex German passages of Hubert Fichte.

6. An alternative view accounting for these differences might lie in the non-canonical and diffused structure of Vodou, which allows some degree of latitude for varying interpretations and localized versions of rituals.

7. While Matory's discussion of transvestism does not entail a disruption, inversion, or ironizing of gender categories, his provocative comments prompt some of my own observations on the carnivalesque, diffused throughout this book, in which I contend that the temporary exchange or assumption of identities that takes place during Carnival is quite different from the all-pervasive effects on subjectivity that trance possession implies for initiates. While a devotee might go into trance for an orisha or lwa for twenty minutes at a ceremony once a week, the personality of this deity informs his routine life, predicting employment, marital circumstances, and overall personality. This life-transforming quality of trance possession is markedly different from the fixed and limited experience of Carnival, which is all over on Ash Wednesday. In this sense, carnivalesque cross-dressing functions as the secular counterpart of sacred transcorporeality. While the carnivalesque merely provides an escape valve and therefore strengthens normative categories, cross-gender possessions and mystic marriages allow for a thorough resubjectification of the individual.

CHAPTER 1. OF DREAMS AND NIGHT MARES

1. For earlier developments of the idea of transcorporeality in Vodou, I would like to direct the reader to two previous articles of mine on the subject: "The Afro-Diasporic Body in Haitian Vodou and the Transcending of Gendered Cartesian Corporeality" and "Transcorporeality in Vodou" (Strongman 2008a, 2008b).

2. Edouard Glissant presents this Carnival tradition as one of the few secular places in which West Indian society is able to critique patriarchal heteronormativity:

> Il est une occasion en Martinique où hommes et femmes se rencontrent d'accord pour donner une semblable représentation de leurs rapports: c'est dans la coutume des mariages burlesques du Carnaval, critique de la structure familiale. L'homme y tient le rôle de l'épouse (le plus souvent enceinte) et la femme celui de l'époux; un adulte y tient le rôle d'un enfant au berceau. . . .

Il n'est pas surprenant que le mariage burlesque soit une des rares formes encore vivaces de ce grand questionnement populaire et collectif qu'était et que ne peut plus être le carnaval martiniquais. (1981, 299)

There is an occasion in Martinique in which men and women meet in order to give a symbolic representation of their relationship. This is the tradition of the burlesque marriage during Carnival, a critique of family structure. The man has the role of the wife (often pregnant) and the woman that of the husband; an adult has the role of an infant in a crib. It is not surprising that the burlesque marriage is one of the rare forms still alive of that great popular and collective questioning that can be none other than the Martinican Carnival.

Glissant's Martinican context prevents him from considering Haitian Vodou as yet another site in which West Indian societies are able to question the dictates of gender and sexual norms. However, this Martinican perspective enables us to consider the ways in which this transcorporeality extends beyond the religious and permeates the entire structure of West Indian society, even of those that have been greatly Europeanized as a result of departmentalization.

3. For an alternative view that ridership involves an egalitarian, symmetrical double mounting, please see Jaqui Alexander's (2006, 324) *Pedagogies of Crossing*.

CHAPTER 2. HECTOR HYPPOLITE ÈL MÊME

1. In his lecture "Lo barroco y lo real maravilloso," Alejo Carpentier argues that unlike European surrealism's dependence on contrived technologies to render the fantastic visible, the Latin American marvelous real expresses the always already interwoven threads of the magical and the factual in the quotidian and everyday. In his own words: "Lo real maravilloso, en cambio, que yo defiendo, y es lo real maravilloso nuestro, es el que encontramos al estado bruto, latente, omnipresente en todo lo latinoamericano. Aquí lo insólito es cotidiano, siempre fue cotidiano" (1981, 127; On the other hand, the marvelous real that I defend and that is our own marvelous real is encountered in its raw state, latent and omnipresent, in all that is Latin American. Here the strange is commonplace, and always was commonplace). "En cuanto a lo real maravilloso, sólo tenemos que alargar nuestras manos para alcanzarlo. Nuestra historia contemporánea nos presenta cada día insólitos acontecimientos" (1981, 132; As far as the marvelous real is concerned, we have only to reach out our hands to grasp it. Our contemporary history presents us with strange occurrences every day).

2. Unclear third-person prounoun.

3. The elusive painting *Erzulie auf einem Delphin* was last exhibited in 2010 at Ramapo College Gallery and can be viewed by typing its title in Google images. It was owned by film director Jonathan Demme (*The Silence of the Lambs*, 1991) until the 2014 auction of his extensive Hyppolite collection.

4. "Kounbit" is a Caribbean work party in which bonds of reciprocal aid cement social bonds.

1. The spelling of this deity's name in this book does not seek to recast it in an Anglophone or "re-Africanizing" manner. The Yorùbá divinity Ọ̀ṣun is revered by the name of Ochún or Oshún in Cuba. As Caribbean Spanish retained the "sh" fricative phoneme from Yorùbá in intervocalic position among the ethno-educational social classes that compose the vast majority of Santeros, I have opted for *Oshún*, the spelling that most closely represents the most common variation of its pronunciation. A similar argument can be made for the Spanish spelling of *orisha* instead of *oricha* and *Regla de Osha* instead of *Ocha*. Notice that the retention of this phoneme only takes place intervocalically. In word initial position, Spanish phonological fortition applies and turns the fricative "sh" into affricate "ch." In Cuba, *Changó* is never pronounced as *Shangó*, as it is in the Bight of Benin and Brazil.

2. Ori-eleda is the master of the head. It is the orisha who governs the destiny of an individual person.

3. This is a patakí, a Yorùbá oral narrative, that is widely known in Ifá circles. Fernández Robaina retells it as it is given to him by babalao Agustín Martinez. For further information on this important patakí, Fernández Robaina (1994, 43–45) directs us to his earlier work, *Hablen Santeros y Paleros*; Natalia Bolívar Aróstegui's (1993, 103–66) *Opolopo Owo*; and Heriberto Feraudy Espino's (1993) *Yoruba: Un acercamiento a las raíces*.

CHAPTER 4. LUCUMÍ DIASPORIC ETHNOGRAPHY

1. The *blanquiamento* (whitening) of Lam parallels that of Mário de Andrade and Machado de Assis discussed in chapter 6.

CHAPTER 5. QUEER CANDOMBLÉ SCHOLARSHIP

1. In contrast to Matory's fleeting presentation of same-sex desire in Yorùbá religions in Nigeria and Brazil, note Oyêwùmí's outright dismissal: "Homosexuality does not seem to have been an option [for African bachelors and husbands with pregnant wives]" (1997, 63), and any presentation of "homosexuality into Yorùbá discourse is nothing but the imposition of yet another foreign model" (117). This can be read as a reinscription of the problematic myth of the nonexistence of homosexuality in sub-Saharan Africa as prescribed by Sir Francis Burton in his treatise on the Sotadic Zone.

2. The film director may not have known that at the time the title of babalaô was not conferred on women. The role was not available to women as Iyaláwo or Ìyánífá until the 1990s. Here, the regendering of the character also likely involves a hierarchical reclassification from babalaô to *mãe-de-santo* or *filha-de-santo*.

1. I have obscured my informants' names in this chapter in order to maintain their anonymity.

2. One more interesting instance of the whitening of black Brazilian literary figures involves the recent representation of Machado de Assis. The idea that money whitens on the bill displaying Mário de Andrade is echoed in a controversial 2011 Caixa Econômica Federal television commercial in which a white actor portrays Machado de Assis. (A clip of this commercial and its "corrected" version can be accessed via this link: Guilherme Howes, "Comercial caixa machado de assis," YouTube, July 5, 2012, https://www.youtube.com/watch?v=OboocxKLfRk.) The co-optation of two national writers and the erasure of their African ancestry by two distinct financial institutions speaks to the degree to which blackness and citizenship are incongruous among elite circles in Brazil and the way in which economic ascendancy redeems an ancestry historically dishonored. For more information on the origins of racial whitening in Latin America, I would like to direct the reader to my article "On the Non-equivalence of Black and Negro" (Strongman 2015).

3. For an extended analysis of the relationship between Candomblé and Umbanda, see Lindsey Hale's (2009) Hearing the Mermaid's Song. In a schematic way, however, let it be said that Candomblé venerates African deities while Umbanda, in a more eclectic manner, acknowledges these African deities plus Amerindian spirits and those of old slaves, infants, and other ethnic and professional archetypes.

REFERENCES

Abodunrin, Femi. 1996. *Blackness, Culture, Ideology and Discourse: A Comparative Study*. Bayreuth: Bayreuth African Studies Breitinger.

Agosto de Muñoz, Nélida. 1976. *El fenómeno de la posesión en la religión "Vudú."* Río Piedras: Instituto de Estudios del Caribe.

Alexander, M. Jacqui. 2006. *Pedagogies of Crossing: Meditations on Feminism, Sexual Politics, Memory, and the Sacred*. Durham, NC: Duke University Press.

Alexis, Gérald. 2004. "Hector Hyppolite: Sa peinture profane." *Journal of Haitian Studies* 10 (2): 135–41.

Alexis, Gérald. 2011. "Images des Loas, Portraits d'Homme." In *Hector Hyppolite*, edited by Comité Hector Hyppolite. Paris: Éditions de Capri.

Alves, Henrique L. 1973. *Mário de Andrade*. São Paulo: Editora do Escritor.

Amado, Jorge. 1966. *Dona Flor e seus dois maridos: História moral e de amor*. São Paulo: Martins.

Amado, Jorge. 1969. *Dona Flor and Her Two Husbands: A Moral and Amorous Tale*. New York: Avon.

Ancona Lopez, Telê Porto. 1983. *Mário de Andrade: Entrevistas e depoimentos*. São Paulo: Queiroz.

Argeliers, León. 2002. "Notas Preliminares." In *Visiones sobre Lam*. Havana: Ortiz.

Aschenbrenner, Joyce. 2002. *Katherine Dunham: Dancing a Life*. Urbana: University of Illinois Press.

Atwood Mason, Michael. 2002. *Living Santería: Rituals and Experiences in an Afro-Cuban Religion*. Washington, DC: Smithsonian.

Barnitz, Jacqueline. 2001. *Twentieth-Century Art of Latin America*. Austin: University of Texas Press.

Bastide, Roger. 1946a. *Estudos afro-brasileiros*. São Paulo: Universidade de São Paulo.

Bastide, Roger. 1946b. "Macunaíma visto por un francés." *Revista de Arquivo Municipal*, no. 106: 45–50.

Bastide, Roger. 1958. *Le candomblé de Bahia*. Paris: Mouton.

Bastide, Roger. 1978. *The African Religions of Brazil: Toward a Sociology of the Inter-penetration of Civilizations*. Baltimore: Johns Hopkins University Press. Originally published as *Les religions afro-brésiliennes: Contribution à une sociologie des interpé-nétrations des civilisations*. Paris: Presses Universitaires de France, 1960.

Bataille, Georges. 1943. *L'expérience intérieure*. Saint-Amand: Gallimard.

Beaubrun, Mimerose. 2010. *Nan Dòmi, le récit d'une initiation vodou*. Quétigny: Vents d'ailleurs.

Beaubrun, Mimerose. 2013. *Nan Dòmi: An Initiate's Journey into Haitian Vodou*. San Francisco: City Lights.

Benson, LeGrace. 2011. "Hector Hyppolite, Maître de la Présence." In *Hector Hyppolite*, edited by Comité Hector Hyppolite. Paris: Éditions de Capri.

Birman, Patricia. 1995. *Fazer estilo criando géneros*. Rio de Janeiro: Relume Dumará.

Birringer, Johannes. 1996a. "Homosexuality and the Nation: An Interview with Jorge Perrugoría." *Drama Review* 40 (1): 61–76.

Birringer, Johannes. 1996b. "La melancolía de la jaula." *Performing Arts Journal* 18 (1): 103–28.

Böhme, Hartmut. 1991. "'Eine Schematisierung von Zerstückelungsphantasien': Über einen Ursprung der Fichte'schen Literatur." In *Leben, um eine Form der Darstellung zu erreichen: Studien zum Werk Hubert Fichte*, edited by H. Böhme and Nikolaus Tiling. Frankfurt am Main: Fischer.

Böhme, Hartmut. 1992. *Hubert Fichte—Riten des Autors und Leben des Literatur*. Stuttgart: Springer.

Bolívar Aróstegui, Natalia. 1993. *Opolopo Owo*. Havana: Ed. de Ciencias Sociales.

Bourguignon, Erika. 1975. *Importante papel de las mujeres en los cultos afroamericanos*. Caracas: Instituto de Investigaciones Historicas.

Breton, André. 2002. *Surrealism and Painting*. Boston: MFA. Originally published by Gallimard, 1928 and 1965.

Brown, David. 2003. *Santería Enthroned*. Chicago: University of Chicago Press.

Butler, Judith. 1993. *Bodies That Matter: On the Discursive Limits of "Sex."* New York: Routledge.

Cabrera, Lydia. 1995. *El Monte*. Miami: Ediciones Universal.

Cachita, Yeyé. 2001. "Ochún in a Cuban Mirror." In *Osun across the Waters: A Yoruba Goddess in Africa and the Americas*, edited by Joseph Murphy and Mei-Mei San-ford. Bloomington: Indiana University Press.

Campa Marcé, Carlos. 2002. *Tomás Gutérrez Alea y Juan Carlos Tabio: Fresa y Choco-late*. Barcelona: Paidós.

Carnicel, Amarlindo. 1994. *O fotógrafo Mário de Andrade*. Campinas: Unicamp.

Carp, Ulrich. 2002. *Rio Bahia Amazonas: Untersuchen zu Hubert Fichtes Roman der Ethnologie mit einer lexicalischen Zusammentstellung zur Erforschung der Religionen Brasiliens*. Würzburg: Königshausen und Neumann.

Carpentier, Alejo. 1981. "Lo barroco y lo real maravilloso." In *La novela latinoameri-cana en vísperas de un nuevo siglo*. Mexico City: Siglo XXI.

Cascudo, Câmara. 1972. *Dicionário do Folclore Brasileiro*, 3rd ed. Rio de Janeiro: INL.

Célius, Carlo Avierl. 2011. "Les vèvè du créateur." In *Hector Hyppolite*, edited by Comité Hector Hyppolite. Paris: Éditions de Capri.

Césaire, Aimé. 1983. *Cahier d'un retour au pays natal*. Paris: Présence Africaine.

Chamberlain, Bobby. 1985. "Deus, deuses e dues ex machina nòs Lusíadas e na ficção contemporânea de Jorge Amado." *Hispania* 68 (4): 716–23.

Chamberlain, Bobby. 1990. *Jorge Amado*. Boston: Twayne.

Clark, Mary Ann. 2005. *Where Men Are Wives and Women Rule: Santería Ritual Practices and Their Gender Implications*. Gainesville: University Press of Florida.

Comité Hector Hyppolite. 2011. "Avant-propos." In *Hector Hyppolite*, edited by Comité Hector Hyppolite. Paris: Éditions de Capri.

Congdon, Kristin G., and Kara Kelley Hallmark. 2002. *Artists from Latin American Cultures: A Biographical Dictionary*. Westport, CT: Greenwood.

Conner, Randy, and David Sparks. 2004. *Queering the Creole Spiritual Traditions: Lesbian, Gay, Bisexual and Transgender Participation in African-Inspired Traditions in the Americas*. Binghamton, NY: Harrington Park.

Cosentino, Donald J. 1995a. "Imagine Heaven." In *Sacred Arts of Haitian Vodou*, edited by Donald Cosentino. Los Angeles: UCLA Fowler Museum of Cultural History.

Cosentino, Donald. 1995b. "Interleaf G: Hector Hyppolite." In *Sacred Arts of Haitian Vodou*, edited by Donald Cosentino. Los Angeles: UCLA Fowler Museum of Cultural History.

Cramer, Silke. 1999. *Reisen und Identität: Autogeographie im Werk Hubert Fichtes*. Bielefeld: Aisthesis.

Cros Sandoval, Mercedes. 1975. *La Religión Afrocubana*. Madrid: Playor.

Cros Sandoval, Mercedes. 2008. "Santería in the Twenty-First Century." In *Òrìṣà Devotion as World Religion: The Globalization of Yorùbá Religious Culture*, edited by Jacob Olupona and Terry Rey. Madison: University of Wisconsin Press.

Csordas, Tom. 1990. "Embodiment as a Paradigm for Anthropology." *Ethos* 18 (1): 5–47.

Cuthrell Curry, Mary. 1997. *Making the Gods in New York: The Yoruba Religion in the African American Community*. New York: Garland.

Daniel, Yvonne. 2005. *Dancing Wisdom: Embodied Knowledge in Haitian Vodou, Cuban Yoruba, and Bahian Candomblé*. Urbana: University of Illinois Press.

Dantas, Beatriz Góis. 2009. *Nagô Grandma and White Papa: Candomblé and the Creation of Afro-Brazilian Identity*. Chapel Hill: University of North Carolina Press. Originally published as *Vovó Nagô e Papai Branco: Usos e abusos da África no Brasil*. Rio de Janeiro: Editora Graal, 1988.

Davenport, Charles Benedict, and Morris Steggerda. 1929. *Race Crossing in Jamaica*. Washington, DC: Carnegie Institution.

Davis, Wade. 1986. *The Serpent and the Rainbow*. New York: Simon and Schuster.

Davis, Wade. 1988. *Passage of Darkness: The Ethnobiology of the Haitian Zombie*. Chapel Hill: University of North Carolina Press.

Dayan, Joan. 1995. *Haiti, History and the Gods*. Berkeley: University of California Press.

de Andrade, Mário. 1965. *Macunaíma: O herói sem nenhum caráter*. São Paulo: Martins.

de Andrade, Mário. 1984. *Macunaíma*. Translated by E. A. Goodland. New York: Random House.

Deleuze, Gilles, and Félix Guattari. 1972. *L'anti-Oedipe*. Paris: Éditions de Minuit.

Depestre, René. 1988. *Hadriana dans tous mes rêves*. La Flèche: Gallimard.

Deren, Maya. 1970. *Divine Horsemen: Voodoo Gods of Haiti*. New York: Chelsea House.

Descartes, René. 1948. *Oeuvres philosophiques et morales: Discours de méthode, méditations, les principes de a philosophie, les passions de l'âme, lettres*. Vienna: Aubin.

Descartes, René. 1996. *Discourse on Method and Meditations on First Philosophy*. New Haven, CT: Yale University Press.

Desmangles, Leslie. 1992. *The Faces of the Gods: Vodou and Roman Catholicism in Haiti*. Chapel Hill: University of North Carolina Press.

de Souza, Eneida Maria. 1999. *A pedra mágica do discurso*. Belo Horizonte: UFMG.

Dianteill, Erwan. 1995. *Le savant et le santero: Naissance de l'étude scientifique des religions afro-cubaines (1906–1954)*. Paris: L'Harmattan.

Dianteill, Erwan. 2000. *Des dieux et de signes: Initiation, écriture et divination dans les religions afro-cubaines*. Paris: Éditions de l'École des hautes études en sciences sociales.

Dunham, Katherine. 1969. *Island Possessed*. New York: Doubleday.

Dunham, Katherine. 1983. *The Dances of Haiti*. Los Angeles: Center for Afro-American Studies, UCLA. Originally published 1947.

Ehrsson, H. Henrik. 2007. "The Experimental Induction of Out-of-Body Experiences." *Science* 317 (5841): 1048.

Eppendorfer, Hans. 1977. *Der Ledermann spricht mit Hubert Fichte*. Frankfurt: Suhrkamp.

Falgayrettes-Leveau, Christiane. 1997. *Avant-Propos: Réceptacles*. Paris: Éditions Dapper.

Fanon, Frantz. 1995. *Peau noire, masques blancs*. Paris: Éditions du Seuil.

Feraudy Espino, Heriberto. 1993. *Yoruba: Un acercamiento a las raíces*. Havana: Ed. Política.

Ferguson, Roderick. 2003. *Aberrations in Black: Toward a Queer of Color Critique*. Minneapolis: University of Minnesota Press.

Fernández, Oscar. 1970. "*Dona Flor and Her Two Husbands* by Jorge Amado." *Modern Language Journal* 54 (5): 386–87.

Fernández Calderón, Alejandro. 2010. "Homosexualidad masculina en la Osha." *Desde Cuba* (blog), May 22. https://desde-cuba.blogspot.com/2010/05/homosexualidad -masculina-en-la-osha.html.

Fernández Olmos, Margarite, and Lizabeth Paravisini-Gebert. 2003. *Creole Religions of the Caribbean: An Introduction from Vodou and Santería to Obeah and Espiritismo*. New York: New York University Press.

Fernández Robaina, Tomás. 1994. *Hablen Santeros y Paleros*. Havana: Editorial de Ciencias Sociales.

Fernández Robaina, Tomás. 1996. "Cuban Sexual Values and African Religious Beliefs." In *Machos, Maricones and Gays: Cuba and Homosexuality*. Philadelphia: Temple University Press.

Fernández Robaina, Tomás. 2005. "Género y orientación sexual en la santería." In *La Gaceta de Cuba*. Havana: UNEAC.

Ferrera-Pena, Maria Alicia. 1987. "*Dona Flor and Her Two Husbands* by Jorge Amado." *Third World Quarterly* 9 (4): 1381–85.

Fichte, Hubert. 1974. *Versuch über die Pubertät*. Hamburg: Hoffmann und Campe.

Fichte, Hubert. 1976. "Die Rasierklinge und der Hermaphrodit." In *Xango*, with Leonore Mau. Frankfurt: Fischer.

Fichte, Hubert. 1979. "Toten Gott und Godmiché." In *Kunst aus Haiti*, edited by Sabine Holburg and Gereon Sievernich. Berlin: Heinemann.

Fichte, Hubert. 1980. *Psyche: Anmerkungen zur Psychiatrie in Senegal*. Frankfurt: Qumran.

Fichte, Hubert. 1985. *Lazarus und die Wash-Maschine: Kleine Einführung in die Afroamerikanische Kultur*. Frankfurt: Fischer.

Fichte, Hubert. 1987. *Homosexualität und Literatur 1: Polemiken*. Frankfurt: Fischer.

Fichte, Hubert. 1988. *Der Kleine Hauptbahnhof oder Lob des Strichs*. Frankfurt: Fischer.

Fichte, Hubert. 1989. *Das Haus der Mina in São Luiz de Maranhão*. Frankfurt: Fischer.

Fichte, Hubert. 1993. *Explosion: Roman der Ethnologue*. Frankfurt: Fischer.

Fichte, Hubert. 1996. "The Mediterranean and the Gulf of Benin: The Description of African and Afro-American Rites in Herodotus." In *The Gay Critic*. Ann Arbor: University of Michigan Press.

Fichte, Hubert. 2007. *Lustverlust: Ansichten eines alten Mannes 1972–1982*. Aachen: Rimbaud.

Fichte, Hubert, and Leonore Mau. 1976. *Xango*. Frankfurt: Fischer.

Fletcher, Valerie. 1992. "Wifredo Lam." In *Crosscurrents of Modernism: Four Latin American Pioneers: Diego Rivera, Joaquín Torres-García, Wifredo Lam, Matta*, edited by Valerie Fletcher. Washington, DC: Smithsonian.

Foster, David William. 2003. "Negociaciones queer en *Fresa y Chocolate*: Ideología y homoerotismo." *Revista Iberoamericana* 69 (205): 985–99.

Foucault, Michel. 1979 [1976]. *The History of Sexuality, Volume 1: An Introduction*. London: Allen Lane.

Fouchet, Max-Pol. 1984. *Wifredo Lam*. Paris: Editions Albin Michel.

Frankétienne. 1987. *Adjanoumelezo*. Port-au-Prince: Imprimerie des Antilles.

Fry, Peter. 1986. "Male Homosexuality and Spirit Possession in Brazil." *Journal of Homosexuality* 11 (3–4): 137–53.

García Lorca, Federico. 1928. *Romancero Gitano: Selección poética*. http://www.paginadepoesia.com.ar/escritos_pdf/lorca_rg.pdf.

Gates, Henry Louis. 1988. *The Signifying Monkey: A Theory of African American Literary Criticism*. New York: Oxford University Press.

Genet, Jean. 2004. *The Declared Enemy: Texts and Interviews*. Edited by Albert Dichy. Palo Alto, CA: Stanford University Press.

Gillett, Robert. 1995. "On Not Writing Pornography: Literary Self-Consciousness in the Work of Hubert Fichte." *German Life and Letters* 48 (2): 222–40.

Glissant, Édouard. 1981. *Le discours antillais*. Paris: Éditions du Seuil.

Görke, Daniela. 2005. *Sexualität im westdeustschen Roman der späten sechziger und frühen siebziger Jahre*. Lübeck: Der Andere.

Gregory, Steven. 1999. *Santería in New York City: A Study in Cultural Resistance*. New York: Garland.

Guillot, Maia. 2009. "Du mythe de l'unité luso-afro-brésilienne: Le candomblé et l'umbanda au Portugal." *Lusotopie* 16 (2): 205–19.

Gyekye, Kuame. 1995. *An Essay on African Philosophical Thought: The Akan Conceptual Scheme*. Philadelphia: Temple University Press.

Haberly, David T. 1983. *Three Sad Races: Racial Identity and National Consciousness in Brazilian Literature*. Cambridge: Cambridge University Press.

Hale, Lindsey. 1997. "Preto Velho: Resistance, Redemption, and Engendered Representation of Slavery in a Brazilian Possession-Trance Religion." *American Ethnologist* 24 (2): 392–414.

Hale, Lindsey. 2001. "Mama Oxum: Reflections of Gender and Sexuality in Brazilian Umbanda." In *Osun across the Waters: A Yoruba Goddess in Africa and the Americas*, edited by Joseph Murphy and Mei-Mei Sanford. Bloomington: Indiana University Press.

Hale, Lindsey. 2009. *Hearing the Mermaid's Song: The Umbanda Religion in Rio de Janeiro*. Albuquerque: University of New Mexico Press.

Hamilton, Russell G. 1967. "Afro-Brazilian Cults in the Novels of Jorge Amado." *Hispania* 50 (2): 242–52.

Hamilton, Russell G. 1970. "The Present State of African Cults in Bahia." *Journal of Social History* 3 (4): 357–73.

Hauschild, Thomas. 2002. "Kat-holos: Hubert Fichtes Ethnologie und die allumfassende Religion." In *Ethno/Graphie: Reiseforme des Wissens*, edited by Peter Braun and Manfred Weinberg. Tübingen: Gunter Narr.

Henry, Paget. 2000. *Caliban's Reason: Introducing Afro-Caribbean Philosophy*. New York: Routledge.

Herzberg, Julia P. 1987. "Afro-Cuban Traditions in the Work of Wifredo Lam." *Review—Latin American Literature and Arts*, no. 37.

Herzberg, Julia P. 1992. "Wifredo Lam: Interrelaciones entre el afrocubanismo y el surrealismo." In *Wifredo Lam 1902–1982: Obra sobre papel*, edited by Lucía García-Noriega et al. Mexico City: Televisa.

Herzberg, Julia P. 2001. "Naissance d'un style et d'une vision du monde: Le séjour à La Havane." In *Lam Métis*, edited by Christiane Falgaryettes-Leveau. Paris: Dapper.

Hoffman, L. G. 1985. "Hector Hyppolite." In *Haitian Art: The Legend and Legacy of the Naïve Tradition*. Davenport, IA: Beaux Arts Funds Committee.

Hoffman-Jeep, Lynda. 2005. "Creating Ethnography: Zora Neale Hurston and Lydia Cabrera." *African American Review* 39 (3): 337–53.

Hucks, Tracey E. 2008. "From Cuban Santería to African Yorùbá: Evolutions in African-American Òrìṣà History, 1959–1970." In *Òrìṣà Devotion as World Religion: The Globalization of Yorùbá Religious Culture*, edited by Jacob Olupona and Terry Rey. Madison: University of Wisconsin Press.

Hurston, Zora. 1990. *Tell My Horse: Voodoo and Life in Haiti and Jamaica*. New York: Harper and Row. Originally published 1938.

Johnson, Paul Christopher. 2002. *Secrets, Gossip, and Gods: The Transformation of Brazilian Candomblé*. New York: Oxford University Press.

Katschthaler, Karl. 2005. *Xenolektographie*. Frankfurt: Peter Lang.

Kulick, Don. 1998. *Travesti: Sex, Gender and Culture among Brazilian Transgendered Prostitutes*. Chicago: University of Chicago Press.

Lachatañeré, Rómulo. 1992. *El sistema religioso de los Afrocubanos*. Havana: Editorial de Ciencias Sociales.

Lafetá, João Luís. 1986. *Figuração da intimidade: Imagens na poesia de Mário de Andrade*. São Paulo: Martins Fontes.

Landes, Ruth. 1940. "A Cult Matriarchate and Male Homosexuality." *Journal of Abnormal and Social Psychology* 35: 386–97.

Landes, Ruth. 1947. *City of Women*. New York: Macmillan.

Leacock, Seth, and Ruth Leacock. 1972. *Spirits of the Deep: A Study of an Afro-Brazilian Cult*. New York: Doubleday.

Le Bouler, Jean-Pierre. 2002. *Pierre Fatumbi Verger: Um homem livre*. Salvador: Fundação Pierre Verger.

Le Clézio, J. M. G. 2011. "Préface." In *Hector Hyppolite*, edited by Comité Hector Hyppolite. Paris: Éditions de Capri.

Leiris, Michel. 1970. *Wifredo Lam*. New York: Abrams.

Lenggenhager, Bigna, T. Tadi, T. Metzinger, and O. Blanke. 2007. "Video Ergo Sum: Manipulating Bodily Self-Consciousness." *Science* 317 (5841): 1096–99.

Lerebours, Michel-Philippe. 2011. "À la recherche d'Hector Hyppolite." In *Hector Hyppolite*, edited by Comité Hector Hyppolite. Paris: Éditions de Capri.

Lorde, Audre. 1982. *Zami: A New Spelling of My Name—a Biomythography*. Berkeley: Crossing Press Feminist Series.

Lowe, Elizabeth. 1969. "The 'New' Jorge Amado." *Luso-Brazilian Review* 6 (2): 73–82.

Lowe, Elizabeth. 2001. "A Character in Spite of Her Author: Dona Flor Liberates Herself from Jorge Amado." In *Jorge Amado: New Critical Essays*, edited by Keith Brower, Earl E. Fitz, and Enrique Martínez-Vidal. New York: Routledge.

Lühning, Angela. 2002. "Introdução." In *Verger-Bastide: Dimensões de uma amizade*, edited by Angela Lühning. Rio de Janeiro: Bertrand Brasil.

Madsen, Bertil. 1990. *Auf der Suche nach einer Identität: Studien zu Hubert Fichtes Romantetralogie*. Stockholm: Germanistisches Institut.

Manalansan, Martin F. 2003. *Global Divas: Filipino Gay Men in the Diaspora*. Durham, NC: Duke University Press.

Manigat, Leslie François. 2011. "L'Époque des Dernières Années d'Hector Hyppolite." In *Hector Hyppolite*, edited by Comité Hector Hyppolite. Paris: Éditions de Capri.

Manning, Susan. 2005. "Watching Dunham's Dances, 1937–1945." In *Kaiso! Writings by and about Katherine Dunham*, edited by Vèvè Clark and Sarah E. Johnson. Madison: University of Wisconsin Press.

Marcelin, Milo. 1950. *Mythologie Vodou (Rite Arada) II: Illustrations de Hector Hyppolite*. Pétionville, Haiti: Éditions Canapé Vert.

Mars, Jean Price. 1928. *Ainsi parla l'oncle: Essais d'ethnographie*. New York: Parapsychology Foundation.

Martínez, Juan. 2002. "Los Paisajes Míticos de un pintor cubano: *La Jungla* de Wifredo Lam." In *Wifredo Lam: De lo circunscrito y eterno.* Havana: Centro de Arte Contemporáneo Wifredo Lam, Consejo Nacional de Artes Plásticas.

Matibag, Eugenio. 1996. *Afro-Cuban Religious Experience: Cultural Reflections in Narrative.* Gainesville: University Press of Florida.

Matory, J. Lorand. 1986. "Vessels of Power: The Dialectical Symbolism of Power in Yoruba Religion and Polity." Master's thesis, University of Chicago. Available online at https://culturalanthropology.duke.edu/people/j-lorand-matory.

Matory, J. Lorand. 2005a. *Black Atlantic Religion: Tradition, Transnationalism, and Matriarchy in the Afro-Brazilian Candomblé.* Princeton, NJ: Princeton University Press.

Matory, J. Lorand. 2005b. *Sex and the Empire That Is No More: Gender and the Politics of Metaphor in Oyo Yoruba Religion.* New York: Berghahn.

Matory, J. Lorand. 2008. "Is There Gender in Yorùbá Culture?" In *Òrìṣà Devotion as World Religion: The Globalization of Yorùbá Religious Culture,* edited by Jacob Olupona and Terry Rey. Madison: University of Wisconsin Press.

Mbiti, John S. 1970. *African Religions and Philosophy.* Garden City, NY: Doubleday.

McCarthy Brown, Karen. 1991. *Mama Lola: A Vodou Priestess in Brooklyn.* Berkeley: University of California Press.

McCarthy Brown, Karen. 2006. "Afro-Caribbean Spirituality: A Haitian Case Study." In *Vodou in Haitian Life and Culture: Invisible Powers.* New York: Palgrave.

Medina, Álvaro. 2002. "Lam y Chango." In *Wifredo Lam: La cosecha de un brujo,* edited by José Manuel Noceda. Havana: Letras Cubanas.

Mellor, Phillip, and Chris Schilling. 2010. "Body Pedagogics and the Religious Habitus: A New Direction for the Sociological Study of Religion." *Religion* 40 (1): 27–38.

Merewether, Charles. 1992. "At the Crossroads of Modernism: A Liminal Terrain." In *Wifredo Lam: A Retrospective of Works on Paper.* New York: Americas Society.

Métraux, Alfred. 1946. "The Concept of the Soul in Haitian Vodu." *Southwestern Journal of Anthropology* 2 (1): 84–92.

Métraux, Alfred. 1958. *Le Vaudou haïtien.* Paris: Gallimard.

Métraux, Alfred. 1959. *Vodou in Haiti.* New York: Schocken.

Métraux, Alfred. 1978. *Itinéraires,* vol. 1: *Carnets de notes et journaux de voyage, 1935–1953.* Paris: Bibliothèque scientifique.

Mielke, Rita. 1981. *Doppel-Perspektivisches Erzählen bei Hubert Fichte: Text + Kritik,* vol. 72. Munich: Richard Boorberg Verlag.

Molloy, Sylvia. 1995. "Disappearing Acts: Reading Lesbian Desire in Teresa de la Parra." In *¿Entiendes? Queer Readings, Hispanic Writings,* edited by Emile L. Bergmann and Paul Julia Smith. Durham, NC: Duke University Press.

Montilus, Guérin C. 2006. "Vodun and Social Transformation in the African Diasporic Experience: The Concept of Personhood in Haitian Vodun Religion." In *Haitian Vodou: Spirit, Myth, and Reality,* edited by Patrick Bellegarde-Smith and Claudine Michel. Bloomington: Indiana University Press.

Moreno Vega, Marta. 2008. "The Dynamic Influence of Cubans, Puerto Ricans, and African-Americans in the Growth of Ocha in New York City." In *Òrìṣà Devotion as World Religion: The Globalization of Yorùbá Religious Culture*, edited by Jacob Olupona and Terry Rey. Madison: University of Wisconsin Press.

Mott, Luiz. 2007. "Historical Roots of Homosexuality in the Lusophone Atlantic." In *Cultures of the Lusophone Black Atlantic*, edited by Nancy Priscilla Naro, Roger Sansi-Roca, and David H. Treece. New York: Palgrave Macmillan.

Munro, Martin. 2007. *Exile and Post-1946 Haitian Literature: Alexis, Depestre, Ollivier, Laferriere, Danticat*. Liverpool: Liverpool University Press.

Murphy, Joseph M. 1988. *Santería: African Spirits in the Americas*. Boston: Beacon.

Noceda, José Manuel. 2002. *Wifredo Lam en las colecciones cubanas*. Havana: Arte Cubano.

Nunes, Maria Luisa. 1973. "The Preservation of African Culture in Brazilian Literature: The Novels of Jorge Amado." *Luso-Brazilian Review* 10 (1): 86–101.

Olomo, Olóyé Àìná. 2009. "Sàngó beyond Male and Female." In *Sàngó in Africa and the African Diaspora*, edited by Joel E. Tishken, Tóyìn Fálolá, and Akíntúndé Akínyemí. Bloomington: Indiana University Press.

Olupona, Jacob, and Terry Rey, eds. 2008. *Òrìṣà Devotion as World Religion: The Globalization of Yorùbá Religious Culture*. Madison: University of Wisconsin Press.

Omari-Tunkara, Mikelle Smith. 2005. *Manipulating the Sacred: Yorùba Art, Ritual, and Resistance in Brazilian Candomblé*. Detroit: Wayne State University Press.

Ortiz, Fernando. 1950. *Wifredo Lam y su obra vista a través de significados críticos*. Havana: Ministerio de Educación.

Ortiz, Fernando. 1973. *Los negros brujos*. Miami: Ediciones Universal.

Ortiz, Fernando. 2002. *Visiones sobre Lam*. Havana: Fundación Fernando Ortiz.

Oyěwùmí, Oyèrónké. 1997. *The Invention of Women: Making an African Sense of Western Gender Discourses*. Minneapolis: University of Minnesota Press.

Paillière, Madeleine. 1975. *Peintres d'Haïti*, vol. 1: *Hector Hyppolite/Lucien Price*. Collection Histoire de l'Art. Port-au-Prince: La Societé des Amis du Musée d'Art Haitien.

Pérez, Elizabeth. 2016. *Religions in the Kitchen: Cooking, Talking, and the Making of Black Atlantic Traditions*. New York: New York University Press.

Pordeus, Ismael, Jr. 2000. *Uma casa luso-afro-portuguesa com Certeza: Emigrações e metamorfoses da Umbanda em Portugal*. São Paolo: Terceira Margen.

Pordeus, Ismael, Jr. 2009. *Portugal em Transe: Transnacionalização das religiões afro-brasileiras: Conversão e performances*. Lisbon: ICS.

Poupeye, Veerle. 1998. *Caribbean Art*. London: Thames and Hudson.

Prandi, Reginaldo. 2008. "Axexê Funeral Rites in Brazil's Òrìsà Religion: Constitution, Significance, and Tendencies." In *Òrìṣà Devotion as World Religion: The Globalization of Yorùbá Religious Culture*, edited by Jacob Olupona and Terry Rey. Madison: University of Wisconsin Press.

Pressel, Esther. 1977. "Negative Spirit Possession in Experienced Brazilian Umbanda Spirit Mediums." *Case Studies in Spirit Possession*, edited by Vincent Crapanzano and Vivian Garrison. New York: John Wiley.

Quiroga, José. 2000. *Tropics of Desire: Interventions from Queer Latino America*. New York: New York University Press.

Raillard, Alice. 1990. *Jorge Amado: Conversations avec Alice Raillard*. Paris: Gallimard.

René, Georges, and Marilyn Houlberg. 1995. "My Double Mystic Marriages to Two Goddesses of Love: An Interview." In *Sacred Arts of Haitian Vodou*, edited by Donald Cosentino. Los Angeles: UCLA Fowler Museum of Cultural History.

Ribeiro, René. 1969. "Personality and the Psychosexual Adjustment of Afro-Brazilian Cult Members." *Journal de la Societé des Americanistes* 58: 109–20. Reprinted in René Ribeiro, *Antropologia da religião e outros estudos*. Recife: Editora Masangana, 1982.

Rodman, Selden. 1948. *Renaissance in Haiti: Popular Painters in the Black Republic.* New York: Peregrini and Cudahy.

Rojas-Jara, Carlos Luis. 1995. "Modernism with a Cuban Accent: A Contextual Approach to *The Jungle* by Wifredo Lam." Master's thesis, University of California, Riverside.

Rosenthal, Judy. 1998. *Possession, Ecstasy, and Law in Ewe Voodoo*. Charlottesville: University Press of Virginia.

Rossetti Batista, Marta. 2004. *Coleçao Mário de Andrade*. São Paolo: Universidade de São Paolo.

Russeff, Ivan. 2001. *Educação e cultura na obra de Mário de Andrade*. Campo Grande, Brazil: UCDB.

Santí, Enrico Mario. 1998. "*Fresa y Chocolate*: The Rhetoric of Cuban Reconciliation." *MLN* 113 (2): 407–25.

Santos, Maria José. 2004. "Pelos caminhos críticos de *Dona Flor e seus dois maridos*." In *Em torno de Gabriela e Dona Flor*, edited by Ivia Alves. Salvador: Casa de Palavras.

Saraiva, Clara. 2007. "African and Brazilian Altars in Lisbon—Some Considerations on the Reconfigurations of the Portuguese Religious Field." In *Cultures of the Lusophone Black Atlantic*, edited by Nancy Priscilla Naro, Roger Sansi-Roca, and David H. Treece. New York: Palgrave Macmillan.

Sartre, Jean-Paul. 1943. *L'être et le néant: Essai d'ontologie phénoménologique*. Paris: Gallimard.

Seljan, Zora. 1999. "Aduni." In *Um Grapiúna no país do carnaval: Atas do I Simpósio Internacional de Estudos sobre Jorge Amado*, edited by Vera Rollemberg. Salvador: Casa de Palabras.

Seltzer Goldstein, Ilana. 2000. *O Brasil Best Seller de Jorge Amado: Literatura e identidade nacional*. São Paolo: Senac.

Serra, Ordep. 2006. "Carnaval dos Travestidos: Verger e as metamorphoses do carnaval." In *Brasil de Pierre Verger*. Rio de Janeiro: Fundação Pierre Verger.

Serres, Michel. 1999. *Variations sur le corps*. Saint-Amand-Montrond: Éditions le Pommier.

Smith, P. J. 1994. "The Language of Strawberry." *Sight and Sound* 4 (December): 31–32.

Sosa, Juan J. 2008. "La Santería: An Integrating, Mythological Worldview in a Disintegrating Society." In *Òrìṣà Devotion as World Religion: The Globalization of Yorùbá Religious Culture*, edited by Jacob Olupona and Terry Rey. Madison: University of Wisconsin Press.

Stebich, Ute. 1978. *Haitian Art*. New York: Brooklyn Museum.

St. Jean, Serge. 1973. *Hector Hyppolite: Une somme*. Port-au-Prince: n.p.

Stokes Sims, Lowery. 2002. "The Painter's Line: The Drawings of Wifredo Lam." *Master Drawings* 40 (1): 57–72.

Stoller, Paul. 2004. "Sensuous Ethnography, African Persuasions, and Social Knowledge." *Qualitative Inquiry* 10 (6): 817–35.

Strongman, Roberto. 2008a. "The Afro-Diasporic Body in Haitian Vodou and the Transcending of Gendered Cartesian Corporeality." *Kunapipi, Journal of Postcolonial Writing and Culture* 30 (2): 11–29.

Strongman, Roberto. 2008b. "Transcorporeality in Vodou." *Journal of Haitian Studies* 14 (2): 4–29.

Strongman, Roberto. 2015. "On the Non-equivalence of Black and Negro: Origins of the Cultural Constructions of New World Blackness in Iberian and Northern European Slave Codices." In *Slavery as a Global and Regional Phenomenon*, edited by Eric Hilgendorf, Jan-Christoph Marschelke, and Karin Sekora. Heidelberg: Universitätsverlag Winter.

Sweet, James H. 1996. "Male Homosexuality and Spiritism in the African Diaspora: The Legacies of a Link." *Journal of the History of Sexuality* 7 (2): 184–202.

Taillandier, Yvon. 1970. *Wifredo Lam*. Paris: Denoël.

Taylor, Charles. 1989. *Sources of the Self: The Making of Modern Identity*. Cambridge, MA: Harvard University Press.

Teixeira dos Santos, Newton Paulo. 1994. *A carta e as cartas de Mário de Andrade*. Rio de Janeiro: Diadorim.

Thompson, Robert Farris. 1983. *Flash of the Spirit: African and Afro-American Art and Philosophy*. New York: Random House.

Vadillo, Alicia E. 2002. *Santería y Vodú: Sexualidad y homoerotismo*. Madrid: Biblioteca Nueva.

van Ede, Yolanda. 2009. "Sensuous Anthropology: Sense and Sensibility for the Rehabilitation of Skill." *Anthropological Notebooks* 15 (2): 51–60.

Veiga, Benedito. 2004. "A Dona Flor de Bruno Barreto." In *Em torno de Gabriela e Dona Flor*, edited by Ivia Alves. Salvador: Casa de Palavras.

Verger, Pierre. 1954. *Dieux d'Afrique: Culte des Orishas et Vodouns à l'ancienne Côte des Esclaves en Afrique et à Bahia, la Baie de tous les Saints au Brésil*. Paris: Hartmann.

Verger, Pierre. 1957. *Notes sur le culte des Orisa et Vodoun: A Bahia, la Baie e tous les Saints au Brésil et L'ancienne Cote des esclaves en Afrique*. Dakar: Ifan.

Verger, Pierre. 1968. *Flux et reflux de la Traite des Nègres entre Le Golfe de Bénin et Bahia de Todos Os Santos du XVII au XIX siècle*. Paris: Mouton.

Verger, Pierre. 1981. *Notícias da Bahia-1850*. Salvador: Corrupio.

Verger, Pierre. 1982. *Orisha: Les Dieux Yorouba en Afrique et au Nouveau Monde*. Paris: Métailié.

Verger, Pierre. 1992a. "A Contribução especial das mulheres ao Candomblé do Brasil." In *Artigos*, vol. 1. São Paolo: Corrupio.

Verger, Pierre. 1992b. *Os Libertos: Sete caminhos na liberdade de escravos da Bahia no século XIX*. São Paolo: Corrupio.

Verger, Pierre. 1993. *Le Messager*. Paris: Editions Revue noire.

Vidal-Ortiz, Salvador. 2005. *Sexuality and Gender in Santería: Towards a Queer of Color Critique in the Study of Religion*. New York: City University of New York.

Wafer, James William. 1991. *The Taste of Blood: Spirit Possession in Brazilian Candomblé*. Philadelphia: University of Pennsylvania Press.

Ward, Graham. 2000. *Cities of God*. London: Routledge.

Weinberg, Manfred. 1995. "Die stupende und bisher noch wenig reflektierte Idee von Bikontinentalität und Bisexualität der afroamerikanischen Kultur: Zu Struktur und Function des 'Zwischen' bei Hubert Fichtes." In *Medium und Maske: Die Literatur Hubert Fichtes zwischen den Kulturen*, edited by Hartmut Böhme and Nikolaus Tiling. Stuttgart: M&P.

Werneck de Castro, Moacir. 1989. *Mário de Andrade: Exílio no Rio*. Rio de Janeiro: Rocco.

Wiredu, Kwasi. 1996. *Cultural Universals and Particulars: An African Perspective*. Bloomington: Indiana University Press.

INDEX

Note: Page numbers in italics refer to illustrations.

anthropology/ethnography: Africanist scholars, 23; ambivalence phase, 104, 106, 110–11, 128, 131–32; Anglophone tradition, 107, 128–30, 155, 170–71; Brazil-Africa dialogue on Candomblé, 219–22; as ceremony, 24, 175–77; from Cuba, the US, and France, 104; Cuban tradition, 107, 121–24, 132, 258n3; cultural conversion, 134; cultural production, influence on, 195; degeneracy phase, 104–7, 131–32, 182–83, 186–87; dialogic quality of field research, 6; essentialist discourses, 104–6; First World researchers, 104, 171–72; French tradition, 125–28, 171–72; lack of knowledge of scholarly tradition, 193; literary theft by foreign ethnographers, 243; nonheteronormativity rejected by, 111–12; passing for gay, 128; patronizing attitudes, 52–53, 112, 225; sexual interactions with informants, 59–60; testimonial ethnographical genre, 115; transcorporeality phase, 104, 194; as transcripturality, 252–53; Western misunderstandings, 15–19; women anthropologists, 27–28, 47–48. See also white art critics; white queer ethnographers

Argeliers, León, 164–65

artists, Caribbean, 51–100; artistic renaissance of 1940s, 93–94; magical realism in writings of, 53–55; patronizing attitudes toward, 52–53. See also de Andrade, Mário; Hyppolite, Hector; Lam, Wifredo

Ashé-power, 2

Asians, 104–5

Atwood Mason, Michael, 128

Augustine, 7

authorial reflexivity, 23

Autoportrait (Hyppolite), 60, 66–70, 68, 74, 76, 87, 91

Axé (divine life force), 218

Axé (divine power), 224

babalorixá, 184, 224, 234, 250

Baron Samedia (lwa), 36, 58

"Baroque and the Marvelous Real, The" (Carpentier), 55

Barreto, Bruno, 6, 195, 208–10

Bastide, Roger, 182–84, 197, 227, 232, 241, 248–49

Bataille, Georges, 9

Batuque. See Candomblé

Beaubrun, Mimerose, 5, 28–32, 35, 37, 45, 253. See also Nan Dòmi

Beaubrun, Theodore "Lòlò," 32, 37

Believers, The (film), 137

Benoit, Rigaud, 81

Benson, LeGrace, 96–97

Between Men (Sedgwick), 206

bicha, 189–90

bicontinentality, 63, 72–73, 76

binarisms, 103–4; Candomblé distinct from Western, 203; of Exu, 206; literacy/illiteracy, 91, 97; in Lucumí, 111, 115–16; middle-class dichotomy, 195; mind-body, 7–11, 182; reason and emotion, 70; saint/orisha, 115–16

bird imagery: in Hyppolite's paintings, 80, 82–83, 115; in Lam's works, 156, 170–71, 175; in Macunaíma, 212, 213, 222–24, 226, 229–30, 243–44; Oxalá and, 212, 213, 223–24; parrot as linguistic trickster, 243–44

Birman, Patricia, 190–91

Birringer, Johannes, 114–15, 118–19

bisexuality, 63, 72–76

Black Atlantic Religion (Matory), 22

black nationalist movements, 138

blackness: erased in discussions of de Andrade, 241; erased in discussions of Lam, 159–68; erased in Fresa y Chocolate, 119–20, 159; erased in Portuguese Candomblé, 214, 218–19; queerness coarticulated with, 141–48, 231; spiritual, 141–42

Black Panthers, 65

body: black, emptied by European imperialism, 4–5; black male, fetishizing of, 62–67; of Christ, 4; divine as a self inside, 9, 17; honam (material body), 11; kòkadav (flesh and blood), 15, 17, 21, 30; leather fetish equated with black body, 84–87; as machine, 20–21; nannanrèv (dream body), 30; as open vessel, 4, 171, 207; regendering of during trance, 35–36; in religious studies, 255–56n4; removable anima, 127; shadow of (ye), 11–12; without organs, 19–20; Yorùbá construction of, 23, 127. See also receptacularity; transcorporeality

Bonfim, Our Lord of (Nosso Senhor do Bonfim), 195, 196, 224; Bonfim-as-Oxalá, 230; hymn to, 227–29; Lavagem do Bonfim, 226–30

Bourguignon, Erika, 188

Brazil, 63–64; Constitution, 214; First Congreso Afro-Brasileiro, 241; homophobia, 187–88; independence struggle, 227–30; Inquisition, 203; ministers of religion, state certification, 213–14; music, state co-optation through, 227–29; nationalism, 240; Quimbanda spiritual tradition, 203; Salvador da Bahia, 181, 192–93, 213; Vodou in, 98–100; whitening of literary figures, 238–39, 239, 258–59n2. See also Candomblé